Moreton Morrell Site

COMPETITIVE ANXIETY IN SPORT

Rainer Martens, PhD
Human Kinetics Publishers

Robin S. Vealey, PhD
Miami University (Ohio)

Damon Burton, PhD
University of Idaho

Library of Congress Cataloging-in-Publication Data

Martens, Rainer, 1942-
    Competitive anxiety in sport / by Rainer Martens, Robin S. Vealey,
Damon Burton.
        p. cm.
    Rev. ed. of: Sport competition anxiety test / R. Martens. 1977.
    Includes bibliographical references and index.
    ISBN 0-87322-264-4
    1. Sports--Psychological aspects.   2. Anxiety--Testing.
    3. Competition (Psychology)--Testing.   I. Vealey, Robin S., 1954-
    . II. Burton, Damon, 1949-   .   III. Martens, Rainer, 1942-   .   Sport
    competition anxiety.   IV. Title.
    GV706.4.M36   1990
    796'.01--dc20   89-38808
                                                                                        CIP

ISBN: 0-87322-935-5 (paper)
ISBN: 0-87322-264-4 (cloth)

The following material was reprinted or adapted from *Sport Competition Anxiety Test* by
Rainer Martens, 1977, Human Kinetics, copyright 1977 by Rainer Martens: chapters 1
through 5; SCAT-A and SCAT-C; Figures 1.1, 1.2, 1.3, 2.1, 2.3, 4.1, 4.2, and 4.3; and
Tables 3.1, 3.2, 3.3, 3.4, 3.5, 3.6, 3.7, 3.8, 4.1, 4.2, 4.3, 4.4, 4.5, 4.6, and 4.7.

Developmental Editor: Christine Drews; **Production Director:** Ernie Noa; **Copyeditor:**
Bruce Owens; **Assistant Editors:** Robert King, Timothy Ryan, and Valerie Hall;
Proofreader: Karin Leszczynski; **Typesetters:** Angela K. Snyder, Cindy Pritchard, and
Yvonne Winsor; **Text Design:** Keith Blomberg; **Text Layout:** Kimberlie Henris; **Cover
Design:** Hunter Graphics; **Illustrations:** David Gregory; **Printed By:** Braun-Brumfield

Printed in the United States of America   10 9 8 7 6 5 4 3 2

Human Kinetics
Web site: http://www.humankinetics.com/

United States: Human Kinetics, P.O. Box 5076, Champaign, IL 61825-5076
1-800-747-4457
e-mail: humank@hkusa.com

Canada: Human Kinetics, 475 Devonshire Road, Unit 100, Windsor, ON N8Y 2L5
1-800-465-7301 (in Canada only)
e-mail: humank@hkcanada.com

Europe: Human Kinetics, P.O. Box IW14, Leeds LS16 6TR, United Kingdom
(44) 1132 781708
e-mail: humank@hkeurope.com

Australia: Human Kinetics, 57A Price Avenue, Lower Mitcham, South Australia 5062
(088) 277 1555
e-mail: humank@hkaustralia.com

New Zealand: Human Kinetics, P.O. Box 105-231, Auckland 1
(09) 523 3462
e-mail: humank@hknewz.com

Contents

Preface

This book is a revision of the *Sport Competition Anxiety Test* (SCAT), published in 1977 by the first author, but it is also substantially more. The book is divided into four parts. Part I contains the revised version of Martens's (1977) original competitive anxiety monograph, including new and more comprehensive norms. In Part II all published studies that have used SCAT are reviewed and conclusions and future research directions discussed. In Part III the development of the Competitive State Anxiety Inventory–2 (CSAI-2) is reported, including the validation research, the scale and instructions for its use, and recently developed norms. In Part IV the 16 studies that have used the CSAI-2 since the scale was released in 1982 are reviewed. On the basis of this literature, conclusions, problems, and suggestions for future research are outlined. Part V concludes with an emerging theory of competitive anxiety. In the preface of the 1977 edition of SCAT, Martens indicated that he was formulating this theory but that it was not sufficiently developed to warrant reporting at that time. Although the theory is not yet developed to the authors' satisfaction entirely, it was deemed sufficiently valuable to report as a concluding chapter to many years of research on competitive anxiety in sport.

For the first author (Martens), this book is a culmination of 20 years of research and study on competitive anxiety. His doctoral dissertation, which examined how individuals were influenced by audience anxiety when performing a motor skill in a competitive situation, revealed the need for better instrumentation to measure the then-vague anxiety construct. Martens decided that a sport-specific competitive trait anxiety scale would likely be a better predictor of competitive state anxiety and behavior than would a general trait scale. And so SCAT was born, and after 6 years of development the scale was published and soon widely used.

Through the validation research for SCAT it became apparent that a sport-specific state anxiety scale was also needed. A modified version of Spielberger's State Anxiety Inventory (SAI) was first developed and was called the Competitive State Anxiety Inventory (CSAI). This scale consisted of 10 items from the SAI that were more applicable to the competitive sport environment. The research using the CSAI verified that it was a more sensitive scale than was the SAI for measuring state anxiety in sport contexts.

As research progressed in the larger field of anxiety, other components of anxiety were identified as having important predictive power in explaining behavior. Two of those components—cognitive and somatic anxiety—appeared to be particularly relevant to sport. Thus, Martens decided to develop a new version of the CSAI that would assess these components, but in a way that was specific to competitive sport. As this work began, the coauthors of this book, Robin Vealey and Damon Burton, began their doctoral studies with Martens at the University of Illinois. As part of their research assistantship duties, they spent many hours developing and testing the revised CSAI, which is now called the CSAI-2.

The initial test validation work for the CSAI-2 was completed in 1982, and the authors, along with Linda Bump and Daniel Smith (also doctoral students), reported the culmination of 3 years of research and 14 studies at the 1982 conference of the North American Society for the Psychology of Sport and Physical Activity (NASPSPA). Due to the enthusiastic response given by the scientists attending that symposium, the authors were invited to submit the work to the *Journal of Sport Psychology*. The paper was submitted to the journal, but the reviews were mixed about the quality of the research, and it was recommended that the 80-page paper be sharply reduced in length.

The authors debated their next move and in the end chose not to chop up the coherent line of research into short articles but rather to publish the manuscript in its entirety. In addition, the authors did not agree with the substance of several recommended changes that would be required by reviewers if the manuscript were to be published in the *Journal of Sport Psychology*.

Another important consideration was the knowledge that personality tests are often misused by individuals who do not understand the theoretical rationale underlying the instruments or the appropriate procedures for administering these tests. The authors also felt that the validation of the CSAI-2, much like the development of SCAT, represented a systematic and rigorous approach to test development that could serve as a model for the development of other sport-specific inventories.

Consequently, Martens, Vealey, and Burton decided to write *Competitive Anxiety in Sport* not only to report the development of the CSAI-2 but also to update the original SCAT monograph and review the studies that have used the scale over the last 12 years. In addition, because researchers were aware of the CSAI-2 after the 1982 NASPSPA presentation, many requests were received for the scale and its supporting validation research. Thus, between 1982 and 1989 several studies have been published using the CSAI-2. This permitted the authors to review these studies and add their findings to the original validation research. The evidence reported in Part IV supports the conclusion that the CSAI-2 has validity as an instrument for use by sport psychologists.

With this brief historical summary of the work reported in this book, we as authors would like to close on a more personal note. We hope that this book will be useful to sport psychologists and spark additional inquiry into the topic of competitive anxiety. We have sought to provide a comprehensive report of the theoretical, psychometric, and validation information. Ultimately, you must decide whether the evidence about SCAT and the CSAI-2 warrant their use.

We invite you to use both instruments. We grant permission, without written approval, by this notice for anyone to reproduce, but not publish, these scales for research purposes. We, of course, would appreciate receiving reports of your findings so that we can stay abreast of the use of the scales.

The publication of this text has been our objective for the past 5 years, but each of us found it difficult because our career paths diverged. Martens left the University of Illinois to devote his full time to the management of Human Kinetics Publishers. Vealey and Burton, after completing their doctoral degrees, began very active careers as sport psychologists at Miami University (Ohio) and the University of Idaho, respectively. It has been particularly the perseverance and work of coauthors Vealey and Burton in revising the SCAT and CSAI-2 manuscripts, developing and revising norms, and reviewing research using both instruments that brought this publication to fruition.

Rainer Martens

Robin S. Vealey

Damon Burton

Acknowledgments

We gratefully acknowledge the valuable assistance of Renee DeGraff, Dan Gould, Wayne Halliwell, Tom Hanson, Julie Simon, Jeff Simons, and Dana Sinclair in helping with the review of the SCAT literature. Our thanks also to Linda Bump and Dan Smith for their contribution to the development of the CSAI-2 and to Diane Gill, Tara Scanlan, and Julie Simon for their work in developing SCAT.

We also thank Brian Williams-Rice for his help in developing SCAT and CSAI-2 norms and Bob Brustad, Rich Cox, Dan Gould, Vikki Krane, Becky Lewthwaite, Shane Murphy, Linda Petlichkoff, Tara Scanlan, Maureen Weiss, and Jean Williams for sharing their SCAT and CSAI-2 data with us for the computation of norms.

Finally, we close by expressing publicly our appreciation for one another for the 10 years of friendship, mutual respect, and satisfaction in working collaboratively in sport psychology.

PART I

Development and Validation of the Sport Competition Anxiety Test

A revised and condensed version of the contents of the Sport Competition Anxiety Test (SCAT) (1977) is presented in Part I, which contains the original theoretical model on which SCAT is based and a revised presentation of the development, validation, and administration of SCAT. Chapter 2 in the original monograph was eliminated because the rationale for the development of SCAT that was based on previous anxiety research no longer seemed necessary. In chapter 5, the scale is printed, and new normative data are reported.

Chapter 1

Anxiety in Sport

Some years ago through an odd set of occurrences I found myself coaching wrestling at the University of Montana. The team's 147-lb wrestler (I will fictitiously name him Jim Macey) was a young man with great ability. In fact, Jim knew considerably more about wrestling than I did, although he never shoved that fact in my face. Jim's teammates admired his talent and early in the season elected him team captain.

Our first meet of the season was at Eastern Washington University in Cheney. After weighing in and seeing Jim's opponent, I was confident that he would have little difficulty winning. One to two hours before the meet, however, I noticed that Jim was very quiet and not his usual smiling, loquacious self. I inquired if he were feeling ill, but he assured me he was not.

That evening we defeated Eastern Washington, 26-20, giving our team its first victory of the season and me my first win as a head coach. But the win was not totally satisfying. Jim won his bout, but by a narrow margin. He wrestled as if he were a different person. Nonaggressive throughout the bout, Jim permitted his opponent to "take the bout to him." Rather than Jim wrestling his usual aggressive, offensive style, he was defensive. It was only his superior skills and a weak opponent that permitted him to eke out a 5-4 win. For several hours after the match he remained quiet and atypically withdrawn. I sensed that he sensed his teammates' and coach's bewilderment as to why he did not "mop up" his opponent.

As the season progressed, I came to know Jim Macey much better. He became incredibly uptight before every bout regardless of how easy or difficult his opponent was. Jim was not enjoying wrestling due to this enormous competitive stress and about midway through the season indicated his desire to quit. After several lengthy conversations, I convinced Jim to stay with the team, although in retrospect I am not sure it was the correct thing to do. At the time I was convinced that the team needed him and that he would be an excellent wrestler if he could overcome his anxieties. I recall talking at length with him about anxiety; I could easily relate and empathize with Jim because I had also experienced high states of anxiety when I wrestled. Although I always believed that these high states of anxiety helped me wrestle better, in Jim's case anxiety was unquestionably detrimental. Through conversations with Jim, I sought to remove the pressure that he felt; but I could not do this because the pressure was self-imposed. Jim, I felt, feared failure so much that he almost panicked before and during a bout. He could not get control of his emotional state as he approached competition.

Although I wanted to help, as a young coach I simply did not know what to do. I did not understand Jim's problem well, nor did I have a clear conception of how to alleviate his extraordinarily high state anxiety. Jim never overcame his competitive anxiety, and he completed the season with a mediocre record, far poorer than his ability warranted.

My inability to help Jim and my frustration from a number of related experiences in sport directed me to the then-obscure field of sport psychology. I believed then and today that what goes on in an athlete's head is just as, if not more, important than are physical talent and skill in determining success and enjoyment in competitive sport. Consequently, I terminated my short coaching career to pursue my curiosity about sport psychology.

Because of the Jim Maceys of the world, sport psychologists need to answer such questions as the following: What causes athletes to become uptight? Why do some athletes rise to the occasion in intense competition while others choke under the pressure? What are the short- and long-term effects of competitive stress? How does competitive anxiety affect the performance of the athlete? Can athletes learn to control their emotional states, and will this help them optimize their performance? What can be done to alleviate hyperanxious states? What can be done to prevent athletes from burning out as a result of the tremendous psychological stress from intense competition over extended periods of time?

Although researchers have made significant progress in recent years toward answering these questions and understanding competitive anxiety, a great deal of work remains to be done. Researchers have sought to identify sources of anxiety and learn how different individuals perceive these sources. Moreover, this improved understanding of the causes of competitive anxiety has allowed sport psychologists to examine the mechanisms that athletes use to cope with competitive anxiety and the consequences of failing to develop such coping skills. Currently, numerous techniques are being utilized to cope with excessive anxiety effectively, including hypnosis (e.g., Unestahl, 1986), biofeedback training (e.g., DeWitt, 1980; Peper & Schmid, 1983; Wenz & Strong, 1980), progressive relaxation (e.g., Weinberg, Seabourne, & Jackson, 1981), visuomotor behavior rehearsal (e.g., Hall & Erffmeyer, 1983; Kolonay, 1977; Lane, 1980; Noel, 1980; Suinn, 1977; Titley, 1980; Weinberg et al., 1981), autogenic training, meditation techniques (e.g., Layman, 1978), positive self-monitoring (e.g., Johnston-O'Connor & Kirschenbaum, 1986; Kirschenbaum & Bale, 1980; Kirschenbaum, Ordman, Tomarken, & Holtzbauer, 1982; Kirschenbaum, Wittrock, Smith, & Monson, 1984), thought stopping (e.g., Meyers & Schleser, 1980; Silva, 1982), various self-talk techniques (e.g., Hamilton & Fremouw, 1985; Meyers, Schleser, Cooke, & Cuvillier, 1979), induced affect (e.g., Smith, 1980), and comprehensive cognitive-behavioral intervention packages (e.g., Kirschenbaum & Bale, 1980; Kirschenbaum et al., 1982; Meyers & Schleser, 1980).

COMPETITIVE ANXIETY TERMINOLOGY

A discussion of competitive anxiety requires the establishment of a common language that allows precise and efficient communication. When students undertake the study of a physical or biological science, they usually encounter a completely new vocabulary with specific nomenclature to describe the new phenomena they are studying. However, when studying a social science, students must frequently learn new meanings to words they already know, giving these familiar terms precise meanings to describe specific phenomena. *Anxiety, stress, arousal,* and *competition* are terms familiar to all of us, but scientific rigor requires that precise definitions for these complex phenomena replace the vague, general meanings that these words have in our everyday vocabularies.

State and Trait Anxiety

Confusion existed for some time in the anxiety literature whether certain anxiety instruments assessed a general tendency to be anxious or immediate anxiety states. Although this distinction between state and trait anxiety was beginning to emerge in the 1950s, Spielberger (1966b) is credited with formalizing the state-trait theory of anxiety. According to Spielberger, *state anxiety* refers to an existing or immediate emotional state characterized by apprehension and tension. *Trait anxiety* is a predisposition to perceive certain situations as threatening and to respond to these situations with varying levels of state anxiety. In Spielberger's (1966b) words,

> anxiety states are characterized by subjective, consciously perceived feelings of apprehension and tension, accompanied by or associated with activation or arousal of the autonomic nervous system. (p. 17)

Trait anxiety, however, is

> a motive or acquired behavioral disposition that predisposes an individual to perceive a wide range of objectively nondangerous circumstances as threatening and to respond to these with state anxiety reactions disproportionate in intensity to the magnitude of the objective danger. (p. 17)

Individuals high in trait anxiety either perceive more situations as threatening, respond to threatening situations with more intense levels of state anxiety, or both. To clarify further the conceptual distinction between state and trait anxiety, Spielberger makes the analogy between anxiety and energy. According to this analogy, state anxiety is like kinetic energy, or an ongoing reaction taking place at some level of intensity, whereas trait anxiety is comparable to potential energy, or a latent predisposition for a kinetic reaction to occur if triggered by appropriate stimuli.

Cognitive Versus Somatic Anxiety

As early as the mid 1960s, researchers were beginning to view anxiety as a multi-dimensional rather than a unidimensional construct. Liebert and Morris (1967) first hypothesized that anxiety comprises cognitive-worry and emotional-arousal components. Subsequent research by Endler (1978), Davidson and Schwartz (1976), and Borkovec (1976) has identified similar components of anxiety that have since been termed cognitive anxiety and somatic anxiety, a distinction applied to both state and trait anxiety.

Cognitive anxiety is the mental component of anxiety and is caused by negative expectations about success or by negative self-evaluation. According to Morris, Davis, and Hutchings (1981), cognitive anxiety is characterized by "conscious awareness of unpleasant feelings about oneself or external stimuli, worry, disturbing visual images" (p. 547). In sport, cognitive anxiety is most commonly manifested by negative performance expectations and thus negative self-evaluation.

Somatic anxiety refers to the physiological and affective elements of the anxiety experience that develop directly from autonomic arousal. Somatic anxiety is reflected in such responses as rapid heart rate, shortness of breath, clammy hands, butterflies in the stomach, and tense muscles.

Although cognitive and somatic anxiety are hypothesized to be conceptually independent, Morris, Davis, and Hutchings (1981) have noted that they likely covary in stressful situations because these situations contain elements related to the arousal of each. Cognitive and somatic anxiety refer to behavior along two dimensions: intensity and direction. Cognitive and somatic anxiety are always negative in direction due to their links with negative affect; high levels of cognitive and somatic anxiety are experienced as unpleasant.

Arousal

Both cognitive and somatic anxiety are closely associated with the concept of *arousal*, which refers to the intensity dimension of behavior, the state of the organism varying on a continuum from deep sleep to intense excitement. Other terms, such as *activation* and *energy mobilization*, have been used to describe the same dimension. Thus, arousal refers only to the intensity dimension of behavior, whereas cognitive and somatic anxiety refer to both intensity and direction, and are often aroused by cues in the environment that are perceived as threatening.

Stress

Stress has historically been one of the most ambiguous psychological constructs in the behavioral sciences. Stress has been defined as stimulus, intervening, and response variables by different researchers. As a stimulus variable, stress is a precipitator; as an intervening variable, a mediator; and as a response variable, a behavior. Thus, McGrath's (1970a) work conceptualizing stress as a process was particularly important in clarifying this semantic jumble. According to McGrath, four events must be considered in studying stress as a social psychological process:

1. The physical or social environment that places some objective demand on the individual
2. The individual's perception of the demand and the decision about how to respond to it
3. The individual's actual response to the perceived demand
4. The consequences resulting from that response

McGrath defined stress as an imbalance between the perceived environmental demand and the perceived response capability of the organism. Furthermore, the consequences of such an imbalance must be perceived as important, so that adverse consequences will be anticipated for failure to meet these demands. Succinctly stated, "stress has to do with a (perceived) substantial imbalance between demand and response capability, under conditions where failure to meet demand has important [perceived] consequences" (McGrath, 1970a, p. 20). McGrath's stress process is illustrated in Figure 1.1.

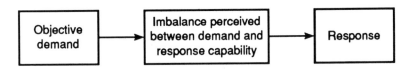

Figure 1.1.   McGrath's (1970a) stress process.

Spielberger's (1966b) state-trait anxiety concepts and Morris, Davis, and Hutching's (1981) cognitive-somatic anxiety concepts are both easily incorporated into McGrath's stress paradigm. Trait anxiety is an important personality disposition that describes how a person is likely to perceive the environmental demand–response capability discrepancy. State anxiety represents the momentary anxiety state precipitated by the interaction between the person's level of trait anxiety and the current discrepancy between environmental demands and response capabilities. Thus, cognitive and somatic anxiety represent separate components of both state and trait anxiety.

Note that in McGrath's definition of the stress process it is not stated that objective demand must exceed response capability; there must only be an imbalance. Normally we think of stress in terms of an overload; demands are made on us, creating uncertainty that we can meet them adequately. Stress may occur, however, when the objective environment does not demand enough, or when there is an underload rather than an overload. In recent years a substantial body of literature has shown that stresslike effects may occur from sensory deprivation, social isolation, or stimulus impoverishment.

Spielberger (1972b) uses the term *stress* somewhat differently to describe a stimulus event in an overall process that he terms *anxiety*. In the temporally ordered sequence of events specified by this anxiety model, a particular level of stress is perceived to involve a specific level of danger, thus prompting a state anxiety reaction of quantifiable magnitude. Thus, *stress* in Spielberger's model is limited to "denoting environmental conditions or circumstances that are characterized by some degree of objective physical or psychological danger" (p. 488). Moreover, Spielberger labels the individual's subjective appraisal of a situation as being physically or psychologically dangerous as *threat*, whereas he terms the response component of the model the *state anxiety reaction*. Thus, Spielberger's process of anxiety may be restated as shown in Figure 1.2.

Figure 1.2.   Spielberger's (1972b) process of anxiety.

The significant differences between the McGrath and the Spielberger models are the terms they use to describe their overall processes and the individual components of their models. In essence, they are describing the same process, but Spielberger refers to it as *anxiety*, whereas McGrath calls it *stress*. Moreover, they use different terms to describe the stimulus, cognition, and response components of their models. Spielberger calls the stimulus *stress*, whereas McGrath refers to it as *objective demand*. Spielberger uses the succinct term *threat* to describe the subjective cognitive appraisal process that McGrath refers to as an *imbalance perceived between demand and response capability*. Finally, Spielberger refers to the response as *state anxiety reaction*, whereas McGrath uses the more general term *response*.

COMPETITIVE ANXIETY MODEL

After having carefully evaluated both models, we have chosen to develop an independent model of competitive anxiety that borrows from the terminology of both Spielberger and McGrath. Although the McGrath and the Spielberger models are in essence the same, we prefer to use McGrath's term *stress* rather than *anxiety* to describe the overall process for two reasons. First, anxiety is too often associated only with personality traits, which constitute only the stimulus portion of the anxiety process as described by Spielberger. Second, stress is often considered to be more than only a stimulus variable. Thus, *stress* here will refer to the overall process that is associated with the occurrence of state anxiety, not only the objective stimulus event that elicits the perception of threat. We also have borrowed McGrath's term *objective demand* to refer to those antecedent variables that may elicit the perceptions of threat, although the objective environmental demand need not necessarily be perceived as dangerous or threatening.

Spielberger's definition of *threat*, however, cogently labels the perception of imbalance between perceived environmental demand and response capability and will be used to describe this cognitive appraisal variable. Finally, Spielberger's term *state anxiety reaction* will be employed to describe the response component of this model. Thus, the terms used to describe the stress process as shown in Figure 1.3 will be used hereafter to obtain consistency in terminology.

Figure 1.3. Terminology used to describe the stress process in this book.

GLOSSARY OF COMPETITIVE ANXIETY TERMS

Terminology in the anxiety literature has not been used consistently because individual researchers have often used different terms to represent the same construct. As a quick reference for readers, the competitive anxiety terminology as defined in this chapter and used throughout the book is summarized in this section.

State anxiety is an existing or current emotional state characterized by feelings of apprehension and tension and associated with activation of the organism. State anxiety is linked with negative affect. Hereafter, state anxiety will be abbreviated as *A-state*.

Trait anxiety is a predisposition to perceive certain environmental stimuli as threatening or nonthreatening and to respond to these stimuli with varying levels of A-state. Hereafter, trait anxiety will be abbreviated as *A-trait*.

Cognitive anxiety is the mental component of anxiety caused by negative expectations about success or by negative self-evaluation. According to Morris, Davis, and Hutchings (1981), cognitive anxiety is characterized by "conscious awareness of unpleasant feelings about oneself or external stimuli, worry, disturbing visual images" (p. 547).

Somatic anxiety refers to the physiological and affective elements of the anxiety experience that develop directly from autonomic arousal. Somatic anxiety is reflected in such responses as rapid heart rate, shortness of breath, clammy hands, butterflies in the stomach, and tense muscles.

Arousal describes a state of the organism and varies on a continuum from deep sleep to intense excitement.

Threat is the perception of physical or psychological danger. It is the perception of an imbalance between environmental demand and response capability.

Stress is the process that involves the perception of a substantial imbalance between environmental demand and response capabilities under conditions in which failure to meet demands is perceived as having important consequences and is responded to with increased levels of cognitive and somatic A-state.

SUMMARY

Experimental and experiential evidence indicates that anxiety is a common occurrence in competitive situations and that the effects of anxiety on sport performance are extremely debilitating. To examine anxiety in sport with greater precision, it is important to define terminology in a systematic way to understand the differences between A-trait and A-state, somatic and cognitive anxiety, and the related constructs of arousal, anxiety, and stress. Also, it is important to build from existing anxiety theory to conceptualize the interrelationships among these constructs into a theoretical framework to serve as the basis for research in the area.

Chapter 2

Competitive Trait Anxiety

Competitive trait anxiety is a situation-specific modification of the more general A-trait construct. *Competitive A-trait* is defined as a tendency to perceive competitive situations as threatening and to respond to these situations with A-state. The operationalization of the competitive A-trait construct is important in understanding behavior in sport, particularly in understanding which competitive situations are perceived as threatening and how persons respond to the threat. The Sport Competition Anxiety Test (SCAT), discussed in chapters 3 through 5, has been developed to assess competitive A-trait, and the construction of SCAT was based on four significant theoretical developments in the field of personality:

- The adoption of an interactional theory of personality that predicts behavior better than do trait or situational paradigms
- The development of situation-specific A-trait instruments that have superior predictive power compared to general A-trait scales
- The trait-state theory of anxiety, which distinguishes between A-trait and A-state
- The development of a conceptual model for the study of competition as a social process

The remainder of this chapter is devoted to a discussion of these developments to provide a theoretical basis for the development of SCAT.

THE INTERACTIONAL PARADIGM

Almost all sport personality research conducted before the mid-1970s used the trait approach. Some researchers explicitly selected to do so, but most implicitly did so as a result of borrowing a particular personality inventory, for example, the Cattell 16-PF, the Minnesota Multiphasic Personality Inventory (MMPI), or the California Psychological Inventory (CPI). The trait approach is based on the assumption that personality traits—the fundamental units of personality—are relatively stable, or consistent, attributes that exert generalized causal effects on behavior. The trait approach considers the general source of behavioral variance to reside within the person, minimizing the role of situational or environmental factors.

In reaction to limitations of the trait approach, as well as to the popularity of behavioral psychology, some personologists have advocated a situational paradigm (Mischel, 1968, 1973), which asserts that human behavior is determined largely by situational factors and that personality variables exert little influence on behavior. Situationism, however, is an extreme reaction to trait psychology. Trait psychology exhalts internal structures to the neglect of the environment, whereas situationism hails the environment as the only important source of behavioral variance and neglects individual differences. Both the trait and the situational paradigms provide limited views of possible sources of behavioral variance, and researchers have increasingly recognized that a third alternative—an interactional approach that views behavior as the joint product of both personality and situational factors—provides better behavior prediction than do paradigms that are limited to either personality or situational variables alone (Bowers, 1973; Carson, 1969; Vale & Vale, 1969).

The interactional paradigm, which has long been advocated by social psychologists and behavioral geneticists, views the situation and the person as codeterminants of behavior without specifying either the situation or the person as primary or subsidiary causes of behavior. Instead, the importance of personality and situational variables is dependent on the sample of people studied and the situational constraints under which they must perform. Lewin (1935) was one of the pioneers of interactionism, expressing as early as the 1940s this now-famous equation:

$$B = f(P, E)$$

$$B = \text{Behavior}$$
$$P = \text{Person}$$
$$E = \text{Environment}$$

Although the differences in these three paradigms should be clear, considerable confusion has arisen over why interactionists use the same traits in their research that trait psychologists use. The answer is that interactionists do not believe that traits such as A-trait, achievement motivation, and internal-external control are nonexistent. On the contrary, they believe that traits are viable constructs and not only the sole or even the primary determinants of behavior. Interactionists are not demanding the abolition of traits or of the instruments used to assess traits, but they consider these traits to function differently than do trait psychologists. Traits (or *dispositions* as interactionists prefer to call them) are *tendencies*, or *predispositions*, to perceive or respond to certain classes of situations with certain behaviors.

To reiterate, trait psychologists view traits as having widespread influence on behavior with little or no concern for situational determinants (i.e., traits are the primary determinants of behavior). The interactionist considers these traits as dispositions or tendencies to behave in certain ways in certain classes of situations (i.e., traits are not necessarily the primary determinants of behavior). Nicholls's (1984) achievement motivation theory and Bandura's (1977) self-efficacy theory (both interactional theories) show how interactionists incorporate traits or dispositions into their theories. Each of these theories contains both a dispositional construct (perceived ability in the former theory and self-efficacy in the latter) and situational constructs (expectancy of success and success/failure history in the former theory and task difficulty in the latter).

GENERAL ANXIETY VERSUS SITUATION-SPECIFIC ANXIETY

Many behavioral scientists have examined the relationship between general A-trait and various behaviors but have failed to obtain anticipated results. One group of psychologists (Mandler & Sarason, 1952; Sarason, Davidson, Lighthall, Waite, & Ruebush, 1960) have suggested that the problem lies with poor measurement technology that attempts to study anxiety as a unitary, general phenomenon. Instead, they claim that anxiety is a learned response to situations. In other words, one person may become quite anxious when taking a math test, sitting in a dentist's chair, or delivering a speech but not when competing in a hockey game, performing at a piano recital, or taking a driver's examination. Thus, we can better predict behavior when we have more knowledge of the specific situation and how persons tend to respond to these types of situations.

Mandler and Sarason (the so-called Yale psychologists) pursued this approach in studying test anxiety in academic situations. Their research has shown improved behavioral prediction when a person's situation-specific anxiety disposition and other relevant situational characteristics are known. As a result of this improved behavioral prediction, other behavioral scientists have developed situation-specific anxiety scales to measure audience anxiety (Paivio & Lambert, 1959), fear of negative evaluation and social avoidance and distress (Watson & Friend, 1969), and fear of snakes, heights, and darkness (Mellstrom, Cicala, & Zuckerman, 1976). After reviewing some of the research using situation-specific A-trait instruments, Spielberger (1972b) concluded that "in general, situation-specific trait anxiety measures are better predictors of elevation in A-state for a particular class of stress situations than are general A-trait measures" (p. 490).

Competitive A-trait is a situation-specific construct that was especially developed to identify A-trait dispositions in competitive sport situations. Its development is based substantially on the evidence that situation-specific A-trait constructs are better predictors of behavior in the particular situation for which the construct was designed.

A TRAIT-STATE THEORY OF ANXIETY

Spielberger's (1966b) conceptual distinction between A-trait and A-state (see chapter 1) is fundamental to his theory of anxiety (see Figure 2.1). Spielberger's (1972a) trait-state theory of anxiety is based on the following assumptions:

1. Stimuli that are either external or internal to the person and that are perceived as threatening evoke A-state reactions. High levels of A-state are experienced as unpleasant through sensory and cognitive feedback mechanisms.
2. The greater the amount of threat perceived, the more intense the A-state reaction.
3. The longer the person perceives threat, the more enduring the A-state reaction.
4. Compared with persons low in A-trait, persons high in A-trait will perceive more situations as threatening, respond with more intense A-state reactions, or both. Evidence indicates that situations involving potential failure or threats to self-esteem are more potent sources of threat than are potentially physically harmful situations. It is primarily through past experiences that some persons acquire high or low A-trait.
5. Elevated levels of A-state have stimulus and drive properties that may be manifested directly in behavior or that may serve to initiate psychological defenses that have been effective in reducing A-states in the past.
6. Stressful situations frequently encountered may cause an individual to develop specific psychological defense mechanisms that are designed to reduce or minimize A-state.

From this theory it is clear that the focus of future research must be on the stimuli or antecedent conditions that evoke A-state, on the cognitive processes that interpret these stimuli as threatening, and on the behaviors that are manifested in response to the perceived threat.

THE COMPETITIVE PROCESS

It is necessary to understand the elements involved in the competitive process to fully understand anxiety in competitive situations. Previously, Martens (1975a) outlined a model that views competition as a process. The model of the competitive process is illustrated in Figure 2.2. It is not unlike the McGrath model of stress or the Spielberger model of anxiety (cf. Figure 2.2 with Figure 1.1 or 1.2). The competitive process model applies a cognitive paradigm (i.e., stimulus-cognition-response) to competition. In contrast to previous research on competition, the important feature of this model is the cognitive emphasis on the organism as a mediator between stimulus and response.

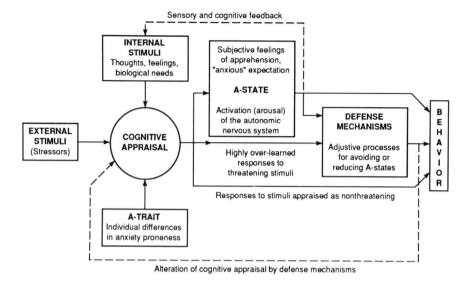

Figure 2.1. A trait-state conception of anxiety in which two anxiety concepts, A-trait and A-state, are posited and conceptually distinguished from the stimulus conditions that evoke A-state reactions and the defenses against A-states. It is hypothesized that the arousal of A-states involves a sequence of temporally ordered events in which a stimulus that is cognitively appraised as dangerous evokes an A-state reaction. This A-state reaction may then initiate a behavior sequence designed to avoid the danger situation, or it may evoke defensive maneuvers that alter the cognitive appraisal of the situation. Individual differences in A-trait determine the particular stimuli that are cognitively appraised as threatening. *Note.* From ''Theory and Research on Anxiety'' by C.D. Spielberger. In *Anxiety and Behavior* (p. 17) by C.D. Spielberger (Ed.), 1966, New York: Academic Press. Copyright 1966 by Academic Press. Adapted by permission.

The four components of this competition model are briefly described and discussed in relation to A-trait and A-state.

The Objective Competitive Situation

The initial element of the model is the *objective competitive situation* (OCS), which defines all the objective stimuli in the competitive process. The OCS specifies the type of task, the difficulty of opponents, the playing conditions and playing rules, and the available extrinsic rewards. In other words, the OCS specifies the environmental demand, or the *objective demand*. In the competitive process, the environmental demand is dictated by what the individual must do to obtain a favorable outcome when compared to a standard. The standard may include another individual's performance (an opponent), an idealized performance level, or the

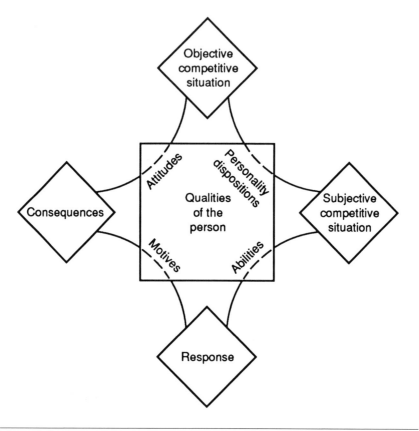

Figure 2.2.   The competitive process. *Note*. From Martens (1975a, p.69).

individual's own past performance. Moreover, criteria defining the conditions under which such a comparison is to be made are clearly specified to include "[a situation] in which the comparison of an individual's performance is made with some standard in the presence of at least one other person who is aware of the criterion for comparison and can evaluate the comparison process" (Martens, 1976, p. 14). It is important to recognize that this definition specifies only the minimal requirements of an OCS.

Because the OCS defines the environmental demands for the person, it is this physical and social environment that may or may not contain sources of threat (perception of danger). The competitive process is an evaluative situation, and most research concerned with the antecedents of A-state have found evaluative situations to be potentially threatening. A number of researchers have suggested that both fear of failure and fear of physical harm are prevalent sources of A-state in competitive sport. Although Spielberger (1972a) has concluded that the former is more threatening than is the latter, no empirical evidence supports this position. In competitive sport, some of the specific elements of the OCS that may affect A-state include the nature of the competitive task, the conditions under which that task must be performed, the ability of performers and their opponents, the available rewards, and the presence of significant others.

The Subjective Competitive Situation

How the person perceives, accepts, and appraises the OCS is termed the *subjective competitive situation* (SCS). The SCS is mediated by such factors as personality dispositions, attitudes and abilities, and other intrapersonal factors. Most studies of the competitive process have assumed that the OCS is perceived identically by everyone, although common sense suggests that this assumption is unfounded. To improve our understanding of how people behave in competitive situations, we must understand differences in how they perceive the same situation. Because the SCS describes a process that occurs within the person, it cannot be directly measured and can be inferred only from other behavioral indices. Competitive A-trait is one important personality predisposition that is hypothesized to affect the SCS. Competitive A-trait is an indicator of a person's tendency to perceive OCS's as threatening or nonthreatening.

Response

How a person responds to the OCS is largely determined by the SCS. Individuals can respond at three levels: behavioral responses such as performing well, physiological responses such as increased palmar sweating, and psychological responses such as increased A-state as measured by the CSAI-2.

Consequences

In competition, the consequences are frequently viewed in terms of success and failure, and success is normally perceived as a positive consequence and failure as a negative one. Understanding an individual's history of participation consequences in previous competitive situations helps determine whether a person approaches or avoids subsequent competition. In large part, the accumulated consequences of participation in the competitive process are thought to determine individual differences in competitive A-trait.

APPLYING THE COMPETITIVE PROCESS MODEL TO COMPETITIVE ANXIETY

This general model may be adapted to the specific study of competitive anxiety as illustrated in Figure 2.3. Competitive A-trait is shown as a personality variable that directly affects the perception of threat, which mediates A-state responses to the OCS.

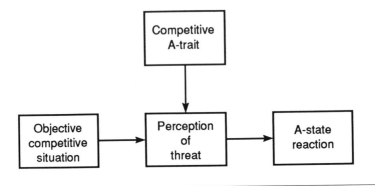

Figure 2.3.   Competitive A-trait as a mediator between competitive stimulus and response.

SUMMARY

This approach to the study and measurement of A-trait in sport is based on the interactional paradigm, the situation specificity of personality characteristics, the distinction between personality traits and states, and the conceptualization of competition as a social evaluation process. Competitive A-trait is the sport-specific modification of the more general A-trait construct and is defined as a tendency to perceive competitive situations as threatening and to respond to these situations with A-state. These developments provide a theoretical basis for the development of SCAT as a measure of competitive A-trait. The accumulated evidence clearly supports the value of measuring trait anxiety specific to competition.

Chapter 3

Development of SCAT

Competitive A-trait is a construct that describes individual differences in (a) perception of threat, (b) A-state response to perceived threat, or (c) both. Thus, individuals differ in their tendency to perceive competitive situations as threatening, in the intensity of A-state reactions they have to these situations, or in both. SCAT was developed for the purpose of providing a reliable and valid measure of competitive A-trait. In this chapter, the development of SCAT is described as is evidence of SCAT's reliability and content and concurrent validity.

SCAT was initially developed, following guidelines outlined in the American Psychological Association's (1974) *Standards for Educational and Psychological Tests and Manuals*, for use with children between the ages of 10 and 15 years. Shortly after this initial version of SCAT was developed, an adult form of the inventory was constructed. These two forms of SCAT are identical except for the instructions and one word of one question. The internal structure, reliability, and validity of SCAT were determined independently for the child and the adult forms on the basis of responses from more than 2,500 athletes.

PLANNING THE INVENTORY

The initial step in developing SCAT was to specify clearly what the inventory was designed to measure (see chapter 2). Next, the format of SCAT was established on the basis of several criteria that were deemed desirable: (a) an objective rather than a projective scale, (b) minimal response bias, (c) unambiguous administration procedures, (d) a short completion time, and (e) easy scoring procedures. Specifically, the format chosen for both the child and the adult forms of SCAT was one adopted by Spielberger (1973) for the State-Trait Anxiety Inventory for Children (STAIC). The inventory is self-administered, and responses on each item are rated on 3-point Likert scales and range from 1 (hardly ever) to 3 (often).

The reactivity of assessing anxiety was a major concern in selecting the inventory format. So that response bias could be minimized, the inventory was not referred to as an anxiety scale, and several spurious items were included to direct attention to other elements of competition. Although the problem of response bias cannot be eliminated, the format used for SCAT had been shown to be minimally affected by response sets when some of the test items were reversed (Smith, 1969; Spielberger, Gorsuch, & Lushene, 1970). Moreover, it was not deemed appropriate to develop social desirability or lie scales in conjunction with the inventory because these scales suffer from the same weakness that they supposedly detect.

ITEM SELECTION

Two criteria were employed in developing a pool of items for assessing competitive A-trait. First, the item needed to be understood by persons taking the inventory. Second, the item needed to have face validity for measuring competitive A-trait. Initially, a pool of 75 items was generated by modifying items from Taylor's (1953) Manifest Anxiety Scale, Spielberger's (1973) STAIC, and Sarason et al.'s (1960) General Anxiety Scales and by composing items especially for the new inventory.

Six judges rated the 75 items on face or content validity and clarity of sentence structure. Items failing to meet selection criteria were eliminated, although some of the retained items were slightly modified to eliminate ambiguity. The 21 items retained from the original item pool and the 9 spurious items were then labeled Version 1 of SCAT.

Version 1

Version 1 was initially administered to 193 male junior high school students in three suburban Chicago schools. Subjects ranged in age from 12 to 15 years and were largely from white, middle-class families. Item discrimination of Version 1 was assessed by computing

- item analyses,
- triserial correlations, and
- discriminant analyses.

Item analyses were computed according to Magnusson's (1966) method for differences between extreme groups. After the upper and lower 27% of the total score distribution were separated, analyses compared the proportion of individuals in each extreme group who answered the item consistent with their total test scores to those who responded to the item opposite to their total test scores. A nomograph was then used to obtain a correlation coefficient between individual items and the total test scores for both upper ($n = 52$) and lower ($n = 52$) extremes. Within the item analyses, two selection criteria for items were established. For inclusion in the scale, an item was required to have a correlation coefficient of .40 with the total test scores for the upper extreme subsample and a correlation coefficient of .40 with the total test scores for the lower extreme subsample. Not only was this criterion more rigorous than the .20 to .30 acceptance level frequently employed, but applying this criterion to both the high and the low SCAT groups insured that each item was sensitive to measuring both A-trait extremes, a characteristic absent in many psychological inventories.

The second selection criterion was triserial correlations computed according to procedures described by Jaspen (1946) and designed to ensure the homogeneity of the inventory. A triserial correlation was used because SCAT scores were considered a continuous variable, whereas responses to individual items were forced into a trichotomy (i.e., hardly ever, sometimes, often). Triserial correlations of at least .40 between individual items and the total SCAT score were necessary for item acceptance.

Finally, discriminant analysis was used to determine the discriminating power of each item while controlling for the correlations between items. Subjects in the upper and the lower thirds of the distribution of SCAT scores were assigned to high A-trait and low A-trait groups, and a discriminant analysis was computed to determine individual items that best discriminated between these two extreme groups. Discriminant function coefficients of at least 0.90 were required for item inclusion.

The results of these three types of analyses yielded fairly consistent patterns for each item. Ten of the 21 items met all selection criteria, and 4 other items met 3 of the 4. On the basis of this composite picture of each item, the 14 most discriminating items were retained for Version 2.

Version 2

The 14 items constituting Version 2 demonstrated the following characteristics: (a) a mean item analysis coefficient of .65 for high SCAT respondents and .54 for low SCAT respondents, (b) a mean triserial correlation coefficient of .61, and (c) a mean discriminant function coefficient of 1.64.

Version 2, consisting of the 14 accepted items and 7 spurious items, was then administered to two additional samples: junior high school males living in Brockport, New York, and junior high school males living in suburban Chicago. Item analyses, triserial correlations, and discriminant analyses were then computed on the responses of the combined samples ($N = 175$). Ten items met all selection criteria except for two items that demonstrated slightly lower discriminant function coefficients. These 10 items were selected with 5 spurious items to constitute Version 3 of SCAT.

Version 3

For the 10 items constituting Version 3, summary statistics revealed mean item analysis coefficients of .64 for the high competitive A-trait respondents and .58 for the low A-trait performers, a mean triserial correlation coefficient of .68, and a mean discriminant function coefficient of 1.39.

Version 3 of SCAT was then administered to two more samples: 106 male and female fifth- and sixth-grade students (ages 10 to 13) in Hutchinson, Kansas, and 98 male and female junior high school students (ages 12 to 15) in the same city. Item analyses, triserial correlations, and discriminant analyses were again computed separately on each sample. The results of these analyses are summarized in Table 3.1. All 10 items in Version 3 satisfied acceptance criteria. A summary of the statistical attributes of the child form of SCAT (hereafter SCAT-C) for Versions 1 through 3 combined are shown in Table 3.1.

Table 3.1 Mean Coefficients for Version 3 and All 10 Test Items Combined From Versions 1 Through 3

Coefficient	5th and 6th graders ($N=106$) (Version 3)	Junior high school ($N=98$) (Version 3)	10 accepted items (Versions 1-3)
Item analysis			
High competitive A-trait	.65	.48	.59
Low competitive A-trait	.57	.79	.66
Triserial correlation	.69	.68	.68
Discriminant analysis	1.11	1.18	1.36

SCAT for Adults

SCAT-C was modified for use with adult samples (hereafter SCAT-A) by making two simple changes: (a) modifying the instructions so they were appropriate for adults and (b) changing one word on one item. SCAT-A was given to 153 male and female university students to assess its item discriminability. Results confirmed that all items exceeded selection criteria, and summary statistics revealed the following characteristics for SCAT-A:

- Mean item analysis coefficients of .61 for high SCAT ($n = 42$) and of .67 for low SCAT ($n = 42$) groups
- A mean triserial correlation coefficient of .64
- A mean discriminant function coefficient of 1.01

Moreover, for the modified item (Number 8 on the inventory), the item analysis coefficient was .52 for low and .57 for high competitive A-trait subjects.

On the basis of these consistent item discrimination results, it was judged that Version 3 of SCAT-C and SCAT-A was sufficiently promising to investigate its reliability and concurrent validity.

RELIABILITY

SCAT's reliability was assessed by test-retest and analysis of variance (ANOVA) techniques. The test-retest reliability of SCAT-C was assessed for four samples of boys and girls, Grades 5 to 6 and 8 to 9, from the Champaign-Urbana, Illinois, public schools. Each sample completed SCAT-C and then was retested at one of four subsequent time intervals: 1 hour, 1 day, 1 week, and 1 month. As shown in Table 3.2, test-retest reliability ranged from .57 to .93 with a mean of .77 for all samples combined. These are acceptable levels of test-retest reliability.

The test-retest reliability procedure always contains some unknown reactivity because subjects invariably recall taking the inventory previously. This reactivity increases the error variance, thus affecting the correlation coefficient. Consequently, obtaining another estimate of reliability through ANOVA procedures that do not require a retest was deemed appropriate. ANOVA reliability was computed using procedures outlined by Kerlinger (1973). This technique calculates the variance between items on the inventory, the variance between individuals (V_{ind}), and the residual, or error, variance (V_e). It then computes the reliability coefficient using the following formula:

$$r_{tt} = \frac{V_{ind} - V_e}{V_{ind}}$$

ANOVA reliability was computed on responses to the initial administration of SCAT-C for the samples used to assess test-retest reliability. These results, summarized in Table 3.3, indicate that ANOVA reliability coefficients (mean $r = .81$) for the combined samples were slightly higher than the reliability coefficients obtained using test-retest procedures. Additionally, an even higher ANOVA reliability coefficient ($r = .85$) was obtained for SCAT-A with subjects used for item analyses.

INTERNAL CONSISTENCY

Internal consistency is concerned with the homogeneity of scale items. Evidence of internal consistency is demonstrated in part by both the item analysis correlations and the triserial correlations that assessed the relationship of each item with the total test score. These correlations were uniformly high for both high and low SCAT subjects across the various samples. A more direct means for determining the homogeneity of SCAT is to compute a Kuder-Richardson formula 20 (KR-20) coefficient from the correlation matrix among the 10 inventory items.

Internal consistency results for the four SCAT-C samples that were used to determine item discriminability of Version 3 and two SCAT-A samples of University of Illinois undergraduates are summarized in Table 3.4. The KR-20

Table 3.2   Test-Retest Reliability for Four Samples and Four Time Intervals for SCAT-C

Sample	1-hour retest				1-day retest				1-week retest				1-month retest			
	r	n	T_1	T_2	r	n	T_1	T_2	r	n	T_1	T_2	r	n	T_1	T_2
Grades 5 and 6																
Male																
M	.90	35	18.89	18.86	.61	35	18.89	18.20	.74	31	18.97	18.94	.65	55	17.69	18.51
SD			4.43	5.03			4.43	5.00			4.06	5.04			4.24	4.15
Female																
M	.85	49	20.22	19.14	.71	43	19.93	18.88	.87	26	19.62	19.19	.73	29	20.59	19.83
SD			4.72	4.51			3.97	4.61			4.41	4.53			3.60	4.33
Grades 8 and 9																
Male																
M	.85	31	18.35	17.23	.78	39	18.82	17.28	.80	36	18.19	17.86	.66	37	19.11	18.30
SD			5.32	5.00			4.15	4.41			4.34	4.64			4.58	4.22
Female																
M	.93	38	20.47	20.21	.80	34	21.44	21.24	.57	34	22.44	21.38	.82	34	18.76	18.00
SD			4.95	5.22			5.29	5.62			4.67	4.85			4.81	4.89
Combined r over samples	.88				.73				.75				.72			

Note. Combined r over samples and time = .77.

Table 3.3   Reliability Through ANOVA for SCAT-C

Sample	1 hour	1 day	1 week	1 month	Combined
Grades 5 and 6					
Males	.81	.79	.71	.81	.78
Females	.80	.73	.79	.68	.75
Grades 8 and 9					
Males	.89	.80	.83	.84	.84
Females	.87	.89	.87	.89	.88
Combined	.84	.80	.80	.80	.81

Table 3.4   Internal Consistency of SCAT

Sample	Form	N	Mean interitem correlation	KR-20 coefficient
Grades 5 and 6; males and females from Kansas	C	98	.32	.96
Grades 7-9; males and females from Kansas	C	105	.32	.95
Grades 5-9; males from Illinois	C	299	.30	.95
Grades 5-9; females from Illinois	C	287	.33	.96
University undergraduate females	A	121	.35	.97
University undergraduate males	A	147	.30	.95

coefficients ranged from .95 to .97 for both SCAT-A and SCAT-C, demonstrating a high degree of internal consistency.

VALIDITY

Although psychometricians have suggested that new psychological inventories must demonstrate a plethora of specific types of validity, consensus suggests that it is most important for new inventories to demonstrate content, concurrent, predictive, and construct validity. Although evidence reviewed in the previous section demonstrated that SCAT was reliable and that reliability is essential for an inventory to be valid, reliability does not ensure validity. The fundamental purpose of the following section is to demonstrate SCAT's content and concurrent validity. Evidence for the predictive and construct validity of SCAT is presented in chapters 4 and 6.

Content Validity

Content (or face) validity essentially refers to expert judgment about the representativeness of SCAT items for measuring competitive A-trait. In the initial construction of SCAT, 75 items were modified for sport competition from standard A-trait scales or were developed by the author specifically for SCAT. Six judges assessed these 75 items for content validity and grammatical clarity. Each of the judges were qualified researchers in sport psychology or motor learning and had either conducted research on anxiety in sport or were known to be knowledgeable on this topic. Item evaluation was facilitated by providing each expert with a concise statement of the purpose of the inventory (i.e., a summary of chapter 2), a list of the 75 items to be rated for content validity on a 1-7 scale, and a yes-no response on each item's grammatical clarity. With two exceptions, only those items that all judges rated as having high content validity (i.e., a score of 6 or 7 from each expert) and being grammatically clear were retained in the item pool. The two exceptions were items that required only minor grammatical changes. Of the 10 items in SCAT-C, all received a mean content validity rating of 6.5 or higher. The one modified item for SCAT-A was not content analyzed.

Concurrent Validity

The American Psychological Association's (1974) *Standards for Educational and Psychological Tests* recommends that self-report inventories be first validated by demonstrating concurrent validity with previously validated scales. Thus, concurrent validity is determined by correlating SCAT with other personality constructs to assess how well empirical relationships match theoretical predictions. Thus, concurrent validity is inferred when a new inventory is convergent with or divergent from theoretically predicted relationships with previously validated inventories.

The concurrent validity of SCAT was examined by investigating relationships between SCAT and four general A-trait inventories and five selected personality inventories that should demonstrate predictable relationships with A-trait.

General A-Trait Inventories

The three general A-trait anxiety inventories used to assess the concurrent validity of SCAT-C included the Children's Manifest Anxiety Scale Short Form (CMAS) (Levy, 1958), the General Anxiety Scale for Children (GASC) (Sarason et al., 1960), and the Trait Anxiety Inventory for Children (TAIC) (Spielberger, 1973). The Trait Anxiety Inventory for Adults (TAI) (Spielberger et al., 1970) was used to determine the concurrent validity of SCAT-A. Separate samples were used to determine SCAT's relationship with each of these general anxiety scales.

A situation-specific A-trait scale such as SCAT was expected to yield low to moderate positive correlations with nonspecific anxiety inventories. High correlations between SCAT and general anxiety scales would indicate that SCAT was measuring the same anxiety construct that general anxiety scales were, thus revealing that SCAT has no unique purpose. Low correlations between SCAT and general anxiety inventories would indicate that SCAT was totally unrelated to general anxiety, making the validity of SCAT questionable. Thus, moderate correlations demonstrated sufficient convergence to infer that similar constructs were being measured yet enough divergence to warrant the development of the new scale.

As shown in Table 3.5, these data conform with theoretical predictions by demonstrating low to moderate positive correlations with these general anxiety scales. Given that the test-retest reliability of SCAT produced correlation coefficients of .70 to .90 and that general A-trait scales when correlated with one another yielded correlation coefficients of .50 to .60, correlation coefficients of .28 to .46 between general A-trait scales and a sport-specific A-trait scale clearly support the concurrent validity of SCAT-A and SCAT-C.

Table 3.5   Correlation Coefficients of SCAT With Other Anxiety Scales

Scale	Sample	Form	Anxiety scales		SCAT		r
			M	*SD*	*M*	*SD*	
CMAS Short Form (*N*=95)	Grades 7-9; males and females from Kansas	C	4.32	2.12	19.23	4.78	.28
GASC (*N*=75)	Grades 7-9; males from Chicago	C	21.29	6.47	18.51	5.48	.46
TAIC (*N*=105)	Grades 7-9; males and females from Kansas	C	42.64	6.12	18.10	4.57	.46
TAIA (*N*=153)	University of Illinois undergraduate males and females	A	43.81	5.91	20.92	5.55	.44

Selected General Personality Inventories

Three additional concurrent validation studies were conducted that examined the relationship between SCAT and each of the following anxiety-related general personality inventories: (a) the Junior-Senior High School Personality

Questionnaire (HSPQ) (Cattell & Cattell, 1969), (b) the Social Avoidance and Distress Scale (SAD) and the Fear of Negative Evaluation Scale (FNE) (Watson & Friend, 1969), (c) the Internal-External Control Scale for children (Bialer, 1961), and (d) the Mehrabian achievement motivation scale (Mehrabian, 1968).

HSPQ. SCAT-A and the HSPQ were given to both male and female high school students in Moline, Illinois. The correlation coefficients between SCAT and each of the 14 primary factors of the HSPQ were computed using the standard scores for each variable. The relationship between SCAT and the second-order factor Anxiety (Q_{II}) was also computed.

Five of the 14 primary factors and the Q_{II} secondary factor of the HSPQ seem to be theoretically related to anxiety. As shown in Table 3.6, each of these anxiety-related factors demonstrated a significant relationship with SCAT, whereas the remaining factors were unrelated to SCAT.

Relationships between SCAT and each of these six HSPQ factors clearly supported theoretical predictions. Factor D measured excitability and Factor Q_4 tenseness, and both clearly contained elements of anxiety. As predicted, these factors showed moderate positive relationships with SCAT for both males and females.

Table 3.6   Relationship Between SCAT-A and the HSPQ

Factor	Label	Males (N=58)			Females (N=98)		
		M	SD	r	M	SD	r
Sizothymia-affectothymia (reserved-warmhearted)	A	10.12	3.32	−.15	10.03	3.12	−.17
Intelligence	B	7.26	2.14	−.04	7.47	1.49	.10
Ego strength[a]	C	10.59	3.46	−.33	7.95	3.56	−.41
Phlegmatic temperament-excitability[a]	D	8.76	3.31	.36	10.12	3.11	.30
Submissiveness-dominant	E	10.78	2.82	−.14	8.41	2.78	−.16
Desurgency-surgency	F	10.98	3.29	.00	9.27	3.74	−.16
Superego strength	G	9.79	3.51	−.10	10.40	2.85	.02
Threctia-parmia (shy-bold)[a]	H	10.17	3.14	−.38	9.61	3.52	−.07
Harria-premsia (tough-tenderminded)	I	7.64	3.83	.10	13.91	3.23	.22
Zeppia-coasthenia (zestful-reflective)	J	9.94	2.60	.07	8.60	3.19	−.09
Untroubled adequacy-guilt proneness[a]	O	8.78	2.94	.15	9.38	3.12	.23
Group dependency–self-sufficiency	Q_2	9.98	3.54	−.03	9.27	3.47	.05
Self-sentiment (lax-exacting)	Q_3	8.79	2.99	−.10	10.29	3.07	−.05
Ergic tension (relaxed-tense)[a]	Q_4	9.29	3.68	.32	9.88	3.22	.41
Anxiety (second-order factor)[a]	Q_{II}	. . .	. . .	.37	. . .	. . .	.36
SCAT		19.53	4.14		21.64	5.19	

[a]Anxiety-related items.

Factor C revealed a moderate negative relationship with SCAT, confirming the predicted link between high SCAT respondents and subjects characterized by Factor C as affected by feelings, emotionally less stable, easily upset, and changeable. Factor H also generally conformed with theoretical predictions, demonstrating a substantial negative correlation with SCAT for males but only a small negative correlation for females. Thus, individuals characterized by Factor H as shy, withdrawn, emotionally cautious, and quick to see danger tend to score high on SCAT. Moreover, these data further revealed that Factor O had a low but positive relationship with SCAT for males and a slightly higher relationship for females. Thus, subjects with high SCAT profiles tend to have a Factor O profile that characterizes them as apprehensive, self-reproaching, insecure, worried, and troubled. Finally, the second-order anxiety factor (Q_{II}) was positively related to SCAT as well. It should be noted, however, that although each of the factors in the HSPQ that contained some element of anxiety correlated significantly with SCAT, the correlation coefficients were not as large as would be predicted.

SAD and FNE.   SCAT-C, the SAD, and the FNE were given to junior high school students from Moline, Illinois. The SAD measures the tendency to avoid being with, talking to, or personally interacting with other people. The FNE measures "apprehension about others' evaluations, distress over negative evaluations, avoidance of evaluative situations, and the expectations that others would evaluate oneself negatively'' (Watson & Friend, 1969, p. 449). Thus, these two scales assess individual dispositions to becoming anxious in social situations. Consequently, it was predicted that these two scales would demonstrate low to moderate positive correlations with SCAT. As shown in Table 3.7, this prediction is supported for females but not for males. There is no apparent reason for the substantial discrepancy in relationships obtained for the male and the female samples, particularly in light of the absence of gender differences among other samples.

Table 3.7   Correlation Coefficients Between SCAT-C and Three Personality Dispositions

Personality disposition	Males				Females			
	N	M	SD	r	N	M	SD	r
Fear of negative evaluation	50	13.92	4.88		43	16.95	6.53	
With SCAT-C		19.86	4.30	.10		21.20	4.38	.36
Social avoidance and distress	50	11.86	4.85		43	11.05	6.30	
With SCAT-C		19.86	4.30	.11		21.20	4.38	.46
Internal-external control	41	38.17	2.33		49	38.08	2.59	
With SCAT-C		19.17	4.41	−.32		21.20	4.29	−.37

Internal-External Control. SCAT-C and the Internal-External Control Scale for children were given to another junior high school sample from Moline, Illinois. Bialer's (1961) scale was developed to measure the degree to which children perceive personal control or responsibility for the outcome of events in their environment. Those students high in internal control perceive that they are generally responsible for personal outcomes, whereas those high in external control perceive that outcomes are controlled by others or are due to luck or chance. The moderate negative relationship between SCAT and internal-external control obtained in this study was consistent with theoretical predictions (see Table 3.7). Those individuals not perceiving control over outcomes tend to become more anxious (high SCAT) in competitive situations in which the uncertainty of outcomes is high, whereas individuals perceiving high control are less anxious (low SCAT) because they have confidence that they can obtain positive outcomes.

Mehrabian Achievement Motivation Scale. The Mehrabian (1968) achievement motivation scale was administered to four samples: male 9th and 10th graders, female 9th and 10th graders (both groups coming from the Moline, Illinois, public schools), undergraduate males from the University of Illinois, and female athletes from five volleyball teams that participated in the 1974 Illinois intercollegiate volleyball tournament. The first two samples responded to SCAT-C and the latter samples to SCAT-A. Samples 1 and 3 completed the male version of the achievement motivation scale, whereas Samples 2 and 4 completed the female version.

Mehrabian's operationalization of achievement motivation is clearly related to anxiety because persons scoring high on the inventory (i.e., high achievers) have a stronger motive to achieve success relative to their motive to avoid failure, whereas low achievers demonstrate the opposite tendency.

In applications of achievement motivation theory (Atkinson & Feather, 1966), Sarason's test anxiety scale has been used as an index of fear of failure. Because test anxiety would be expected to be moderately related to competitive anxiety, it may be predicted that persons scoring high on SCAT would demonstrate a significant negative relationship with low achievement motivation as measured by Mehrabian's scale. This prediction, however, is theoretically incorrect. The test anxiety scale measures only the strength of the motive to avoid failure and does not assess the strength of the motive to achieve success. Those persons scoring low in achievement motivation on Mehrabian's scale are both high in the fear of failure and low in the motive to achieve success, whereas persons high in achievement motivation are low in the fear of failure and high in the motive to achieve success. Nevertheless, it is equally possible to be low or high in both dimensions of achievement motivation; consequently, fear of failure may be obscured in overall resultant achievement motivation by the influence of the motive to achieve success. Thus, it was expected that resultant achievement motivation would be unrelated to SCAT.

Data shown in Table 3.8 confirm this hypothesis. Results from these four samples give no indication that high competitive A-trait individuals are more or less motivated to achieve than are low competitive A-trait individuals.

Table 3.8   Correlation Coefficients Between SCAT and Achievement Motivation

Sample (SCAT form)	N	M	SD	r
Male 9th and 10th graders (SCAT-C)	66	103.20	16.30	
		19.97	4.31	.15
Female 9th and 10th graders (SCAT-C)	50	101.80	13.20	
		20.30	4.28	.02
University undergraduate males (SCAT-A)	155	109.06	13.45	
		19.64	4.38	−.11
Female volleyball players (SCAT-A)	52	104.04	12.46	
		20.27	4.41	−.07

Conclusions Regarding Concurrent Validity

In summary, the concurrent validation research just reviewed has determined the relationship between SCAT and certain selected personality dispositions to assess whether competitive A-trait fits into the constellation of other personality dispositions consistent with theoretical predictions. With only minor exceptions, the accumulated evidence firmly supports SCAT's concurrent validity. SCAT was moderately related to general anxiety scales and to those factors on the HSPQ that contain some dimension of anxiety. Moreover, the relationships observed between SCAT and the FNE, the SAD, the internal-external control, and the achievement motivation inventories were consistent with the hypotheses with two exceptions: Both the FNE and the SAD correlated very weakly with SCAT among males, although the relationship was much stronger for females. No explanations are apparent for these findings.

SUMMARY

The development of SCAT followed guidelines set by the American Psychological Association for the development of psychological inventories. Initial phases included inventory planning, item selection, content validation by expert judges, and four different types of item analyses. These initial analyses yielded an adult form of SCAT (SCAT-A) to be used with subjects 15 years and older and a children's form of SCAT (SCAT-C) to be used with subjects between 10 and 14 years of age. Support for the reliability and internal consistency of SCAT was obtained using test-retest, ANOVA, and KR-20 analyses. Evidence for the concurrent validity of SCAT was obtained by demonstrating significant relationships between competitive A-trait as measured by SCAT and other personality constructs in accordance with theoretical predictions.

Chapter 4

Construct Validation of SCAT

The most important step in the development of SCAT is to demonstrate the inventory's construct validity. This is demonstrated by an accumulation of evidence that competitive A-trait, as operationalized by SCAT, is related to other constructs consistent with theoretical predictions. Thus, construct validity carefully marshals evidence demonstrating that SCAT really measures competitive A-trait, the construct it purports to measure.

CONSTRUCT VALIDATION MODEL

Much of the evidence for the construct validation of SCAT is derived from demonstrating that SCAT predicts A-state in competitive situations in accordance with theoretical expectations. It may appear that construct validity is simply predictive validity. A subtle difference, however, exists between construct and predictive validity and is illustrated in the model developed for the construct validation of SCAT in Figure 4.1.

In Figure 4.1, the theoretical constructs and their relationships are shown above the broken line and the relevant operational definitions of these constructs and their relationships below the broken line. The theoretical relationship between competitive A-trait and A-state is shown as Link 1. As discussed in chapter 2, individuals high in competitive A-trait are expected to perceive more competitive situations as threatening, perceive greater degrees of threat in competitive situations and hence respond with higher levels of A-state, or both. No difference in A-state is predicted between high and low competitive A-trait persons in noncompetitive situations.

Construct validity for SCAT is determined by examining Link 3 through the assessment of the relationship shown in Link 4. Predictive validity is represented by Link 4 (the operational level of Link 1), and construct validity is shown as Link 3 (the linkage between the theoretical construct and its operationalization). To the extent that Link 4 is supported (i.e., SCAT predicts A-state), it is possible

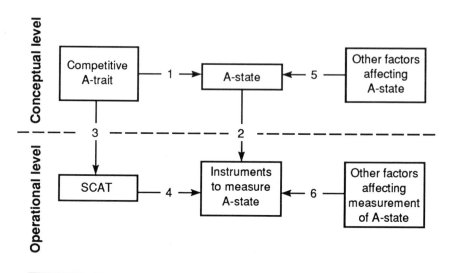

Figure 4.1.   Construct validation model for SCAT.

to infer construct validity, assuming that Links 1 and 2 are valid and Links 5 and 6 properly controlled. In any validation process, it is necessary to make assumptions about the validity of some links in order to test other links. In this model the assumption that Links 1 and 2 are valid is based on previous experimental evidence. Spielberger et al. (1970) and Spielberger (1972a) summarized substantial research evidence showing that Link 1 is valid for general A-trait and that Spielberger's A-state inventory is a valid method of assessing A-state (Link 2). It is assumed here that Link 1 is equally valid for competitive A-trait (see discussion in chapter 2).

The factors shown to affect A-state and its measurement (Links 5 and 6) must be controlled or systematically manipulated in empirical testing. Factors affecting Link 5 include all environmental conditions that may change A-state, for example, the presence of evaluative others, failure, and unanticipated changes in routine. Factors affecting Link 6 include such measurement artifacts as recording errors, response sets, social desirability, acquiescence, and insensitivity of instrumentation.

In demonstrating the construct validity of SCAT, Link 4 can be tested in a number of ways. The original validation of SCAT was based on testing six specific theoretical predictions from the model:

- High SCAT subjects will manifest higher A-state than will low SCAT subjects in competitive but not in noncompetitive situations.
- SCAT will predict precompetitive but not noncompetitive A-state better than will other person, task, and situation variables.
- SCAT will correlate more strongly with A-state in competitive than in noncompetitive situations.

- SCAT will correlate more strongly with competitive A-state as the level of situational threat increases.
- SCAT will predict competitive but not noncompetitive A-state better than will other A-trait measures.
- High SCAT subjects will perform poorer than will low SCAT subjects in competitive but not in noncompetitive situations.

ORIGINAL CONSTRUCT VALIDATION RESEARCH

Eleven experimental and field studies were originally conducted by Martens (1977) and his colleagues to assess the construct validity of SCAT by testing these six specific theoretical predictions. Although these studies were reported in some detail in the original SCAT monograph, this section briefly reviews the findings of these 11 studies as the basis for SCAT's original construct validity. Subsequent research by other investigators is summarized that directly supports the construct validity of SCAT.

Impact of A-Trait Level on Competitive A-State

The first two original construct validation studies were carried out in a contrived competitive situation to determine whether differences in A-trait would lead to differential levels of A-state by examining the observed relationship between their two operational constructs: SCAT and Spielberger et al.'s (1970) STAI. The major hypothesis of these studies was that high SCAT performers would manifest higher A-state than would low SCAT performers in stressful competitive situations.

Study 1

As part of her doctoral dissertation, Scanlan (1975) administered SCAT to 306 10- to 12-year-old males in a baseline condition. Forty-one high and 42 low SCAT subjects, constituting the upper and the lower quartiles of the distribution of SCAT-C scores, were selected and randomly assigned to three success-failure conditions: a success condition (i.e., won 80% of their matches), a neutral condition (i.e., won 50% of their matches), and a failure condition (i.e., won 20% of their matches), yielding a SCAT × Success-Failure (2 × 3) factorial design. A-state was assessed by Spielberger's State Anxiety Inventory for Children (SAIC) scale at four time intervals during the experiment: (a) baseline before testing, (b) precompetition, (c) postcompetition, and (d) postdebriefing. Several weeks after the initial selection, subjects were brought to a mobile van in the school parking lot, where they competed on a complex motor maze for 20 contests. Subjects were cleverly deceived into believing that they were competing against an opponent who was performing the same task under similar circumstances at another school with ongoing performance comparisons provided by means of a computer hookup.

Success-failure was manipulated by the experimenter and evaluation potential maximized through instructions, knowledge of results, and attributional emphasis.

The impact of subjects' levels of A-trait and success-failure histories on their subsequent A-states was assessed by means of a 2 × 3 ANOVA with A-state difference scores the dependent variable. Although the SCAT main effect was nonsignificant, the interaction effect for the SCAT × A-state repeated measures ANOVA was significant $F(2, 156) = 4.88, p < .01$, indicating that high SCAT subjects had a somewhat larger ($p < .10$) increase in A-state scores precompetitively than did low SCAT subjects, whereas postdebriefing high SCAT subjects showed a somewhat greater ($p < .10$) reduction in A-state than did low SCAT subjects. Moreover, success-failure manipulations had the expected impact on performers' A-states. As predicted, subjects in the failure condition exhibited a significantly greater increase in A-state than did subjects in the success or neutral conditions. In summary, differences in A-trait in this investigation generally yielded expected differences in A-state, although these findings only approached statistical significance. Moreover, subjects' A-states were higher in the threatening failure conditions than they were in the success or neutral conditions.

Study 2

Martens and Gill (1976) replicated and extended the findings in Study 1 by adding a gender factor and a fourth, no-competition control (NC) success-failure condition, yielding a Gender × SCAT × Success-Failure (2 × 2 × 4) factorial design. Similar experimental procedures were employed, first administering SCAT-C to 490 male and female 10- to 12-year-olds and then selecting 45 males and 45 females who scored in the upper quarter of the SCAT-C distribution and a similar number of low SCAT males and females to compete in the bogus motor maze competition. An equal number of subjects of each gender were then randomly assigned to the four success-failure groups. A-state was assessed by the SAIC at four time periods: (a) basal several weeks before competition, (b) precompetition, (c) midcompetition, and (d) postcompetition. All the remaining procedures were identical to Study 1.

Data were analyzed using multivariate analysis of covariance, with the initial A-state measure as the covariate and the three subsequent measures of A-state as dependent variables. The results revealed significant main effects for SCAT, $F(3, 77) = 3.04, p < .04$, and for success-failure, $F(9, 187.55) = 4.50, p < .0001$, across pre-, mid-, and postcompetition A-states. Univariate analyses of variance and discriminant function analyses showed that high SCAT subjects were higher in A-state than were low SCAT subjects, particularly for pre- and midcompetition A-states. The adjusted means for these conditions are shown in Table 4.1.

Success-failure results also demonstrated expected relationships. For mid- and postcompetition measures, A-states increased linearly with increased failure. Gender and interaction effects were nonsignificant. Overall, Study 2 provided

Table 4.1   Study 2: Adjusted Means for Low and High SCAT Subjects for Pre-, Mid-, and Postcompetition A-States

SCAT level	Precompetition	Midcompetition	Postcompetition
Low	30.17	30.55	28.37
High	32.83	35.30	30.88

consistent theoretical support for the construct validity of SCAT by demonstrating that (a) high SCAT subjects manifested higher levels of A-state than did low SCAT subjects during competitive but not noncompetitive situations and (b) A-states increased as threat increased, particularly during and after competition.

Prediction of A-State: SCAT Versus Other Variables

Gill and Martens (1977) designed Study 3 to evaluate the construct validity of SCAT by assessing how well SCAT could directly predict A-state compared to other person, task, and situation variables in competitive versus noncompetitive situations.

Study 3

Ninety-six fifth- and sixth-grade boys and girls were selected as subjects to represent equally the full range of SCAT-C scores. Each subject was paired with another subject of similar grade and gender, and this two-person team then competed in 20 contests on the complex motor maze. Half the teams were assigned to a so-called conjunctive scoring system, in which the poorer of the two partners' scores was used as the team score; the remaining teams used a so-called disjunctive scoring system, in which the better of the two partners' score was selected. The 24 teams assigned to each scoring system were then randomly assigned to one of three success-failure conditions: success (i.e., win 80% of their matches), failure (i.e., win 20% of their matches), or a no-competition control. A-state was assessed by the SAIC at four time intervals during the experiment: (a) basal, (b) precompetition, (c) midcompetition, and (d) postcompetition.

Multiple regression analyses were employed to predict A-state scores at each of the four time intervals, using SCAT, gender, task type, and success-failure condition as predictor variables. Significant F ratios were obtained for each of the four regression analyses, and, somewhat surprisingly, SCAT was a significant predictor of A-state at each of the four time periods. SCAT was the only significant predictor of basal and precompetitive A-states, although, as predicted, success-failure became a more significant predictor than did SCAT for mid- and postcompetition A-states.

Similar multiple regression analyses were computed for Studies 1 and 2 to assess the validity of the results of Study 3. The data shown in Table 4.2 only partially confirm theoretical predictions. The results of Study 1 were highly consistent with predictions and demonstrated that SCAT was a significant predictor of precompetitive but not of basal or postcompetitive A-state.

Results of Studies 2 and 3 are more troublesome, however, because SCAT predicted not only pre- and midcompetition A-states but also noncompetitive and postcompetitive A-states. Theoretically, SCAT was developed to identify individuals responsive to competitive threat, a condition that should not be present in noncompetitive or postcompetitive situations. Although SCAT predicted pre- and midcompetition A-states substantially better than did noncompetitive or postcompetitive ones, these findings were unexpected. Nevertheless, recent research on the CSAI-2 would suggest a plausible explanation for these results (see Part III). Because SCAT predominantly measures somatic anxiety (i.e., autonomic arousal) and because participating in an experiment was probably arousing for these children, A-state was probably already elevated when baseline measures were taken, thus accounting for its significant relationship with SCAT. Moreover, heightened competitive arousal seems to take some time to dissipate (e.g., it is not uncommon for athletes to require several hours to "come down" after participating in a stressful competition). Thus, continued elevated arousal levels may have accounted for the significant relationship between SCAT and postcompetition A-state.

Competitive Versus Noncompetitive SCAT–A-State Relationships

Although the internal validity of Studies 1 through 3 was high, these lab studies offered little evidence of the external validity of the relationship between SCAT and A-state in competitive situations. Therefore, in an effort to maximize external validity in assessing the construct validity of SCAT, Martens and Simon (1976b) conducted three field studies to test the hypothesis that SCAT would be more significantly related to A-state in competitive than in noncompetitive situations.

Studies 4 and 5

The subjects in Study 4 were 52 players from five collegiate volleyball teams from the state of Illinois who were competing in the state tournament. Spielberger et al.'s (1970) State Anxiety Inventory (SAI) was employed to assess A-state at three different time periods: (a) baseline, (b) precompetition before a match in pool play, and (c) precompetition before a quarter- or semifinal match. Subjects from four teams completed baseline measures of the SAI and SCAT the evening before the tournament began, whereas players from the fifth team completed these measures the first day of the tournament several hours before their first match. Both precompetition SAI measures were obtained courtside immediately before the match.

Table 4.2 Studies 1 Through 3: Summary of Multiple Regression Results

	Dependent variables											
Standardized regression coefficients	Initial			Precompetition			Midcompetition			Postcompetition		
	Study			Study			Study			Study		
	1	2	3	1	2	3	1	2	3	1	2	3
SCAT	.17	.42**	.42**	.27*	.45**	.49**	...	.33**	.42**	.16	.24**	.22**
Success-failure	−.07	.02	−.02	−.02	.05	−.12	...	.31	.37**	.45	.46**	.55**
Gender	...	−.03	−.02	...	.10	.06	...	.27*	.02	...	.14	.03
Task type	...	...	−.03	...	...	.02	...	...	.16	...	...	.08
Multiple R	.18	.42	.42	.27	.46	.51	...	.53	.57	.48	.54	.60
R^2	.03	.18	.18	.07	.21	.26	...	.28	.32	.23	.29	.36
F ratio	1.37	4.90**	4.96**	3.18*	6.18**	7.94**	...	8.92**	11.13**	11.88**	9.29**	12.55**
df	2,8	3,68	3,92	2,80	3,68	3,92	...	3,68	3,92	2,80	3,68	3,92

$*p < .05.$ $**p < .01.$

In Study 5, 115 male students in physical education boxing classes were selected as subjects due to of the highly competitive structure of these classes and the high importance placed on the outcome of a boxing tournament at the end of the course in determining students' grades. Students completed SCAT and the noncompetitive A-state measure at the beginning of a regular class in which a film was shown, and precompetitive A-state was assessed immediately before a competitive tournament bout.

The results of Study 4 shown in Table 4.3 reveal that SCAT was significantly related to precompetition A-state for the quarter- or the semifinal match but not for basal or pool-play precompetition A-state. Surprisingly, actual A-states did not increase substantially from basal to either precompetition situation. Comparison with norms for college females reported by Spielberger et al. (1970) indicated that the basal A-state mean of 41.06 was in the 75th percentile. Thus, apparently players' A-states were already elevated 6 to 18 hours before competition and did not increase noticeably immediately before their matches.

Table 4.3   Study 4: Means and Correlation Coefficients for SCAT and A-State Scores

Measure	*M*	*r* with SCAT (corrected)
SCAT	20.27	. . .
Basal A-state	41.06	.22
Precompetitive A-state 1	41.46	.28
Precompetitive A-state 2	42.79	.44*

*$p < .01$.

In contrast, A-states observed in Study 5 increased substantially from basal to precompetitive situations (see Table 4.4), although the magnitude of the correlation between SCAT and A-state increased only slightly from the noncompetitive to the precompetitive situation. Moreover, contrary to theoretical predictions, SCAT was significantly correlated not only to precompetitive A-state but also to noncompetitive A-state.

Again these studies proved only somewhat helpful in demonstrating the construct validity of SCAT. Although SCAT significantly predicted precompetitive A-states in both studies, the failure to find a significant link between SCAT and the initial precompetitive A-state in Study 4 and the demonstration of a significant relationship between SCAT and noncompetitive A-state in Study 5 directly contradicted theoretical predictions. Moreover, both studies revealed that SCAT and A-state scores did not share a substantial amount of common variance (approximately 16%).

Table 4.4   Study 5: Means and Correlation Coefficients for SCAT and A-State Scores

Measure	M	r with SCAT (corrected)
SCAT	21.56	. . .
Basal A-state	37.48	.42*
Precompetitive A-state	52.70	.49*

*$p < .01$.

Several subjects and the research assistants involved in Studies 4 and 5 reported that they felt that Spielberger et al.'s (1970) SAI contained items that were not particularly applicable to competitive sport situations. After some initial analyses and comparisons with other instruments, factor analysis was used to modify the SAI by identifying 10 items most sensitive to competitive situations (see Martens, Burton, Rivkin, & Simon, 1980). This new state anxiety instrument was called the Competitive State Anxiety Inventory (CSAI).

Study 6

Study 6 was designed to determine whether measurement problems associated with using the 20-item SAI to measure A-state in competitive situations and measuring basal A-state too close to competition were responsible for the inconsistencies in the findings for Studies 4 and 5. Martens and Simon (1976b) investigated the relationship between SCAT and A-state among 136 female interscholastic basketball players in competitive and noncompetitive situations by using the CSAI. In an effort to obtain a truer baseline measure of A-state, Martens and Simon had the players complete the CSAI and SCAT after school at least 3 days before their next game, whereas precompetitive measures of A-state were obtained at courtside immediately before a regular-season game.

The results of this study provide consistent and impressive evidence for the construct validity of SCAT. Players demonstrated a substantial increase in A-state from noncompetitive ($M = 18.44$) to precompetitive ($M = 27.96$) situations. Moreover, the relationship between SCAT and A-state was nonsignificant in the noncompetitive situation ($r = .28$) but was highly significant in the precompetitive situation ($r = .73$), accounting for over 53% of the A-state variance.

Conclusions From Studies 4, 5, and 6

The overall results from these three studies provide mixed support for the construct validity of SCAT. Nevertheless, it is believed that methodological problems confounded results in Studies 4 and 5, resulting in inconsistencies in expected relationships between SCAT and noncompetitive and precompetitive A-states.

Study 6, which utilized a more sensitive competitive A-state measure and obtained a truer baseline measure of A-state, demonstrated impressive evidence of SCAT's ability to predict precompetitive but not noncompetitive A-state.

Impact of Level of A-Trait and Threat on Competitive A-State

Another way of providing evidence for the construct validity of SCAT is to demonstrate that SCAT's ability to predict competitive A-state increases as the level of situational threat increases. Thus, the next study attempted to evaluate the construct validity of SCAT by testing the two theoretical predictions that were assessed in Studies 1 and 2 but by employing a different type of methodology.

Study 7

The purpose of Study 7 was to investigate the A-state reactions of basketball players with differential levels of competitive A-trait to a series of competitive and noncompetitive situations that varied in level of threat. Simon and Martens (1977) modified Endler, Hunt, and Rosenstein's (1962) S-R Anxiety Inventory for the sport of basketball, creating 12 noncompetitive, precompetitive, competitive, and postcompetitive situations that varied from nonthreatening to highly threatening. The questionnaire was administered to players from the same nine interscholastic girls' basketball teams used in Study 6. Players read each situation and completed the CSAI to indicate their perceived A-state levels when in that hypothetical situation.

The mean A-state scores of all subjects for each of the 12 situations are reported in Table 4.5. Simple linear regression equations (computed between SCAT and A-state scores for each of the 12 situations) and the *t* tests to determine their significance are also provided. All regressions were significant except for Situation 1, the only noncompetitive situation. Moreover, the pattern of results suggests that SCAT best predicts precompetitive A-state, predicts midcompetition A-state somewhat less well, predicts postcompetition A-state only marginally, and predicts noncompetitive A-state quite poorly. These findings closely parallel theoretical predictions and lend solid support to the construct validity of SCAT.

The pattern of regression coefficients provided only partial support for the hypothesis that SCAT is a better predictor of A-state as threat increases. An examination of the 8 situations describing precompetitive and competitive situations reveals that those situations occurring immediately before the basketball game (4, 9, and 10) had the highest correlations between SCAT and A-state ($rs = .57$, .63, and .52, respectively). Furthermore, as the other 3 precompetitive situations (2, 6, and 8) demonstrate, the magnitude of the relationship between SCAT and A-state decreased ($rs = .32$, .49, and .35, respectively) the greater the interval between the situation and competition. Thus, the general trend among the 6

Table 4.5   Study 7: Means and Regression Equations for Predicting A-State From SCAT for the 12 Situations in the Basketball S-R Anxiety Inventory

Situation	Nature of situation	A-state mean	Regression equation	t test
1	Noncompetitive	15.27	$y = 11.99 + .14x$	1.85
2	Prepractice	19.04	$y = 9.77 + .41x$	3.96***
3	Postcompetitive	21.69	$y = 15.44 + .27x$	2.93**
4	Precompetitive	22.04	$y = 7.93 + .62x$	8.11***
5	Competitive—no challenge	22.18	$y = 10.68 + .50x$	6.13***
6	Precompetitive	24.86	$y = 10.05 + .65x$	6.57***
7	Postcompetitive	26.68	$y = 19.85 + .30x$	3.24**
8	Uncertainty about playing	31.21	$y = 22.32 + .39x$	4.27***
9	Precompetitive	31.48	$y = 16.10 + .68x$	9.28***
10	Precompetitive	32.57	$y = 20.00 + .55x$	7.04***
11	Postcompetitive	33.04	$y = 29.46 + .16x$	2.24*
12	Competitive	34.15	$y = 23.65 + .46x$	6.49***

*$p < .05$.   **$p < .01$.   ***$p < .001$.

precompetitive situations was for SCAT to become a better predictor of A-state as threat increased, although Situation 2 offers a notable exception to this pattern. In relatively nonthreatening Situation 2, SCAT's prediction of A-state was second best among the 12 situations.

It was also unexpected that SCAT did not improve as a predictor as A-state increased. Subsequent analyses suggested as one possible explanation for this finding that a ceiling effect may have existed for high SCAT subjects that lowered the relationship between SCAT and A-state in highly threatening situations. Thus, overall this study provided mixed support for the construct validity of SCAT, which again demonstrated itself to be a better predictor of A-states in precompetitive and competitive situations than in noncompetitive or postcompetitive situations. However, only partial support was provided for the prediction that SCAT would become a better predictor of competitive A-state as threat increases.

Prediction of A-State: SCAT Versus Other A-Trait Measures

Another technique to assess the construct validity of SCAT is to compare SCAT with alternative measures of A-trait to determine whether SCAT can predict A-state more effectively in competitive situations.

Study 8

Study 8 tested these theoretical predictions by having the same 136 female high school basketball players used in Studies 6 and 7 complete two A-trait measures: SCAT and Spielberger et al.'s (1970) TAI. These measures were then compared with coaches' ratings of A-trait. Coaches' ratings were selected as an alternative measure of competitive A-trait because coaches are interested in maximizing players' performance, and knowing how players will respond to stressful competitive situations is often critical to individual and team success. Thus, it was reasoned that coaches are highly motivated to know their players well and that careful scrutiny of players should make coaches' ratings good alternative measures of competitive A-trait.

Subjects completed the two A-trait measures in after-school sessions at least 3 days before competition, whereas coaches completed the rating forms assessing each player's level of A-trait several weeks later at the conclusion of the season. Players also completed the CSAI in (a) a noncompetitive after-school session and (b) precompetitively at courtside immediately before a regular-season game.

Theoretical predictions suggest that SCAT should predict competitive A-state better than should a general A-trait measure such as the TAI, whereas the reverse should be true for noncompetitive A-state. The patterns of results depicted in Figure 4.2 were highly congruent with theoretical predictions.

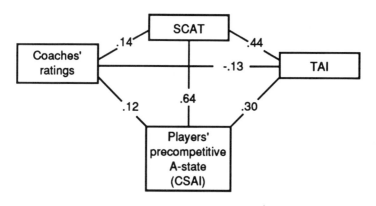

Figure 4.2. Study 8: Relations among three measures of A-trait and players' CSAI scores.

These correlational data also corroborated previous pilot data with a volleyball sample that suggested that coaches' ratings did not correlate very highly with SCAT. This finding should not be surprising because coaches' ratings appear to be very inaccurate predictors of A-state as evidenced by the minimal correlation with players' A-states ($r = .12$). The TAI was not significantly related to coaches' ratings either, but correlations between the TAI and SCAT do corroborate previous concurrent validity research by demonstrating a moderate relationship between the two A-trait measures ($r = .44$). More important, as predicted, SCAT correlated much higher with players' precompetitive A-state ($r = .64$) than with the TAI ($r = .30$), but the TAI demonstrated a stronger relationship with noncompetitive A-state ($r = .44$) than did SCAT ($r = .25$).

Overall, these data further enhance the construct validity of SCAT by demonstrating that SCAT is a better predictor of competitive A-state than is either another measure of competitive A-trait such as coaches' ratings or a general A-trait inventory such as the TAI.

Study 9

The purpose of Study 9 was to extend the results of Study 8 by comparing SCAT and the TAI as predictors of A-states by using the S-R Anxiety Inventory modified for basketball described in Study 7. The two major hypotheses of this investigation were (a) that SCAT would predict competitive A-state better than would the TAI in precompetitive and competitive situations but not in noncompetitive or postcompetitive ones and (b) that as the level of competitive threat increased, the better SCAT would predict A-state than would the TAI.

The results of this investigation are summarized in Table 4.6. All correlation coefficients were corrected for attenuation because predictions were being made

Table 4.6 Study 9: Comparison of SCAT With the TAI as Predictors of A-State in the 12 Situations in the Modified S-R Anxiety

Situation	Nature of situation	TAI and A-state (CSAI) r	SCAT and A-state (CSAI) r	t test for difference between rs
1	Noncompetitive	.25	.18	.67
2	Prepractice	.47	.36	1.09
3	Postcompetitive	.35	.28	.69
4	Precompetitive	.35	.65	3.46***
5	Competitive—no challenge	.44	.53	1.02
6	Precompetitive	.35	.56	2.27*
7	Postcompetitive	.33	.31	.23
8	Uncertainty about playing	.33	.40	.71
9	Precompetitive	.34	.72	4.63***
10	Precompetitive	.27	.59	3.57***
11	Postcompetitive	.06	.22	2.69**
12	Competitive	.24	.56	3.50***

Note. $N = 136$. All correlation coefficients are significant at the .05 level except that of the TAI-CSAI coefficient for Situation 11.

*$p < .05$.   **$p < .01$.   ***$p < .001$.

about hypothetical situations. These data demonstrate that SCAT was a significantly better predictor than was the TAI in 6 of 12 situations, whereas the TAI was never a significantly better predictor of A-state. Scrutiny of these 6 situations shows them to include the four true precompetitive situations as well as stressful competitive and postcompetitive situations. Moreover, the five highest correlations for the SCAT–A-state relationship were for Situations 4, 6, 9, and 10 (the precompetitive situations) and Situation 12 (the stressful competitive situation) whereas the lowest four correlations were for Situation 1 (the noncompetitive situation) and Situations 3, 7, and 11 (the postcompetitive situations).

Although the TAI was never a better predictor of A-state than was SCAT, these data supported theoretical predictions by demonstrating higher correlations between the TAI and A-state in four situations: (a) the noncompetitive situation (i.e., Situation 1), (b) two of the three postcompetitive situations (i.e., Situations 3 and 7), and (c) Situation 2, which describes a prepractice situation that is likely viewed as noncompetitive as well. Thus, these data generally support the construct validity of SCAT by demonstrating that SCAT significantly predicts A-state better than does the TAI in precompetitive and competitive situations but not in noncompetitive or postcompetitive ones, whereas the TAI is more strongly correlated to A-state in noncompetitive and postcompetitive situations than is SCAT. Again, no consistent support was provided for the prediction that SCAT would become a better predictor of competitive A-state as threat increases.

A-Trait, A-State, and Motor Performance

Although it was important to demonstrate the link between competitive A-trait and A-state, it is critical to take the next step and examine how these constructs interact to influence motor performance.

Studies 10 and 11

Studies 10 and 11 are extensions of Studies 1 and 2, with the focal point being motor performance rather than A-state responses. The major hypothesis of these two studies was that high competitive A-trait subjects perform poorer than do low competitive A-trait subjects in competitive but not in noncompetitive situations. This hypothesis is based on the assumption that high competitive A-trait subjects manifest higher A-state levels than do low competitive A-trait persons in competitive situations and on the drive theory notion that higher A-state interferes with task execution during the initial stages of performance on complex motor tasks.

In Studies 10 and 11, subjects from Studies 1 and 2 performed 20 complex motor maze trials. As reported in Studies 1 and 2, high competitive A-trait subjects in both experiments manifested higher A-state than did low competitive A-trait subjects in competitive situations. Motor performance results for these same subjects, however, indicated no significant differences between high and low

SCAT groups. Subjects' SCAT and A-state scores were used as predictors in a multiple regression analysis in which motor performance scores were the dependent variable to ascertain whether the A-state scores for the high and the low SCAT subjects mediated the relationship between motor performance and competitive A-trait. Two different multiple regression models were used for each experiment. The first, using a linear equation, determined whether SCAT and A-state scores predicted motor performance, whereas the second determined whether SCAT predicted motor performance linearly and A-state scores predicted motor performance curvilinearly. The results from each of these multiple regression analyses for both experiments indicated that neither SCAT nor A-state scores were able to predict subjects' motor performance significantly.

Does this failure of SCAT to predict motor performance in Studies 10 and 11 mean that SCAT lacks construct validity? Probably not. Figure 4.3 shows a simple model of the relationship among A-trait, A-state, and motor performance. The model reveals that competitive A-trait is theorized to predict A-state (Link 1) and that A-state is hypothesized to predict motor performance (Link 2). Thus, the prediction of motor performance by competitive A-trait is mediated by A-state. In the nine previous studies, evidence has been presented that competitive A-trait is predictably and reliably related to A-state in competitive situations (Link 1). This evidence reflects SCAT's construct validity.

Figure 4.3. Relationship between competitive A-trait and motor performance as mediated by A-state.

Rather than interpreting the failure of SCAT and A-state to predict motor performance in Studies 10 and 11 as negative evidence of SCAT's validity, we see that these results demonstrate that a simple measure of A-state is not an adequate predictor of motor performance (Link 2). Methodological problems, individual and task differences, and experiments of low sensitivity all may have accounted for the failure of A-state to predict motor performance in Studies 10 and 11. For example, as noted in Studies 1 and 2, the A-state levels created in laboratory experiments are not nearly as great as they are in field studies. This may explain why Studies 10 and 11 failed to find A-state and hence competitive A-trait to be significant predictors of motor performance. It also may be that a number of intervening variables need to be added to the model in Figure 4.3 to discern accurately the relationship between A-state and motor performance.

Weinberg's Work in Predicting Motor Performance

Although typically it is postulated that the ineffective measurement of A-state is the primary reason for the failure to understand Link 2, it also needs to be recognized that we often use weak measures of motor performance. To obtain a better understanding of Link 2, we must measure not only performance outcome (the end product of the movement) but also the movement itself. An experiment by Weinberg (1977) illustrates this point in a study that obtained noteworthy results.

Weinberg selected 10 high and 10 low A-trait subjects who scored on the extremes of Spielberger's TAI. Using Spielberger's SAI, he obtained all subjects' A-states in a resting condition. He then gave them motivating instructions for throwing a tennis ball at a target. The subjects received 10 trials and then received negative feedback about their performance, threw another 10 trials, and then retook the A-state scale.

Weinberg compared the A-state scores of the low and the high A-trait subjects by computing an analysis of covariance using the initial A-state scores as covariates. The results showed that high A-trait subjects were significantly higher in A-state after the experiment than were low A-trait subjects (see Table 4.7). These findings are not surprising, but the performance results were. As shown in Table 4.7, the performance of high A-trait subjects was compared to the performance of low A-trait subjects on the last 10 trials, using performance on the first 10 trials as a covariate. The low A-trait subjects performed over 50% better than did the high A-trait subjects.

Table 4.7 A-State and Performance Results Obtained by Weinberg (1977)

TAI level	A-state		Performance	
	Basal	Postexperimental	Trials 1-10	Trials 11-20
Low	28.2	33.4	10.3	16.5
High	35.9	46.4	10.2	9.3

Although this dramatic difference in performance warrants attention and replication, the unique part of Weinberg's study is that he monitored the subjects' performance through several electromyographic (EMG) measures that assessed the electrical activity of the muscles involved in throwing the tennis ball. These measures of the movement itself revealed that high A-trait subjects used more energy over a longer period of time after the throw than did low A-trait subjects (perseveration). In addition, for performance both before and after failure feedback, high A-trait subjects exhibited cocontraction of agonists and antagonists, whereas low A-trait subjects employed more sequential contraction of these muscle groups.

Thus, although Weinberg's performance differences are probably the largest yet reported for any motor task, what makes his study unique is the clear EMG differences between high and low A-trait subjects. Further research using such measures of the movement process, especially in conjunction with competitive A-trait instead of general A-trait, appears promising.

Conclusions Regarding the Prediction of Motor Performance

The findings of Studies 10 and 11 indicate that knowledge of A-states alone does not provide an adequate base for predicting motor performance. Some of the reasons that A-state does not predict motor performance were identified. Nevertheless, the inability of SCAT to predict motor performance does not lower SCAT's construct validity. In fact, when we understand the relationship expressed by Link 2 in Figure 4.3, only then will competitive A-trait become an important predictor of motor performance. In other words, there is no theoretical reason to believe that competitive A-trait is directly related to motor performance. Competitive A-trait will predict performance only to the extent that high competitive A-trait athletes manifest higher levels of A-state than do low competitive A-trait athletes.

Finally, the prediction of motor performance is not the only dependent variable worthy of study. Predicting satisfaction from sport participation, personality development as a consequence of sport participation, and interpersonal behaviors in sport are alternative dependent variables of importance. The relationship between competitive A-trait and these variables is equally worthy of study by sport psychologists.

SUMMARY

Evidence gathered in 11 experimental and field studies supports the construct validity of SCAT as a valid measure of competitive A-trait by providing results in accordance with theoretical predictions. High SCAT subjects manifested higher A-states than did low SCAT subjects in competitive situations but not in noncompetitive situations. SCAT was also found to be a better predictor of A-state than were other person, task, and situational variables in competitive situations but not in noncompetitive situations. Similarly, SCAT was found to correlate more strongly with A-state in competitive than in noncompetitive situations, and partial support was provided for the prediction that the correlation between SCAT and A-state would grow stronger as the level of situational threat increased. In competitive conditions, SCAT was a better predictor of A-state than were coaches' ratings of their players' A-states or a general A-trait scale. However, SCAT was not a better predictor of A-state in noncompetitive conditions. Spielberger et.

al.'s SAI was modified in this phase of studies to provide an A-state instrument more sensitive to competitive situations. This new sport-specific A-state scale, the CSAI, enabled the researchers to demonstrate a more consistent and strong relationship between competitive A-trait (SCAT) and competitive A-state. Finally, neither SCAT nor the CSAI were able to predict subjects' motor performance significantly. These nonsignificant findings may have been the result of methodological problems and individual and task differences.

Chapter 5

Using SCAT and SCAT Norms

As already explained, SCAT is an A-trait inventory designed to measure a predisposition to respond with varying levels of A-state in competitive sport situations. SCAT was constructed primarily for research purposes to identify subjects varying in competitive A-trait. SCAT has both a child form (SCAT-C) for children ranging in age from 10 through 14 and an adult form (SCAT-A) for persons aged 15 and older (or the reading level of the average 15-year-old). The usefulness of SCAT as a diagnostic instrument for clinical purposes has not been established. Revised norms are available, however, for both males and females ranging in age from 10 years through college-age adults.

Currently, SCAT has been translated into Spanish, French, German, Russian, Japanese, and Hungarian. Nevertheless, the reliability and validity of these foreign versions of SCAT must be independently determined to ensure that translation has not altered the basic meaning of individual items and that these items validly tap the construct of A-trait. Other cultures may view competition quite differently (Duda, 1985, 1986; Maehr & Nicholls, 1980), which could substantially alter the relationships postulated in the construct validation model for SCAT. Such a revalidation of SCAT has not been done to our knowledge.

ADMINISTRATION OF SCAT

Both forms of SCAT are self-administering and may be taken either alone or in groups. The inventory has no time limits, but normally less than 5 minutes is required for its completion. Instructions for taking the inventory are printed on the form.

Because SCAT has considerable face validity among the 10 anxiety items, 5 spurious statements were added to reduce response bias. These 5 items are not scored. The scale should also be presented to subjects as the Illinois Competition Questionnaire (or state of your choice). To alleviate possible response biasing, the innocuous title and spurious items should always be used.

When administering SCAT it is important to make sure that subjects respond to each item according to how they generally feel in competitive sport situations. If A-state scales such as the CSAI-2 (see Part III) are used in conjunction with SCAT, respondents should be aware of how these scales differ; A-state inventories require respondents to report how they feel at the moment, not how they generally feel.

Recent research with the CSAI-2 has revealed that anti–social desirability instructions are very beneficial in reducing response bias to that scale. These anti–social desirability instructions have since been modified for SCAT and should be standardly employed when administering the inventory to minimize response distortion problems. These instructions should be committed to memory and convincingly communicated to respondents each time SCAT is administered. These instructions, along with both forms of the SCAT inventory, are printed on pages 52 to 54.

Before allowing subjects to begin SCAT, make sure the instructions are completely understood. Answer questions by reiterating or clarifying the instructions. Do not offer any information regarding the purpose of the inventory. Be sure to instruct the respondent to answer all items.

When both the CSAI-2 and SCAT are used, it is recommended that the CSAI-2 be given before SCAT; otherwise, responses to the CSAI-2 may be influenced by having responded to SCAT immediately before.

Anti–Social Desirability Instructions

The effects of highly competitive sports can be powerful and very different among athletes. The inventory you are about to complete measures how you generally feel about competition. Please complete this inventory as honestly as you can. Sometimes athletes feel they should not admit any nervousness, anxiety, or worry about competition because this is undesirable. Actually, these feelings are quite common, and to help us understand them we want you to share your feelings with us candidly. If you are worried about the competition or have butterflies or other feelings that you know are signs of anxiety, please indicate these feelings accurately on the inventory. Similarly, if you feel calm and relaxed, indicate these feelings as accurately as you can. Your answers will not be shared with anyone. We will be looking only at group responses.

The Sport Competition Anxiety Test for Adults (SCAT-A) appears on the facing page.

Illinois Competition Questionnaire

Form A

Directions: Below are some statements about how persons feel when they compete in sports and games. Read each statement and decide if you HARDLY EVER, or SOMETIMES, or OFTEN feel this way when you compete in sports and games. If your choice is HARDLY EVER, blacken the square labeled A, if your choice is SOMETIMES, blacken the square labeled B, and if your choice is OFTEN, blacken the square labeled C. There are no right or wrong answers. Do not spend too much time on any one statement. *Remember* to choose the word that describes how you *usually* feel when competing in *sports and games*.

	Hardly Ever	Sometimes	Often
1. Competing against others is socially enjoyable.	A ☐	B ☐	C ☐
2. Before I compete I feel uneasy.	A ☐	B ☐	C ☐
3. Before I compete I worry about not performing well.	A ☐	B ☐	C ☐
4. I am a good sport when I compete.	A ☐	B ☐	C ☐
5. When I compete I worry about making mistakes.	A ☐	B ☐	C ☐
6. Before I compete I am calm.	A ☐	B ☐	C ☐
7. Setting a goal is important when competing.	A ☐	B ☐	C ☐
8. Before I compete I get a queasy feeling in my stomach.	A ☐	B ☐	C ☐
9. Just before competing I notice my heart beats faster than usual.	A ☐	B ☐	C ☐
10. I like to compete in games that demand considerable physical energy.	A ☐	B ☐	C ☐
11. Before I compete I feel relaxed.	A ☐	B ☐	C ☐
12. Before I compete I am nervous.	A ☐	B ☐	C ☐
13. Team sports are more exciting than individual sports.	A ☐	B ☐	C ☐
14. I get nervous wanting to start the game.	A ☐	B ☐	C ☐
15. Before I compete I usually get uptight.	A ☐	B ☐	C ☐

Illinois Competition Questionnaire

Form C

Directions: We want to know how you feel about *competition*. You know what competition is. We all compete. We try to do better than our brother or sister or friend at something. We try to score more points in a game. We try to get the best grade in class or win a prize that we want. We all compete in sports and games. Below are some sentences about how boys and girls feel when they compete in sports and games. Read each statement below and decide if *you* HARDLY EVER, or SOMETIMES, or OFTEN feel this way when you compete in sports and games. Mark A if your choice is HARDLY EVER, mark B if you choose SOMETIMES, and mark C if you choose OFTEN. There are no right or wrong answers. Do not spend too much time on any one statement. *Remember* to choose the word which describes how you *usually* feel when competing in *sports and games*.

	Hardly Ever	Sometimes	Often
1. Competing against others is fun.	A ☐	B ☐	C ☐
2. Before I compete I feel uneasy.	A ☐	B ☐	C ☐
3. Before I compete I worry about not performing well.	A ☐	B ☐	C ☐
4. I am a good sport when I compete.	A ☐	B ☐	C ☐
5. When I compete I worry about making mistakes.	A ☐	B ☐	C ☐
6. Before I compete I am calm.	A ☐	B ☐	C ☐
7. Setting a goal is important when competing.	A ☐	B ☐	C ☐
8. Before I compete I get a funny feeling in my stomach.	A ☐	B ☐	C ☐
9. Just before competing I notice my heart beats faster than usual.	A ☐	B ☐	C ☐
10. I like rough games.	A ☐	B ☐	C ☐
11. Before I compete I feel relaxed.	A ☐	B ☐	C ☐
12. Before I compete I am nervous.	A ☐	B ☐	C ☐
13. Team sports are more exciting than individual sports.	A ☐	B ☐	C ☐
14. I get nervous wanting to start the game.	A ☐	B ☐	C ☐
15. Before I compete I usually get uptight.	A ☐	B ☐	C ☐

SCORING SCAT

The procedure for scoring SCAT is identical for both forms. For each item one of three responses is possible: (a) Hardly ever, (b) Sometimes, and (c) Often. The 10 test items (2, 3, 5, 6, 8, 9, 11, 12, 14, and 15) are scored according to the following directions, whereas the spurious items (1, 4, 7, 10, and 13) are not scored:

1 = Hardly ever

2 = Sometimes

3 = Often

Scoring for Items 6 and 11 is reversed according to the following key:

1 = Often

2 = Sometimes

3 = Hardly ever

Thus, the range of possible SCAT scores extends from 10 to 30. SCAT questionnaires in which one test item is omitted can still be scored, but any inventory in which two or more test items are omitted should be invalidated. To obtain the SCAT score for a questionnaire in which a single test item has been omitted, compute the mean item score for the nine items answered, multiply this value by 10, and then round the product to the nearest whole number.

For ease in hand scoring, a scoring template can be made. When SCAT is used with large numbers, machine-scored answer sheets may be preferable.

SCAT NORMS

Updated normative information on SCAT is provided for male and female youth sport, high school, and college athletes (see Tables 5.1 and 5.4 through 5.6) as well as for the sports of baseball, basketball, football, soccer, swimming, tennis, volleyball, and wrestling (see Tables 5.2, 5.3, and 5.7 through 5.10). It should be noted that over half the data used in computation of these norms were obtained from colleagues who have conducted independent competitive A-trait research with such sports as baseball (Brustad & Weiss, 1987), basketball (Brustad, 1986), golf (Krane & Williams, 1987), sailing (Petlichkoff, 1986), shooting (Gould, Petlichkoff, Simons, & Vevera, 1987), soccer (Lewthwaite, 1988; Scanlan & Passer, 1979a, 1979b), swimming (Rinehart, 1981), volleyball (Cox, in press), and wrestling (Scanlan & Lewthwaite, 1984, 1985, 1986; Scanlan, Lewthwaite, & Jackson, 1984).

The Sport Competition Anxiety Test for Children (SCAT-C) appears on the facing page.

Percentile ranks and standard scores are provided for each norm group. The percentile rank of a person's score indicates the percentage of people in the norm group who scored lower on SCAT. Thus, a percentile rank of 63 indicates that 63% of the respondents in the norm group had lower SCAT scores.

Standard scores are also provided because percentile ranks represent measurement on an ordinal scale only, whereas standard scores are expressed on an interval scale. A standard score is simply the deviation of a raw score from the mean expressed in standard deviation units:

$$z = \frac{x - M}{s}$$

where z = a standard score, x = a specified raw score, M = the mean, and s = the standard deviation of the raw score distribution. The z scores were transformed by setting the mean to 50 and the standard deviation to 10. Thus, the transformed z is

$$z = 50 + 10z$$

This transformation is linear in contrast to an area transformation, which is used to obtain a normalized standard score. The normalized standard score permits reference to a standard distribution (the normal curve) and direct conversion to percentiles. If the norm group closely approximates a normal distribution, then both the unnormalized and the normalized standard scores will be the same. Both standard scores were computed, and for all norm groups the two standard scores were identical for the first two places.

The interpretation of the standard scores is based on standard deviation units. A standard score of 60 indicates a score of 1 standard deviation above the mean of the distribution. A score of 35 represents a score 1-1/2 standard deviations below the mean.

A summary of the test statistics for male and female youth sport, high school, and college athletes is presented in Table 5.1, and summary test statistics for eight different sports and the composition of each sport group by competitive level are presented in Tables 5.2 and 5.3. The norms reveal a trend for competitive A-trait to increase with age through high school and then to decrease for collegiate competitors. Females were higher in competitive A-trait than were males at the youth sport level, but high school and college males demonstrated higher SCAT scores than did their female counterparts. Finally, consistent with social evaluation theory, competitive A-trait was higher for individual than for team sport athletes.

Table 5.1 Summary of Test Statistics for Norm Samples by Competitive Level and Gender

Sample	N	M	SD
Youth sports (SCAT-C)			
Male	903	17.82	4.33
Female	191	18.74	4.82
High school (SCAT-A)			
Male	159	23.03	3.93
Female	193	22.45	4.36
College (SCAT-A)			
Male	97	20.92	4.40
Female	468	19.79	4.37

Table 5.2 Summary of Test Statistics for Norm Samples by Sport

Sample	N	M	SD
Baseball/softball	130	18.88	4.59
Basketball	565	19.77	4.95
Football	181	17.94	4.30
Soccer	303	17.04	4.30
Swimming	121	20.74	3.71
Tennis	109	20.89	4.92
Volleyball	358	19.82	4.29
Wrestling	239	20.91	4.43

Table 5.3 Summary of Competitive Levels Constituting Sport Samples

Sample	N	Youth sports	High school	College	Elite
Baseball/softball	130	108	. . .	22	. . .
Basketball	565	371	155	39	. . .

(cont.)

Table 5.3 (Continued)

Sample	N	Youth sports	High school	College	Elite
Football	181	181	. . .	. . .	. . .
Soccer	303	303	. . .	. . .	. . .
Swimming	121	. . .	. . .	51	70
Tennis	92	. . .	62	47	. . .
Volleyball	358	. . .	28	330	. . .
Wrestling	239	155	84	. . .	. . .

Table 5.4   SCAT-C Norms for Youth Sport Athletes

	Standard score (percentile)	
Raw score	Males (N = 903)	Females (N = 191)
30	781 (99)	734 (99)
29	758 (99)	713 (99)
28	735 (99)	692 (99)
27	712 (98)	671 (96)
26	689 (96)	651 (91)
25	666 (94)	630 (86)
24	643 (91)	609 (80)
23	619 (87)	588 (77)
22	596 (82)	568 (72)
21	573 (75)	547 (66)
20	550 (67)	526 (60)
19	527 (59)	505 (54)
18	504 (52)	485 (46)
17	481 (44)	464 (37)
16	458 (36)	443 (30)
15	435 (29)	423 (24)
14	412 (22)	402 (18)
13	389 (15)	381 (12)
12	366 (9)	360 (9)
11	343 (4)	340 (7)
10	319 (1)	319 (3)

Table 5.5   SCAT-A Norms for High School Athletes

Raw score	Standard score (percentile)	
	Males (N = 122)	Females (N = 168)
30	677 (98)	673 (98)
29	652 (96)	650 (95)
28	627 (93)	627 (89)
27	601 (88)	604 (83)
26	576 (78)	581 (77)
25	550 (65)	559 (70)
24	525 (53)	536 (60)
23	499 (43)	513 (51)
22	474 (33)	490 (43)
21	448 (24)	467 (34)
20	423 (17)	444 (26)
19	397 (12)	421 (19)
18	372 (9)	398 (14)
17	346 (7)	375 (11)
16	321 (6)	352 (9)
15	295 (5)	329 (6)
14	270 (5)	307 (5)
13	245 (4)	284 (4)
12	219 (2)	261 (2)
11	194 (1)	238 (1)
10	168 (0)	215 (0)

Table 5.6   SCAT-A Norms for College Athletes

Raw score	Standard score (percentile)	
	Males (N = 80)	Females (N = 443)
30	696 (97)	734 (99)
29	674 (93)	711 (98)
28	652 (93)	688 (96)
27	629 (88)	665 (93)
26	607 (82)	642 (90)

(cont.)

Table 5.6   (Continued)

Raw score	Standard score (percentile)	
	Males (N = 80)	Females (N = 443)
25	585 (77)	619 (86)
24	563 (70)	596 (82)
23	541 (63)	573 (77)
22	519 (56)	550 (69)
21	496 (51)	527 (62)
20	474 (43)	504 (53)
19	452 (34)	481 (43)
18	430 (27)	458 (34)
17	408 (21)	435 (25)
16	386 (16)	412 (18)
15	363 (8)	389 (14)
14	341 (4)	366 (10)
13	319 (2)	343 (6)
12	297 (1)	320 (3)
11	275 (0)	297 (1)
10	253 (0)	274 (0)

Table 5.7   SCAT-A Norms for Baseball and Basketball

Raw score	Standard score (percentile)	
	Baseball (N = 130)	Basketball (N = 565)
30	737 (99)	707 (99)
29	714 (98)	687 (98)
28	691 (95)	666 (96)
27	667 (93)	646 (92)
26	644 (90)	626 (88)
25	621 (86)	606 (82)
24	597 (82)	585 (76)
23	574 (77)	565 (70)
22	551 (70)	545 (65)
21	527 (62)	525 (57)
20	504 (53)	505 (50)
19	481 (43)	484 (44)
18	458 (34)	464 (37)
17	434 (25)	444 (31)

Raw score	Standard score (percentile)	
	Baseball (N = 130)	Basketball (N = 565)
16	411 (18)	424 (25)
15	388 (14)	404 (19)
14	364 (9)	383 (13)
13	341 (5)	363 (10)
12	318 (3)	343 (7)
11	294 (1)	323 (4)
10	271 (0)	302 (1)

Table 5.8   SCAT-A Norms for Football and Soccer

Raw score	Standard score (percentile)	
	Football (N = 181)	Soccer (N = 303)
30	780 (99)	801 (99)
29	757 (99)	778 (99)
28	734 (98)	755 (99)
27	711 (98)	732 (98)
26	687 (96)	708 (96)
25	664 (95)	685 (94)
24	641 (92)	662 (92)
23	617 (87)	639 (90)
22	594 (80)	615 (86)
21	571 (74)	592 (81)
20	548 (65)	569 (73)
19	525 (56)	546 (66)
18	501 (48)	522 (60)
17	478 (41)	499 (53)
16	455 (34)	476 (44)
15	432 (29)	453 (36)
14	408 (23)	429 (28)
13	385 (15)	406 (20)
12	362 (9)	383 (12)
11	339 (4)	360 (6)
10	315 (1)	336 (2)

Table 5.9   SCAT-A Norms for Swimming and Tennis

Raw score	Standard score (percentile)	
	Swimming (N = 121)	Tennis (N = 92)
30	750 (99)	685 (98)
29	723 (99)	665 (95)
28	696 (98)	645 (94)
27	669 (96)	624 (91)
26	642 (92)	604 (83)
25	615 (88)	584 (74)
24	588 (79)	563 (68)
23	561 (68)	543 (60)
22	534 (61)	523 (54)
21	507 (53)	502 (50)
20	480 (40)	482 (44)
19	453 (29)	462 (33)
18	426 (22)	441 (25)
17	399 (18)	421 (21)
16	372 (13)	401 (18)
15	345 (7)	380 (16)
14	318 (3)	360 (13)
13	291 (2)	340 (8)
12	264 (1)	319 (4)
11	237 (1)	299 (1)
10	210 (0)	279 (0)

Table 5.10   SCAT-A Norms for Volleyball and Wrestling

Raw score	Standard score (percentile)	
	Volleyball (N = 358)	Wrestling (N = 239)
30	737 (99)	705 (98)
29	714 (98)	683 (97)
28	691 (95)	660 (95)
27	667 (93)	638 (92)
26	644 (90)	615 (87)
25	621 (86)	592 (81)
24	597 (82)	570 (73)
23	574 (77)	547 (64)
22	551 (70)	525 (56)

	Standard score (percentile)	
Raw score	Volleyball (N = 358)	Wrestling (N = 239)
21	527 (62)	502 (47)
20	504 (53)	480 (38)
19	481 (43)	457 (31)
18	458 (34)	434 (26)
17	434 (25)	412 (21)
16	411 (18)	389 (15)
15	388 (14)	367 (11)
14	364 (9)	344 (7)
13	341 (5)	321 (5)
12	318 (3)	299 (2)
11	294 (1)	276 (2)
10	271 (0)	254 (1)

PART II

Sport Competition Anxiety Test: Literature Review, Current Status, and Future Directions

The considerable research that has been reported in the scientific literature using SCAT is reviewed in this part. The review focuses on two objectives: (a) to obtain a better understanding of how competitive anxiety and behavior are related and (b) to examine the accumulated evidence for the reliability and validity of SCAT as a measure of competitive A-trait. This review is based on an expanded model of competitive anxiety and discusses additional psychometric research, individual differences in competitive A-trait, and the relationship between competitive A-trait and (a) perceived threat, (b) state responses, (c) performance, and (d) performance outcomes. On the basis of the review, conclusions are drawn, psychometric and theoretical problems identified, and guidelines for future research suggested.

Chapter 6

Research Using SCAT: Review and Analysis

The original psychometric process followed in the development of SCAT was outlined in Part I. That process is significant for several reasons. First, the construct of competitive anxiety was conceptualized within a theoretical framework based on the interactional paradigm, situation-specificity, and the distinction between personality traits and states. Second, systematic research studies were conducted to develop SCAT as a reliable and valid operationalization of the competitive A-trait construct. Indeed, in carefully controlled laboratory settings as well as more generalizable field settings, these studies provided evidence for the reliability, content validity, concurrent validity, and construct validity of SCAT. Third, on the basis of this original research, norms for different populations and detailed guidelines for the administration of SCAT were established. Thus, a theoretically based, valid operationalization of competitive A-trait was successfully developed. Ostrow and Ziegler (1978) lauded SCAT as the "first known sport-specific behavioral scale that combines a substantive theoretical base with rigorous psychometric construction" (p. 139).

Since the original conceptualization of competitive anxiety and operationalization of SCAT, many studies have used the scale. An extensive search of the psychology and sport-psychology literature provided 217 citations of the original SCAT monograph (Martens, 1977). Included in these citations are 88 published empirical studies and 35 doctoral dissertations using SCAT. Clearly, SCAT has been a well-used instrument, and as Sonstroem (1984) states, "In its short history SCAT has uniquely advanced an understanding of anxiety in motor learning and sport" (p. 113).

The purpose of this chapter is to summarize and review the findings of all published anxiety research using SCAT to measure competitive A-trait. This review includes articles published in journals, books, and conference proceedings.[1] A reference table of all published studies using SCAT is provided in Appendix A. This review does not include unpublished doctoral dissertations or conference presentations (an annotated bibiliography of the doctoral dissertations that have used SCAT is provided in Appendix B). In this chapter, additional psychometric research on SCAT is reviewed, an expanded model of competitive anxiety is introduced on the basis of the existing literature, and the published research using SCAT is reviewed on the basis of theoretical predictions from the competitive anxiety model.

ADDITIONAL PSYCHOMETRIC RESEARCH

Three studies have replicated various phases of the original psychometric validation of SCAT (Hanin, 1982; Ostrow & Ziegler, 1978; Rupnow & Ludwig, 1981). Specifically, these studies examined the item discrimination, internal consistency, and generalizability of SCAT.

Item Discrimination

To assess item discrimination, Ostrow and Ziegler (1978) conducted item analyses using Magnusson's (1966) method for differences between extreme groups. Subjects whose scores fell in the upper (high competitive A-trait, $n = 523$) and lower (low competitive A-trait, $n = 441$) quartiles of the total SCAT score distribution were examined to determine whether their responses to each SCAT item were consistent with their total SCAT score classification. The results produced correlation coefficients ranging from .67 to .82 with a mean coefficient of .79, indicating that subjects at each extreme of the distribution answered each SCAT item consistent with their SCAT score classification. Also, correlation analyses between SCAT items and total SCAT scores were computed for the entire sample $(N = 1,991)$, producing coefficients ranging from .60 to .82 with a mean coefficient of .71. Finally, to determine the discriminating power of the SCAT items, a discriminant analysis was conducted between the high and the low competitive A-trait groups. The discriminant analysis was significant (Bartlett's χ^2 (55) = 481.10, $p < .001$), indicating that the SCAT items significantly discriminated between subjects in these extreme groups.

---

[1]The breakdown of published studies by source included in the review is as follows: *Journal of Sport and Exercise Psychology* (21), *International Journal of Sport Psychology* (18), conference proceedings (11), *Perceptual and Motor Skills* (9), *Research Quarterly for Exercise and Sport* (8), *Journal of Sport Behavior* (6), other sport journals (6), psychology journals (6), and foreign journals (3). Unpublished studies by Scanlan (1975) and Martens and Simon (1976b) are discussed in the review because they were original validation studies conducted during the development of SCAT.

Internal Consistency

The internal consistency, or reliability, of SCAT was estimated using several different methods. Ostrow and Ziegler (1978) examined the homogeneity of the SCAT items using interitem correlations. For the female sample, the interitem correlations ranged from .26 to .66 with a mean correlation of .46. For the male sample, the interitem correlations ranged from .23 to .64 with a mean correlation of .43.

Analyses using the Kuder-Richardson formula 20 produced internal consistency coefficients of .89 for females and .88 for males (Ostrow & Ziegler, 1978). Rupnow and Ludwig (1981) demonstrated internal consistency estimates of .81 and .80 for two separate samples ($n = 375$ and $n = 361$) of fourth, fifth, and sixth graders using SCAT-C. In addition, split-half reliability estimates of .92 (females) and .91 (males) for SCAT were indicated by Ostrow and Ziegler (1978) as well as estimates of .84 (Sample 1) and .82 (Sample 2) for SCAT-C by Rupnow and Ludwig (1981). Finally, principal component factor analyses resulted in a single-factor structure, indicating that the SCAT items represent a unidimensional competitive A-trait construct (Ostrow & Ziegler, 1978). Overall, these results replicate the original validation research and support the item discrimination ability and internal consistency of SCAT.

Generalizability

Generalizability means that research evidence has indicated that an inventory is appropriate, or generalizable, to a particular population. Although SCAT-C was originally validated for children aged 10 and older, Rupnow and Ludwig (1981) extended the generalizability of SCAT-C to include 9-year-olds (fourth graders).

Perhaps opening the doors to cross-cultural research in competitive anxiety, Hanin (1982) completed a systematic set of studies to develop and validate the Russian form of SCAT. Hanin's standardization procedures began with the preliminary Russian translation of SCAT and continued through phases of content validity, reliability, concurrent validity, and construct validity analyses. This research shows that the Russian form of SCAT is stable and valid; mean scores are comparable to American samples.

AN EXPANDED MODEL OF COMPETITIVE ANXIETY

Chapter 2 presented the theoretical model of competitive anxiety, originally conceptualized by Martens (1977), in which competitive A-trait is viewed as the mediator between the competitive situation and the state anxiety (A-state) reaction (see

Figure 2.3). This model is based on the interactional paradigm, situation-specificity, and the distinction between personality traits and states. The key construct in the model is perception of threat, which is the result of the interaction between the competitive situation and the individual's level of competitive A-trait. This theoretical model of competitive anxiety was derived from Martens's (1975a) model of the competitive process, which was also presented in chapter 2 (see Figure 2.2).

When reviewing the numerous research studies using SCAT, it seemed useful to categorize the studies on the basis of the type of theoretical predictions that were tested. To facilitate the categorization of theoretical predictions, the model of the competitive process and the competitive anxiety model (Figures 2.2 and 2.3) were combined to form an expanded model of the competitive anxiety process as it occurs in sport. This review is organized around this expanded model (see Figure 6.1). The model consists of four links. The process begins in Link 1 as situational factors in the objective competitive situation (OCS) and intrapersonal factors (A-trait) interact to create a perception of threat that is part of the subjective competitive situation (SCS). This perception of threat then interacts with other intrapersonal factors to influence the individual's state responses (A-state) as well as performance (Link 2). These cognitive, somatic, and behavioral responses then interact with intrapersonal factors to create different performance outcomes, or

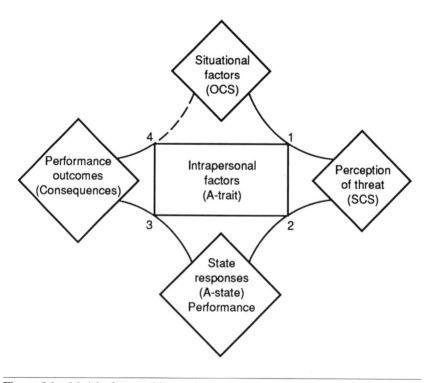

Figure 6.1.   Model of competitive anxiety.

consequences (Link 3). Link 4 completes the cycle of the model as it represents the reciprocal influence of performance outcomes on intrapersonal factors. This expanded model of competitive anxiety is supported by theory and research that emphasize the reciprocity of personality, situational, and behavioral factors (Bandura, 1978; Martens, 1975a, 1975b; Vealey, 1986). The following six sections of this chapter review the research that has used SCAT to measure competitive A-trait. The review is organized to examine the theoretical predictions set forth in the expanded competitive anxiety model.

RELATIONSHIP BETWEEN COMPETITIVE A-TRAIT AND OTHER INTRAPERSONAL FACTORS

In the competitive anxiety model (see Figure 6.1), intrapersonal factors include competitive A-trait, other personality dispositions, and other individual difference factors such as gender, age, ability, and experience. In this section, research that has examined the relationship between competitive A-trait and other intrapersonal factors is reviewed.

Sport-Specific Personality Dispositions

Several studies have employed SCAT to provide evidence for the concurrent or construct validity (or both) of newly developed sport-specific inventories. Willis (1982) demonstrated a significant relationship between competitive A-trait, as measured by SCAT, and the sport-specific motives of fear of failure ($r = .65$, $p < .01$) and power ($r = -.32$, $p < .05$). It is significant that competitive A-trait, or the tendency to feel threatened by competition, is positively related to Willis's fear-of-failure motive and negatively related to power, which is described by Willis as the need to establish control or influence over others. Competitive A-trait was not related to Willis's sport-specific motive to achieve success. Similarly, competitive A-trait was unrelated to the sport-specific achievement motives of competitiveness, win orientation, and goal orientation as measured in Gill's (1986a) Sport Orientation Questionnaire (Gill, Dzewaltowski, & Deeter, 1988). These results support the independence between sport-specific anxiety and achievement measures.

Vealey (1986) found a significant relationship between competitive A-trait and trait sport confidence (SC-trait) in the development of the Trait Sport-Confidence Inventory (TSCI), $r = -.28$, $p < .001$. As predicted, competitive A-trait was negatively related to the disposition of SC-trait. Passer (1983) and Gould, Horn, and Spreeman (1983a) examined the relationship between competitive A-trait and self-confidence/perceived ability in youth athletes by asking them to rate their ability and confidence using Likert scales. Gould et al. found that, compared to high competitive A-trait athletes, low competitive A-trait athletes rated themselves higher in ability, predicted they would finish higher in the competition, and were more confident in their performance prediction. However, Passer found no differences between high and low competitive A-trait athletes in perceived ability. Supporting Passer, Brustad and Weiss (1987) found no differences between high and low competitive A-trait youth athletes in perceived baseball/softball competence using a sport-specific modification of Harter's (1979) Perceived Physical Competence Scale for Children.

The equivocal findings regarding the relationship between competitive A-trait and self-confidence/perceived ability may have resulted from the different experience levels of subjects used in the studies. Vealey's (1986) and Gould et al.'s (1983a) samples included collegiate, high school, and junior elite athletes as compared to the younger athletes playing in seemingly less competitive situations in the Passer (1983) and Brustad and Weiss (1987) studies. It may be that the relationship between competitive A-trait and other personality constructs becomes more sharply defined with age, competitive experience, or both.

In their development of a baseball/softball batting version (B-TAIS) of Nideffer's (1976) Test of Attentional and Interpersonal Style (TAIS), Albrecht and Feltz (1987) hypothesized that competitive A-trait would be related to breadth and focus of attention. As hypothesized, competitive A-trait as measured by SCAT was significantly related to the reduced attention $(r = .45, p < .05)$, overload external $(r = .41, p < .05)$, and overload internal $(r = .37, p < .05)$ subscales on the B-TAIS. Because these three subscales reflect an ineffective focus of attention, these findings suggest that competitive A-trait is related to the tendency to adopt an ineffective attentional focus.

Albrecht and Feltz (1987) also used a trait version of the CSAI-2, the CTAI-2, in conjunction with the B-TAIS to examine the anxiety-attentional–style relationship (the CSAI-2 is discussed at length in chapters 9 through 13). These results are discussed further in chapter 12, but it is important to note that the predicted anxiety-attentional relationships were not as clear with the CTAI-2 as they were with SCAT. As predicted, SCAT was positively correlated with cognitive $(r = .37)$ and somatic $(r = .22)$ anxiety and negatively related to self-confidence $(r = -.33)$ as measured by the CTAI-2.

General Personality Dispositions

SCAT as a measure of competitive A-trait has also been correlated with several general personality dispositions. Consistent with original concurrent validity findings, Ostrow and Ziegler (1978) found a low positive relationship between competitive A-trait and general A-trait as measured by the State-Trait Anxiety Inventory (STAI) (Spielberger et al., 1970) $(r = .42$ and $r = .41, p < .01)$. Cooley (1987) found a similar relationship between SCAT and the STAI $(r = .30)$. Competitive A-trait also showed a positive relationship with test anxiety $(r = .35, p < .05)$ (Stadulis, 1977) as well as with sensitization $(r = .39, p < .01)$, which is the tendency to be aware of potentially threatening internal signals (McKelvie, Valliant, & Asu, 1985).

Several researchers have examined the relationship between competitive A-trait and locus of control (Rotter, 1966). Betts (1982) found a significant negative relationship between competitive A-trait and internal locus of control $(r = -.31, p < .03)$ but no relationship between competitive A-trait and powerful others or chance locus of control. McKelvie et al. (1985) found a significant positive relationship between competitive A-trait and external locus of control $(r = .22, p < .05)$ which differed from an earlier study in which no relationship between these two personality dispositions was indicated (McKelvie & Huband, 1980). Although the results are equivocal, it may be suggested that the tendency to feel threatened by competition is related to the lack of perceived control over life events.

Passer (1983) found that high competitive A-trait children were lower in self-esteem than were low competitive A-trait children using the self-worth subscale from Harter's (1979) Perceived Competence Scale for Children. Also using Harter's scale, Brustad and Weiss (1987) found that high competitive A-trait male youth baseball players were lower in self-esteem than were low competitive A-trait male players, but these differences were not apparent in female youth softball players. However, a follow-up study by Brustad (1988) indicated that lower self-esteem was associated with higher competitive A-trait for both girls and boys participating in youth basketball. In all three of these studies, self-esteem was a better predictor of competitive A-trait in children than was sport-specific perceived competence, indicating that overall feelings of self-worth are more related to competitive A-trait than are the more domain-specific measures of perceived competence.

Gender

Normative data compiled by Martens (1977) during the development of SCAT indicated that the means for competitive A-trait were higher for females than for males across all age-groups. However, the new norms presented in chapter 5 indicate that females are higher in competitive A-trait than males at the youth sport level, but that this trend is reversed for high school and college subjects. Since the original norms were established, several researchers have investigated differences in competitive A-trait between males and females. Hogg (1980), Krotee (1980), and Gill (1988) found that females were higher in competitive A-trait than were males, but Smith (1983), Feltz and Albrecht (1986), Rainey, Conklin, and Rainey (1987), Rainey and Cunningham (1988), and Burhans, Richman, and Bergey (1988) found no differences in competitive A-trait based on gender. Durtschi and Weiss (1984) reported that elite female runners $(M = 17.2)$ were significantly lower than were elite male runners in competitive A-trait $(M = 24.5)$.

An important finding regarding gender differences in competitive anxiety involves the relationship between competitive anxiety and gender role. The literature on gender roles states that masculine and feminine personality characteristics are neither linked to nor determined by biological sex (Bem, 1974). Bem has stated that most individuals possess both masculine (e.g., independent, willing to take risks) and feminine (e.g., affectionate, sensitive) personality characteristics and engage in both masculine and feminine behaviors depending on the situation. Both masculinity and femininity are positive sets of characteristics that are separate, independent dimensions rather than opposite extremes of a single dimension. Bem also defined *androgyny*, which is characterized by high levels of both feminine and masculine characteristics. Androgynous individuals are predicted to have greater flexibility in behavior, as they are not as rigidly sex typed as are masculine or feminine individuals. Bem (1974, 1978) developed the Bem Sex Role Inventory (BSRI) to measure individual differences in gender roles.

Using the BSRI, Wark and Wittig (1979) demonstrated that college males scoring high in masculinity (masculine males) were lower in competitive A-trait than were college females scoring high in femininity (feminine females). However, Wark and Wittig reported differences between only two of the possible six gender-by-gender role combinations, so it was impossible to determine whether differences in competitive A-trait were due to gender or to gender role differences. In follow-up studies, Owie (1981) and Wittig (1984) concurred that masculine males were significantly lower in competitive A-trait than feminine females, but, more important, found no differences between males and females based on gender alone. Wittig, Duncan, and Schurr (1987) indicated that males were lower in competitive A-trait than were females, masculine individuals (regardless of gender) were lower in competitive A-trait than were feminine individuals, and masculine males had the lowest and feminine females the highest competitive A-trait. Also, Wittig et al. found that masculine males were higher in perceived physical self-efficacy (Ryckman, Robbins, Thornton, & Cantrell, 1982), thus providing more evidence for differential socialization based on gender role.

Anderson and Williams (1987) found that feminine females were higher in competitive A-trait than were all other groups and that androgynous females were higher in competitive A-trait than were masculine males. The means of SCAT scores by gender group found in the Anderson and Williams study are illustrated in Figure 6.2. These results indicate that greater endorsement of a feminine gender role, regardless of gender, is associated with higher levels of competitive A-trait. The relationship between gender role and competitive A-trait may help explain the Durtschi and Weiss (1984) finding that elite female runners scored lower on SCAT than did elite males. It may be that elite female athletes possess more of the masculine personality characteristics that are generally associated with success in sport. However, this does not explain why the mean for the elite male runners was extremely higher (86th percentile) than the mean for college males reported in Martens's (1977) normative tables.

Conflicting results have been reported for differences in competitive A-trait based on gender and gender role (Colley, Roberts, & Chipps, 1985; Segal & Weinberg, 1984). Colley et al. reported no significant differences in competitive A-trait between males and females or between masculine males and feminine females. Segal and Weinberg found that males were lower in competitive A-trait

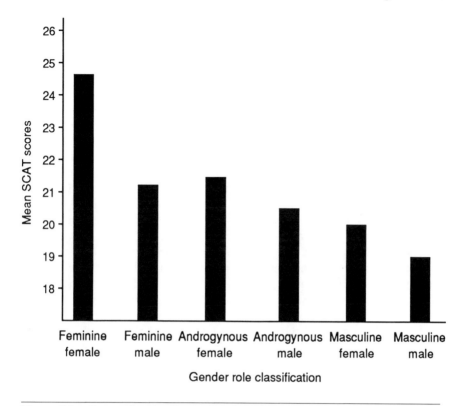

Figure 6.2. Competitive A-trait as a function of gender and gender role. *Note.*
Adapted from Anderson and Williams (1987, p.55).

than were females regardless of gender role as measured by the BSRI. Segal and
Weinberg predicted that gender differences in competitive A-trait may be a function
of how often individuals compete, how competitive they view themselves, and
how important competition is to them. However, a significant gender effect was
indicated even when frequency, competitiveness, and importance of competition
were held constant. Segal and Weinberg qualified their findings by pointing out
that although the gender differences in competitive A-trait were statistically significant, both groups reported moderate and similar levels of competitive A-trait
(20.03 for males and 21.55 for females).

Clearly, additional research is needed to refine our understanding of the relationship between competitive A-trait and gender. On the basis of the changing
social status of women in sport, individual difference factors such as ability, gender
role, and other personality dispositions and situational factors such as type of
sport, level of competition, and social support should be accounted for in examining the relationship between competitive A-trait and gender.

Age

Normative data compiled by Martens (1977) during the development of SCAT indicated that competitive A-trait increased slightly with age with the exception of college males, who were slightly lower than were high school males. Similarly, the new norms reported in chapter 5 show that competitive A-trait increases with age until college, at which point both males and females are lower in competitive A-trait than the younger age groups. Subsequent research examining differences in competitive A-trait based on age has been equivocal. Three studies support the original norms by demonstrating that younger athletes are lower in competitive A-trait than are older athletes (Hogg, 1980; Power, 1982; Watson, 1986). However, the findings by Power and Watson do not provide a true representation of the relationship between competitive A-trait and age due to small sample sizes and the exclusive use of adult subjects.

Hogg (1980) examined competitive A-trait differences according to age in female youth swimmers and found that swimmers under the age of 11 were lower in competitive A-trait than were all other age-groups. Hogg also examined the A-state responses of the swimmers and found that older swimmers (15 years and older) increased in A-state as the competitive meets increased in importance but that younger swimmers (under 15 years) responded similarly to all the meets. Hogg suggested that perhaps competition was less significant to younger swimmers than it was to older swimmers and that this may explain the differences in competitive A-trait due to age.

Smith (1983) found no differences in competitive A-trait based on age for 159 children aged 10 to 13 participating in recreational youth sports. Feltz and Albrecht (1986) found no differences in competitive A-trait between younger (9 to 11 years) and older (12 to 15 years) long-distance runners. However, Gould et al. (1983a) reported that younger athletes were higher in competitive A-trait than were older athletes using 458 junior elite wrestlers aged 13 to 19 years (M = 17 years).

To understand the equivocal findings regarding the relationship between age and competitive A-trait, situational factors, as well as the age range of various samples, must be taken into account. Although the findings of Gould et al. (1983a) are contrary to those of Hogg (1980), the youngest athletes in the Gould et al. study were 13 years old and were competing in an elite, highly structured situation. Gould et al. reported that all athletes in their sample were highly successful and representative of elite athletes in youth wrestling. This is in contrast to Hogg's sample, which was comprised of younger, more recreational athletes. Thus, although the younger athletes in Hogg's study may have been less concerned with competition, that does not seem to have been the case with the younger athletes in Gould et al.'s study. This interpretation is supported by Gould et al.'s additional finding that less experienced wrestlers were higher in competitive A-trait than were wrestlers with more experience.

A similar interpretation may be applied to the Smith (1983) and Feltz and Albrecht (1986) studies. Smith found no differences in competitive A-trait based on age, but her sample was comprised of recreational participants and represented a narrow age range. Although no differences in competitive A-trait based on age emerged in the Feltz and Albrecht study, runners who had been competing longer indicated that they were more worried about performing well and about participating in championship races. To further our understanding of the relationship between competitive A-trait and age, research is needed that accounts for situational differences in competitive structure as well as for the age range and cognitive maturity of subjects.

Ability

Most researchers, coaches, and athletes would agree that anxiety negatively influences sport performance. But does that indicate a negative relationship between sport ability and competitive A-trait? Gravelle, Searle, and St. Jean (1982) reported that candidates for the Canadian national team volleyball team had a mean SCAT score of 18 (18th percentile) with all subjects scoring under the 50th percentile, indicating low levels of competitive A-trait for these subjects. However, these results do not indicate differences based on ability within the team.

No differences in competitive A-trait were found between successful and less successful elite adult male track-and-field athletes (Power, 1982), elite youth wrestlers (Gould et al., 1983a), and elite male netballers (Miller & Miller, 1985). Passer (1983) found no relationship between competitive A-trait and youth sport athletes' ability as evaluated by coaches. Smith (1983) found that young athletes chosen for an all-star team were lower in competitive A-trait than were substitute players. These equivocal results provide no support for a significant relationship between competitive A-trait and ability.

Participation Status

Four studies using SCAT have indicated no significant differences in competitive A-trait between different types of sport participants and nonparticipants. Stadulis (1977) reported no differences in competitive A-trait between nonparticipants, physical education class participants, and universitywide participants in a competitive billiards tournament. McKelvie and Huband (1980) found no differences in competitive A-trait between collegiate athletes and nonathlete university students. Colley et al. (1985) indicated no significant competitive A-trait differences between individuals that did not regularly participate in sport or recreation, individuals that participated in noncompetitive recreational activities, competitive individual sport athletes, and competitive team sport athletes.

Robinson and Carron (1982) examined several intrapersonal and situational factors in an attempt to predict dropout or continuation behavior in high school football. None of the intrapersonal factors, including competitive A-trait, need achievement, self-motivation, and self-esteem, could differentiate between sport starters (athletes that started in games), sport survivors (athletes that participated in less than 10% of the games), and sport dropouts (athletes that quit the team of their own volition). Robinson and Carron concluded that personality dispositions may not be predisposing factors to dropout and continuation behavior in sport.

Two studies, however, have demonstrated differences in competitive A-trait based on participation status in sport. Magill and Ash (1979) compared the competitive A-trait levels of 108 fourth- and fifth-grade youth sport participants and nonparticipants. No differences emerged between groups for the fourth-grade sample. However, nonparticipants were significantly higher in competitive A-trait than were participants in the fifth-grade sample. Using high school subjects, Gill et al. (1988) found that nonparticipants in competitive sport were higher in competitive A-trait than were participants in competitive sport. The equivocality of these findings regarding differences in competitive A-trait based on participation status may be resolved only through further research that accounts for the moderator variables (other individual difference constructs or situational influences) that seem to impinge on the research and prevent clear interpretation of the differential findings.

Additional Intrapersonal Factors

Differences in competitive A-trait have also been examined with regard to race, type of sport, and physiological capacity. Smith (1983) reported no differences in competitive A-trait between black and white youth sport athletes. Power (1982) found no differences with regard to type of event for adult male track-and-field athletes. Thirer, Knowlton, Sawka, and Chang (1978) examined whether competitive A-trait level could be distinguished by physiological workload capacity. They reported that physiological workload indicators accurately distinguished moderate competitive A-trait subjects but could not accurately distinguish high and low competitive A-trait subjects. These results confirm that physiological workload capacity has no apparent connection to competitive A-trait.

Finally, Passer and Seese (1983) examined the relationship between positive and negative life change and subsequent athletic injury in 104 collegiate football players. Competitive A-trait was examined as a possible moderator variable in the relationship between life change and injury and was found to have no significant effects.

Conclusions About the Relationship Between Competitive A-Trait and Intrapersonal Factors

In these studies, which examined the relationship between various intrapersonal factors and competitive A-trait as measured by SCAT, many of the relationships between competitive A-trait and other personality dispositions (both general and sport specific) were as predicted, thus providing further evidence for the concurrent validity of SCAT. Many studies describing differences in competitive A-trait based on gender, age, ability, participation status, and other person factors are largely descriptive and atheoretical. Clearly, SCAT has been used to examine group differences in almost every sample imaginable. The equivocal findings and lack of a conceptual focus indicates the need for additional research to provide theoretical understanding of why these differences in competitive A-trait occur.

PERCEPTION OF THREAT: A RESULT OF COMPETITIVE A-TRAIT AND SITUATIONAL FACTORS

Link 1 in the competitive anxiety model (see Figure 6.1) predicts that situational factors and intrapersonal factors (primarily competitive A-trait) interact to create a perception of threat. The studies reviewed here examine how competition is perceived differently by high and low competitive A-trait individuals to create differential perceptions of threat.

Underlying Sources of Perceived Threat

Researchers have attempted to identify the underlying characteristics of competition that high competitive A-trait individuals find threatening. Fisher and Zwart (1982) identified outcome uncertainty, outcome certainty in a negative direction (losing), and ego threat as sources of threat in sport competition. On the basis of the literature in clinical psychology and test anxiety, Passer (1983) proposed that sources of threat could be labeled as either fear of failure or fear of evaluation. Passer is supported by Rainey and Cunningham (1988), who demonstrated a significant relationship between competitive A-trait and fear of failure and fear of evaluation. Rainey and Cunningham also found a significant relationship between importance of sport and competitive A-trait in female athletes, indicating that perhaps another source of threat in sport is the importance of sport to athletes.

Gould, Horn, and Spreeman (1983b) identified 33 sources of threat (or stress) in junior elite wrestlers. In a factor analysis, these sources of threat loaded on three factors: fear of failure/feelings of inadequacy, social evaluation, and external control/guilt. High competitive A-trait was the most significant predictor of fear of failure/feelings of inadequacy and fear of evaluation. Competitive A-trait was not related to the external control/guilt factor.

Behavioral Indicants of Perceived Threat

On the basis of the underlying sources of perceived threat just discussed, researchers have identified several behavioral differences in perceptions of threat found between high and low competitive A-trait individuals. Using 316 male youth soccer players as subjects, Passer (1983) found that high competitive A-trait players expected to play less well in the upcoming season and worried more frequently about making mistakes, not playing well, and losing than did low competitive A-trait players. Also, high competitive A-trait players expected to experience greater emotional upset, shame, and criticism from parents and coaches after failing than did low competitive A-trait players. Significantly, even when differences in expectancies and self-esteem were controlled statistically, high competitive A-trait players still showed greater performance- and evaluation-related worries than did low competitive A-trait players. Passer's findings support his contention that the manifestation of perceived threat from competitive A-trait and situational factors involves not only performance-related worry (fear of failure) but also fear of evaluation. Passer's findings were corroborated by Rainey et al. (1987), who demonstrated that high competitive A-trait athletes had more frequent performance and evaluation worries as well as more anticipated negative feelings regarding competition than did low competitive A-trait athletes at the junior high level.

Using junior elite wrestlers, Gould et al. (1983a) found that high competitive A-trait wrestlers predicted that they would finish lower in the tournament and worry in a greater number of matches, felt that their nervousness would more often hurt their performance, had more trouble sleeping, and felt that it was less important to their parents that they wrestle well than did low competitive A-trait wrestlers. Using a Likert scale, the wrestlers also predicted what they felt their anxiety would be like 1 week before competition, 24 hours before competition, 1 hour before competition, 2 minutes before competition, during competition against their toughest opponent, and during competition against their weakest opponent. High competitive A-trait wrestlers predicted higher anxiety for themselves for the 24-hour, 1-hour, 2-minute, and against-toughest-opponent measures than did the low competitive A-trait wrestlers. No differences emerged between high and low competitive A-trait wrestlers for the 1-week and the against-weakest-opponent anxiety measures, suggesting that these situations were not perceived as threatening enough to bring out differences in competitive A-trait. These findings provide excellent corroboration for the predicted interaction of situational factors and competitive A-trait in the creation of perceived threat.

Using a sample of young long-distance runners, Feltz and Albrecht (1986) found that the more competitive trait-anxious males worried more than less competitive trait-anxious males about performing up to their levels of ability, improving on their last performance, participating in championship races, not performing well, and being able to get mentally ready to run. For females, the only source of stress that significantly correlated with competitive A-trait was worry about participating in championship races. This gender difference in the perception of threat was substantiated by Brustad and Weiss (1987) using young baseball and softball players. They found that high competitive A-trait boys reported significantly more worries about performance than did low competitive A-trait boys. No differences emerged for any perceptions of threat between high and low competitive A-trait

girls and between high and low competitive A-trait boys or girls on fear of evaluation. However, a follow-up study by Brustad (1988) using a larger sample of
children found that high competitive A-trait boys and girls worried more about
performance and evaluation than did low competitive A-trait boys and girls. Thus,
although some studies have indicated gender differences in manifestations of perceived threat, overall the evidence supports Passer's (1983) contention that perceived threat is based on performance-based worries and also worries about being
evaluated by others.

Fisher and Zwart (1982) examined the relationship between several intrapersonal factors (including competitive A-trait) and responses to different anxiety-
eliciting situations for 40 male college basketball players. The S-R Inventory of
Anxiousness (Fisher, Horsfall, & Morris, 1977) was used to tap subjects' recall
of sources of anxiety during pregame, game, and postgame periods. Athletes'
anxiety responses varied with their perceptions of the situations, and SCAT as
a measure of competitive A-trait accounted for 46% of the anxiety response variance. These findings lend support to the interactional model of competitive anxiety by demonstrating the combined importance of situational factors and
competitive A-trait in creating differential levels of perceived threat.

INFLUENCE OF PERCEPTION OF THREAT ON STATE RESPONSES

In this section, studies that represent Link 2 in the competitive anxiety model
(see Figure 6.1) are examined. Link 2 represents the influence of perception of
threat on individual responses. These responses include A-state, other state
responses (e.g., self-confidence), and performance. The studies reviewed in this
section examined the relationship between competitive A-trait and various state
responses. Perception of threat is a psychological construct that results from the
interaction of situational factors and competitive A-trait. Thus, perception of threat
is assumed to be operationalized by measuring competitive A-trait with SCAT
and examining how competitive A-trait influences behavior in various situations.

Clearly, the most well documented link in the competitive anxiety model is
the ability of SCAT (competitive A-trait) to predict A-state. Overall, 30 published
studies have supported SCAT as a valid predictor of A-state. The remainder of
this section is organized around the various A-state measures that have been used
in SCAT research and concludes with a discussion of the relationship between
SCAT and the additional state characteristics of expectancy, self-confidence, and
physiological arousal.

Influence of Perception of Threat on A-state

Because SCAT was the first sport-specific anxiety inventory conceptualized, there
was no sport-specific A-state inventory available for use in the early SCAT validation studies. Thus, Spielberger's SAI and SAIC were used in these studies and

have continued to be used in studies in which competitive A-state inventories are deemed inappropriate.

Laboratory Studies

The three original laboratory studies reported in chapter 4 established that SCAT was a significant predictor of A-state (SAIC) in competitive situations (Gill & Martens, 1977; Martens & Gill, 1976; Scanlan, 1975). These studies also supported the competitive anxiety model, as SCAT best predicted A-state in precompetitive and midcompetitive measures and as performance factors became the best predictor of postcompetitive A-state.

These original findings have been substantiated by several researchers in laboratory settings. Weinberg (1978, 1979) tested high and low competitive A-trait subjects on a throwing task under different feedback conditions. Weinberg's results indicated that high competitive A-trait subjects exhibited more A-state (SAI) than did low competitive A-trait subjects. Also, emphasizing the influence of competitive A-trait and situational factors on perception of threat, the highest A-state was exhibited by high competitive A-trait subjects in the failure condition. Similarly, Poteet and Weinberg (1980) found that high competitive A-trait subjects were higher in A-state than were low competitive A-trait subjects and that the variance in A-state between groups was higher in competitive than in noncompetitive conditions. Murphy and Woolfolk (1987) found a significant relationship between competitive A-trait and A-state on the SAI ($r = .29, p < .05$) and the Tension scale (Anderson, 1970)($r = .43, p < .001$) on a golf putting task. A significant Trials × Competitive A-Trait interaction indicated that low competitive A-trait subjects were more tense before the posttest than they were before the pretest and that moderate and high competitive A-trait subjects were more tense before the pretest than they were before the posttest.

Field Studies

As stated in chapter 4, it is important to extend the generalizability of SCAT's ability to predict A-state from laboratory settings into the field of competitive sport. The original SCAT field validation studies using the SAI (Martens & Simon, 1976b) supported SCAT's ability to predict A-state in competitive sport settings. These findings have been supported repeatedly throughout the literature.

Using the SAIC to measure A-state in youth soccer players, Scanlan and Passer (1977, 1978, 1979b) demonstrated that (a) SCAT was a significant predictor of both basal and precompetitive A-state and (b) SCAT and precompetitive A-state were more strongly related than were SCAT and basal A-state. These findings were substantiated with the SAI by Weinberg and Genuchi (1980), who studied 30 golfers participating in a collegiate tournament. Watson (1986) combined elite Australian hockey players' scores on SCAT and Alderman's (1976) Alberta Incentive Motivation Inventory to categorize them as approachers and avoiders of achievement behavior and found that avoiders were higher in precompetitive A-state (SAI) than were approachers. In a study conducted in Japan, Koyama, Inomata, and Takeda (1980) reported that the TAI predicted A-state (SAI) of 44 college tennis players better than did SCAT. However, their A-state measures were taken 2 months and 1 day before the competitive event. This finding supports the competitive anxiety model, as SCAT is theorized to predict A-state in anticipation of and during competition rather than in noncompetitive conditions.

Influence of Perception of Threat on Competitive A-State

In the initial field validation studies of SCAT (Martens & Simon, 1976b), it became apparent that Spielberger's general SAI contained items that had little relevance to anticipatory competitive A-state. Therefore, Martens, Burton, Rivkin, and Simon (1980) modified the SAI by identifying 10 items that were more sensitive to A-state changes in competitive situations. Through factor analysis, concurrent validity analysis, and face validity analysis, the SAI was modified to include five activation items measuring high levels of A-state and five deactivation items measuring low levels of A-state typically manifested in competitive situations. The new scale represents a measure of *competitive* A-state and was named the Competitive State Anxiety Inventory (CSAI). Extensive psychometric analyses of the CSAI demonstrated reliability and validity for both the adult and the child (CSAI-C) forms (Martens, Burton, Rivkin, & Simon, 1980). Importantly, the CSAI was demonstrated to be a more appropriate operationalization of A-state in competitive situations (competitive A-state) than was the SAI.

Laboratory Studies

The development of the CSAI, coupled with Martens's (1979) urging for more externally valid research, created a trend toward field studies in competitive anxiety research. However, two carefully controlled laboratory studies provided evidence for the ability of SCAT to predict competitive A-state in accordance with the theoretical model of competitive anxiety.

Scanlan (1978) assessed competitive A-state in 27 high and 27 low competitive A-trait men performing a ring-peg task in three conditions: basal (at rest), noncompetitive (performance evaluation deemphasized), and competitive (competing against an opponent of equal ability). Scanlan found a significant interaction between situation and competitive A-trait as competitive A-state was higher in the competitive condition than in the basal and noncompetitive conditions, and high competitive A-trait subjects exhibited the greatest increase in competitive A-state in the competitive condition (see Figure 6.3). The findings illustrated in Figure 6.3 support the competitive anxiety model by demonstrating that the A-trait groups were affected differently by the situation in which they were performing.

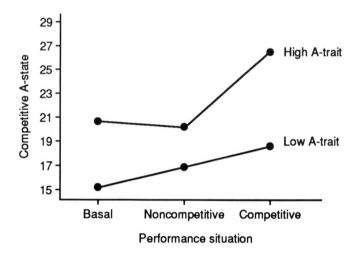

Figure 6.3.   Effects of competitive A-trait and situation on competitive A-state. *Note.* From "Perceptions and Responses of High- and Low-Competitive Trait-Anxious Males to Competition" by T.K. Scanlan, 1978, *Research Quarterly*, **49**, p. 525. Copyright 1978 by the American Alliance for Health, Physical Education, Recreation and Dance. Adapted by permission.

Scanlan and Ragan (1978) used SCAT and Mehrabian's (1968) Measure of Achieving Tendency for Men (MAT) to measure the motives to avoid failure (Maf) and to achieve success (Mas), respectively. The investigators dichotomized 24 subjects as high nACH (low SCAT, high MAT) and 24 subjects as low nACH (high SCAT, low MAT) to participate in the same ring-peg task and used the same procedures used in Scanlan's (1978) study. Supporting Scanlan, both groups increased in competitive A-state from the noncompetitive to the competitive condition, and the increase was significantly greater for low nACH subjects.

Field Studies

The initial validation field studies for SCAT conducted by Martens, Burton, Rivkin, and Simon (1980) using the CSAI established that (a) SCAT is a significant predictor of competitive A-state; (b) SCAT's ability to predict competitive A-state is greatest in situations in which competitive evaluation is anticipated, such as precompetition or midcompetition; (c) SCAT is a better predictor of competitive A-state in competitive situations than is Spielberger et al.'s (1970) TAI; and (d) SCAT is better able to predict athletes' precompetitive A-state than are coaches (Martens & Simon, 1976a, 1976b; Simon & Martens, 1977).

Several field studies have supported SCAT's ability to predict competitive A-state. Martens, Rivkin, and Burton (1980) replicated the Martens and Simon

(1976a) study in which SCAT's ability to predict competitive A-state was compared to coaches' ability to predict competitive A-state. Similar to the earlier findings, Martens and colleagues found that SCAT was better able to predict competitive A-state in precompetitive conditions $(r = .53)$ than were coaches $(r = -.10)$. Amusingly, athletes were very good at predicting the competitive A-state of their coaches $(r = .51)$.

Huband and McKelvie (1986) measured the competitive A-state of 42 collegiate athletes and found that high A-trait athletes were higher in competitive A-state in competitive conditions than were low competitive A-trait athletes. Also, competitive A-state for high competitive A-trait athletes increased more sharply between practice and competition than it did for low competitive A-trait athletes. Moreover, there were no differences in competitive A-state during practice between high and low competitive A-trait athletes, indicating that in baseline situations competitive A-trait is not associated with differences in competitive A-state. Although other studies have cited differences in competitive A-state based on competitive A-trait in baseline conditions (Martens, Burton, Rivkin, & Simon, 1980; Scanlan, 1978; Scanlan & Ragan, 1978), it may be that these competitive A-state measures were not truly baseline measures. The important point, however, is that SCAT's ability to predict competitive A-state increases under competitive conditions. This finding has been supported extensively in the literature and is in accordance with competitive anxiety theory (see chapter 4).

Using the CSAI-C with 76 youth wrestlers, Scanlan and Lewthwaite (1984, 1988) demonstrated that competitive A-trait and personal performance expectancies were the most influential and stable predictors of competitive A-state in precompetitive situations. Other researchers have supported competitive A-trait as a significant predictor of competitive A-state in competitive situations (Cooley, 1987; Gerson & Deshaies, 1978; Wandzilak, Potter, & Lorentzen, 1982). However, the findings of Gerson and Deshaies (1978) and Wandzilak et al. (1982) should be viewed with caution because SCAT was administered immediately before and 3 hours before competition, respectively. Although SCAT is a dispositional measure, it seems likely that subjects' responses as to how they *generally* felt when competing would be influenced by how they felt at that moment due to the proximity of competition.

A particularly provocative study examining the relationship between competitive A-trait and competitive A-state was conducted by Sonstroem and Bernardo (1982) on 30 female collegiate basketball players. Subjects were trichotomized into high, moderate, and low competitive A-trait groups. Three pregame competitive A-state measures were taken, from which lowest, median, and highest values were obtained and categorized as low, moderate, and high competitive A-state *for that subject across the three games.* Thus, competitive A-state measures were trichotomized into low, moderate, and high *intraindividual* competitive A-state scores. This is significant because competitive A-state was defined relative to an individual's own degree of anxiety responsiveness rather than in terms of absolute magnitude. Figure 6.4 illustrates the linear increase of absolute competitive A-state mean values across intraindividual competitive A-state categories. Also, the significant competitive A-trait main effect extends the predictive validity of SCAT, as competitive A-trait predicted the competitive A-state linear relationships between intraindividual categories and absolute scores.

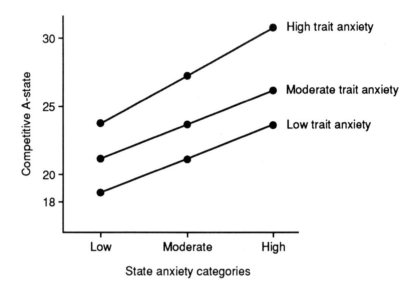

Figure 6.4. Effects of competitive A-trait on competitive A-state. *Note.* From "Individual Pregame State Anxiety and Basketball Performance: A Re-examination of the Inverted-U Curve" by R.J. Sonstroem and P. Bernardo, 1982, *Journal of Sport Psychology*, **4**, p. 240. Copyright 1982, by Human Kinetics Publishers. Adapted by permission.

Validity Generalization

To examine the relationship between competitive A-trait and competitive A-state with greater statistical precision, a meta-analysis based on the validity generalization model was employed. The validity generalization model was proposed by Schmidt, Hunter, and Urry (1976) as a meta-analytic approach to a higher order analysis of studies of predictive validity. Schmidt and Hunter (1977) laid the groundwork for the validity generalization model during the late 1970s. They cited evidence that much of the variability in the outcome of validity studies is due to statistical artifacts. To test the hypothesis that variation in *true* validities is zero, sources of error variance due to artifacts are subtracted from the variance of observed validity coefficients. Although Schmidt and Hunter identified eight sources of between-study variation in observed validity coefficients, only four are usually quantifiable: sample size, criterion reliability, predictor test reliability, and range restriction. Following an example of validity generalization used in a study of motor behavior (Safrit, Costa, & Hooper, 1986), range restriction was not included as an artifact of interest.

To apply the validity generalization model to the relationship between competitive A-trait and competitive A-state, the validity coefficient (bivariate correlation coefficient between competitive A-trait and competitive A-state), sample size, criterion (CSAI) reliability, and predictor test (SCAT) reliability were obtained from 11 studies (see Table 6.1). For inclusion in the analyses, studies must have used SCAT to predict competitive A-state (CSAI) and reported the bivariate correlation between the two measures. Also, only precompetitive measures of competitive A-state were used in the analyses. Because the reliability of SCAT and the CSAI were not reported in the studies, these reliabilities were estimated from assumed frequency distributions following procedures outlined by Hunter, Schmidt, and Jackson (1982). The reliability coefficients computed from these distributions were .87 for SCAT-A (adult version), .82 for SCAT-C (child version), .86 for CSAI-A (adult version), and .78 for CSAI-C (child version).

Table 6.1 Data From Studies Included in Validity Generalization Analysis

Study	Measure	N	R_{tc}
Cooley (1987)	CSAI	53	.52
Gerson & Deshaies (1978)	CSAI	107	.59
Martens, Burton, Rivkin, & Simon (1980)	CSAI	148	.68
Martens, Burton, Rivkin, & Simon (1980)	CSAI	113	.45
Martens, Burton, Rivkin, & Simon (1980)	CSAI-C	468	.56
Martens, Rivkin, & Burton (1980)	CSAI	105	.53
Martens & Simon (1976b)	CSAI	136	.64
Scanlan & Lewthwaite (1984)	CSAI-C	76	.57
Scanlan & Lewthwaite (1984)	CSAI-C	76	.38
Wandzilak, Potter, & Lorentzen (1982)	CSAI	48	.45
Wandzilak, Potter, & Lorentzen (1982)	CSAI	45	.54

Note. R_{tc} = validity coefficient (correlation between SCAT and CSAI/CSAI-C).

The summary data from the validity generalization analyses are outlined in Table 6.2. The three artifacts accounted for 79% of the variance in the observed validity coefficients. Sampling error accounted for 76% of this variance, but this was predicted because the data were analyzed under the conservative assumption that all criterion and predictor test reliabilities were constant at their mean values computed in the assumed frequency distributions. The mean true validity, when artifactual variance was taken into account, was .61. This is the generalized validity coefficient that represents SCAT's ability to predict competitive A-state using the CSAI. The 90% confidence interval ranged from .56 to .66, meaning that

Table 6.2 Summary Data From the Validity Generalization Analysis

Statistic	Value
Weighted mean of observed validity coefficients	.556
Fully corrected mean validity	.666
% variance due to CSAI/CSAI-C reliabilities	1.69
% variance due to SCAT reliabilities	.96
% variance due to sampling error	75.86
% variance accounted for by artifacts	78.52
Mean true validity	.6123
Standard deviation of true validity	.038
90% confidence interval	.563-.661

if another study was conducted using SCAT to predict competitive A-state, the confidence level that the correlation between the two measures would fall within this interval would be 90%.

These analyses have attempted to use meta-analysis to generalize the results of several studies to provide stronger support for the ability of SCAT to predict competitive A-state. Although the results are favorable, they should be viewed with caution due to the small number of studies included in the analyses. Schmidt, Hunter, Pearlman, and Hirsh (1985) recommended using 100 to 200 coefficients in validity generalization studies, although they have used as few as 6. Thus, although preliminary and cautionary, the results of the validity generalization analyses support the predictive ability of SCAT in accordance with theoretical predictions.

Multidimensional Competitive A-State

In 1982, Martens, Burton, Vealey, Bump, and Smith modified the CSAI on the basis of research and theory indicating that anxiety is a multidimensional construct (first published in Part III of this book). This modified instrument, the CSAI-2, measures both somatic and cognitive components of competitive A-state. The original CSAI-2 validation studies indicated that SCAT was a significant predictor of both cognitive (.45) and somatic (.62) competitive A-state. SCAT's stronger relationship with somatic than with cognitive competitive A-state was predicted, as SCAT contains more items that appear to describe somatic manifestations. Although the research using the CSAI-2 is detailed in Parts III and IV, four additional studies that have employed SCAT as a predictor of the CSAI-2 are discussed here.

In a field study of 22 male collegiate rugby players, Maynard and Howe (1987) corroborated the original CSAI-2 validation findings by Martens, Burton, Vealey,

Bump, and Smith (see Part III) that competitive A-trait and somatic competitive A-state were more strongly related than were competitive A-trait and cognitive competitive A-state in two separate matches. However, different findings were reported by Gould, Petlichkoff, and Weinberg (1984) after they measured the competitive A-state of 37 collegiate wrestlers before two tournament matches and found a moderate relationship between competitive A-trait and cognitive competitive A-state for both Matches 1 and 2 but a moderate relationship between competitive A-trait and somatic competitive A-state only in Match 1.

Using a pegboard task in a laboratory setting, Karteroliotis and Gill (1987) examined the relationship between competitive A-trait, cognitive competitive A-state, and somatic competitive A-state in baseline, precompetitive, midcompetitive, and postcompetitive situations. Significant correlations were found between competitive A-trait and cognitive competitive A-state at baseline, midcompetition, and postcompetition, but somatic competitive A-state was significantly related to competitive A-trait only at midcompetition.

Crocker, Alderman, and Smith (1988) examined the relationships between competitive A-trait and CSAI-2 anxiety components at both pretreatment and posttreatment while implementing Smith's (1980) Cognitive-Affective Stress Management Training with elite youth volleyball players. Significantly positive relationships were found at both pre- and posttreatment between competitive A-trait and cognitive and somatic competitive A-state.

The equivocal findings of these four studies using the CSAI-2 indicate that more research is needed to examine the relationship between competitive A-trait and the multidimensional components of competitive A-state. Of paramount interest is the influence of situational factors on these relationships. For example, Karteroliotis and Gill (1987) admitted that the contrived competition in a laboratory failed to produce the type of tension normally experienced in more ego-threatening sport environments. Also, the study by Gould et al. (1984) measured competitive A-state in back-to-back performances the same day, and this may have made the athletes respond differently than they would have in a one-time-performance situation. Clearly, the modification of competitive A-state into cognitive and somatic components has increased the complexity of examining the relationship between competitive A-trait and competitive A-state.

Influence of Perception of Threat on Additional State Characteristics

Although the relationship between competitive A-trait and A-state is of central importance in the competitive anxiety model (see Figure 6.1), competitive A-trait is also predicted to influence other state characteristics. Specifically, research has been conducted examining the relationship between competitive A-trait and expectancy, self-confidence, and physiological measures of arousal.

Expectancy

In two studies, Scanlan and Passer (1979a, 1981) examined the relationship between competitive A-trait and performance expectancies in female and male youth soccer players, respectively. For both samples, soccer ability and self-esteem were significantly related to performance expectancies, but competitive A-trait was not. Thus, competitive A-trait does not appear to be related to individual performance expectancies in precompetitive situations. Interestingly, although high competitive A-trait children find competition threatening and respond with higher competitive A-state, Scanlan and Passer's findings indicated that these children still expected to perform as well as did low competitive A-trait children. However, additional research is needed to confirm these results, as Passer (1983) and Gould et al. (1983a) found that low competitive A-trait youth athletes had higher expectancies about how they would perform in an upcoming season and tournament, respectively, than did high competitive A-trait youth athletes. However, expectancy was measured in these studies in noncompetitive situations in conjunction with the administration of SCAT, and so the expectancy measures are not representative of state characteristics.

Self-Confidence

Using the State Sport-Confidence Inventory (SSCI) to measure precompetitive self-confidence (SC-state), Vealey (1986) found a low yet significant negative relationship between competitive A-trait and SC-state ($r = -.20$). The negative relationship indicates that athletes high in competitive A-trait tend to be low in SC-state before competition.

Self-confidence can also be measured by the CSAI-2. In the development of the CSAI-2, a subscale of items representing state self-confidence emerged from the factor analyses. Although the CSAI-2 is thought of as an anxiety measure, the serendipitous emergence of the state self-confidence factor warranted its inclusion as a subscale in the inventory. In two field studies that used the CSAI-2 (Gould et al., 1984; Maynard & Howe, 1987), competitive A-trait was not related to state self-confidence. However, Karteroliotis and Gill (1987) found a significant negative relationship between competitive A-trait and state self-confidence at midcompetition and postcompetition. Also, Crocker et al. (1988) found significant negative relationships between competitive A-trait and state self-confidence before and after a stress management intervention program. Again, it is difficult to interpret these equivocal findings, and additional research is recommended to examine the situational influences on the relationship between competitive A-trait and state self-confidence.

Physiological Measures of Arousal

Cheatham and Rosentswieg (1982) examined the relationship between competitive A-trait and heart rate of 15 female collegiate softball coaches throughout competition. No relationship was found between the measures. Certainly, many interpretations could be offered for this finding. Heart rate is but one physiological indicator of arousal and has been shown in physiological research to be influenced by many confounding variables. Also, SCAT was developed to measure competitive A-trait in athletes, and coaches may have responded as they felt when competing instead of when coaching. These weaknesses in the study make untenable Cheatham and Rosentswieg's conclusion that SCAT is not a valid and reliable measure of competitive A-trait.

COMPETITIVE A-TRAIT
AND MOTOR PERFORMANCE

In the previous two sections, research using SCAT has been reviewed that represents Links 1 and 2 in the competitive anxiety model. Individual responses are directly influenced by perception of threat, which is influenced by both situational and person factors (particularly competitive A-trait). According to the interactional paradigm, state responses should be the best predictors of performance because performance is the product of both situational and person factors. Thus, SCAT is not predicted to influence performance directly. However, several studies have examined the ability of SCAT to predict performance, and these are reviewed in this section. A detailed examination of the relationship between competitive A-state and performance may be found in Part IV.

Laboratory Studies

In the original SCAT validation studies, Martens, Gill, and Scanlan (1976) found no significant differences in motor performance between high and low competitive A-trait individuals. Three other laboratory studies (Broughton & Perlstrom, 1986; Murphy & Woolfolk, 1987; Poteet & Weinberg, 1980) found no significant relationship between competitive A-trait and motor performance, respectively, on a computerized dice game task, golf putting, and a flexed-arm hang-strength task. Interestingly, Murphy and Woolfolk found that cognitive-behavioral techniques were effective in reducing A-state but that even the reduction of A-state did not result in improved performance.

The failure to demonstrate a significant relationship between competitive anxiety and motor performance may be based on the complex factors involved in performance prediction. That is, it is not that competitive anxiety and performance are unrelated. Anyone who has performed a motor skill in competitive conditions can attest to the adverse effects of anxiety on performance. However, the prediction of motor performance requires precise measurement of variables and control over the multiple factors that impinge on performance.

As discussed in chapter 4, one way to improve performance prediction is to measure performance more precisely by focusing on qualitative aspects instead of performance outcomes, or quantitative aspects. A good example is Weinberg's (1977) measurement of EMG activity in subjects' arm muscles as they competed on a throwing task as an example of qualitative performance measurement. Using SCAT in a follow-up study, Weinberg (1978) found that high competitive A-trait subjects used more EMG energy before, during, and after performance on a competitive throwing task. In the execution of a proper overhand throw, the antagonist muscles should act first as the subject prepares to throw and be followed sequentially by the contraction of the agonist muscles. Finally, the contraction of the antagonists should end the movement. This sequential contraction provides for free phasic movement and was displayed by low competitive A-trait subjects in Weinberg's study. Conversely, high competitive A-trait subjects exhibited cocontraction, in which the agonists and antagonists contracted simultaneously. This cocontraction represents an inefficient movement pattern. Weinberg concluded that high competitive A-trait subject's organization of muscular energy for performance is inhibited due to their perceived threat in competitive situations. Even after success feedback, high competitive A-trait subjects were much more inefficient in their use of neuromuscular energy than were low competitive A-trait subjects.

Weinberg (1978) also demonstrated a significant interaction between competitive A-trait and feedback for performance. Performance was measured as intraindividual improvement from pretest to posttest. Low competitive A-trait subjects performed best after receiving failure feedback, and high competitive A-trait subjects performed best after receiving success feedback. Weinberg (1979) partially replicated these findings by again demonstrating that low competitive A-trait subjects performed better than did high competitive A-trait subjects after failure feedback. In the success condition, no significant differences emerged between high and low competitive A-trait subjects, although the means were in the predicted direction (similar to his 1978 findings).

Weinberg (1979) suggested that the relationship between attentional focus and anxiety may have accounted for the performance differences found in these studies. That is, under threatening (failure) conditions, high competitive A-trait individuals may have directed their attention inward to perceive their anxiety whereas low competitive A-trait individuals may have been motivated more by the competitive challenge to concentrate more optimally. Conversely, success feedback may have altered the perceived threat and the inward attentional focus of high competitive A-trait individuals to allow them to concentrate on task-relevant cues. The lower performance of low competitive A-trait individuals in the success condition suggests that these individuals became overconfident and bored with the lack of challenge and attended to task-irrelevant cues. Certainly, these findings suggest that there is an optimal arousal state for performance and that the interaction between competitive A-trait and success/failure feedback influences the achievement of this optimal arousal state.

Field Studies

Similar to the laboratory studies, field studies examining the relationship between competitive A-trait and motor performance have provided equivocal results. Maynard and Howe (1987) found no relationship between competitive A-trait and performance in 22 male rugby players. Similarly, McKelvie et al. (1985) found no relationship between competitive A-trait and performance in 105 adult marathoners. Thirer and O'Donnell (1980) also found no relationship between competitive A-trait and performance and erroneously used SCAT as a precompetitive anxiety measure over the course of a season. Gerson and Deshaies (1978) reported a significant relationship between competitive A-trait and batting average, but these results should be viewed with caution because SCAT was administered precompetitively and the performance measure was *team* batting average.

The most widely accepted theory regarding the relationship between anxiety (in this case arousal is operationalized as anxiety) and performance is the inverted-U hypothesis (Yerkes & Dodson, 1908). The inverted-U hypothesis states that performance will improve as arousal increases up to an optimal point, after which further increases in arousal debilitate performance. Furthermore, Oxendine (1970) has suggested that gross motor skills such as weight-lifting and football require higher levels of arousal for optimal performance than do fine motor skills such as archery and golf, which require lower levels of arousal for optimal performance. Three field studies have employed SCAT to examine the anxiety-performance relationship on the basis of these theories.

As discussed earlier, Sonstroem and Bernardo (1982) trichotomized 30 female college basketball players into high, moderate, and low competitive A-trait groups and high, moderate, and low intraindividual competitive A-state categories. Performance was computed as a composite of overall basketball playing performance by combining several positive statistics (points, assists, steals, shot percentage) and subtracting negative statistics (turnovers, personal fouls). The effects of competitive A-trait and competitive A-state on performance are illustrated in Figure 6.5. Although the main effect for competitive A-trait was not significant (a significant main effect did emerge for competitive A-state), the results support the inverted-U theory, the effect being especially pronounced in the high competitive A-trait group. In controlling for individual differences in competitive A-state responsiveness by using intraindividual measures, Sonstroem and Bernardo provided excellent support for the inverted-U hypothesis.

Weinberg and Genuchi (1980) trichotomized 30 collegiate golfers into high, moderate, and low competitive A-trait groups and recorded precompetitive A-state (SAI) and performance for a practice round and two competitive rounds. The performance measure used was each golfer's 18-hole total score. For performance, a 3 (competitive A-trait) × 3 (competitive condition) ANOVA indicated a main effect for competitive A-trait, as low competitive A-trait golfers performed

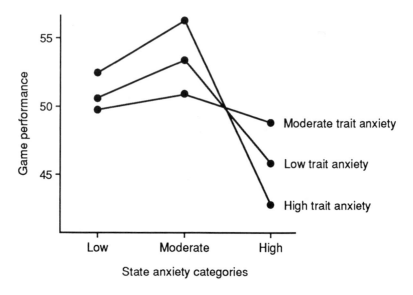

Figure 6.5. Effects of competitive A-trait and A-state on performance. *Note.* From "Intraindividual Pregame State Anxiety and Basketball Performance: A Reexamination of the Inverted-U Curve" by R.J. Sonstroem and P. Bernardo, 1982, *Journal of Sport Psychology*, **4**, p. 242. Copyright 1982 by Human Kinetics Publishers. Adapted by permission.

better than did moderate and high competitive A-trait golfers. No significant differences in performance were found between moderate and high competitive A-trait golfers, although moderate competitive A-trait golfers displayed higher performance means than did high competitive A-trait golfers in both competitive rounds. These results provide partial support for the inverted-U theory and clearly support Oxendine's (1970) hypothesis, as the complex skill of golf was performed best by low competitive A-trait golfers. Weinberg and Genuchi also noted that the relationship between A-state and performance was stronger than was the relationship between competitive A-trait and performance for both days of competition.

Taylor (1987) examined the relationship between several trait personality constructs and performance in 84 collegiate athletes from six different sports. For gross motor sports, athletes who were higher in competitive A-trait and trait self-confidence (modified from the CSAI-2) were ranked higher by their coaches at the end of the season. For fine motor sports, moderate levels of competitive A-trait, trait self-confidence, and trait cognitive anxiety (modified from the CSAI-2) were related to higher performance ratings by the coaches and to their end-of-season rankings. Taylor's results support Oxendine's (1970) theory in that levels of competitive A-trait and other personality dispositions were found to be related to performance differently, depending on the type of sport. However, Taylor's use of coaches' ratings as performance measures is less desirable than are the actual performance measures used in the studies of Sonstroem and Bernardo (1982) and Weinberg and Genuchi (1980).

INFLUENCE OF COMPETITIVE A-TRAIT AND PERFORMANCE ON PERFORMANCE OUTCOMES

Link 3 in the competitive anxiety model represents the influence of responses and intrapersonal factors (competitive A-trait) on performance outcomes (see Figure 6.1). After performing, individuals have different thoughts, feelings, and behaviors (performance outcomes) based not only on the performance but also on intrapersonal factors (especially competitive A-trait) that differentially influence how individuals perceive their performance. In this section, research examining the influence of performance and competitive A-trait on different performance outcomes is reviewed.

Postcompetition A-State

In the original SCAT validation studies conducted in laboratory settings (Gill & Martens, 1977; Martens & Gill, 1976; Scanlan, 1975), competitive A-trait and performance factors (degree of success or failure) were found to be significant predictors of postcompetition A-state as measured by the SAIC (Spielberger, 1973). Performance factors accounted for more of the A-state variance, however, than did competitive A-trait.

Three subsequent field studies using the SAIC examined the effects of several intrapersonal and situational factors on the postcompetition A-state of youth soccer players. Scanlan and Passer (1977) reported that game win-loss was a significant predictor of postcompetition A-state; losing players demonstrated greater A-state after competition than did winning players. SCAT as a measure of competitive A-trait was not a significant predictor of postcompetition A-state.

In a follow-up study, Scanlan and Passer (1978) again found game win-loss to be the most powerful predictor of postcompetition A-state, accounting for 40% of the variance in this situation. Losing players demonstrated higher A-state after competition than did winning players. With regard to game closeness, losing players were higher in A-state than were winning players for very close games, for moderately close games, and for games that were not close. Also, players who lost very close games were higher in A-state than were players who lost moderately close games or games that were not close. Although competitive A-trait was not a significant predictor, Scanlan and Passer found that three other intrapersonal factors did predict postcompetition A-state. Higher basal A-state was associated with higher postcompetition A-state. Players who indicated they had less fun during games were higher in postcompetition A-state than were players who reported having more fun. Finally, players who perceived winning to be more important to their coach evidenced higher A-state than did players who perceived winning to be less important to their coach. Although significant, this last intrapersonal factor accounted for only 1% of the variance in postcompetition A-state.

Because only male youth sport athletes were used in the first two studies, Scanlan and Passer (1979b) replicated these studies using young female soccer players. The results were similar. Game outcome accounted for 40% of the variance in postcompetition A-state, as losing players were more anxious than were winning players. Also, tying players were more anxious than were winning players but less anxious than were losing players. Players experiencing less fun during games evidenced higher postcompetition A-state than did players experiencing more fun. Less satisfied players were more anxious than were more satisfied players, and players who perceived their team performance as poorer were more anxious than were players who had more positive perceptions about team performance. Respectively, these factors accounted for 16%, 1%, and 1% of the variance in postcompetition A-state. Again, competitive A-trait was not a significant predictor of postcompetition A-state. Although the effects of competitive A-trait on A-state were nonsignificant, the Scanlan and Passer studies provide excellent corroboration of the interacting influence of situational and other intrapersonal factors on postcompetition A-state.

Postcompetition Competitive A-State

As discussed previously, the development of the CSAI and the CSAI-C (Martens, Burton, Rivkin, & Simon, 1980) created a distinction between *competitive* A-state and A-state as measured by Spielberger's SAI and SAIC. For that reason, and to be congruent with previous sections of this review, the studies using the CSAI and the CSAI-C are reviewed separately here.

As part of the original SCAT validation process, Simon and Martens (1977) indicated that SCAT was a better predictor of competitive A-state in precompetition and competition situations than in postcompetition situations. Two subsequent field studies using the CSAI have examined the relationship between competitive A-trait and postcompetition competitive A-state.

Scanlan and Lewthwaite (1984) examined individual and situational influences on competitive A-state after two consecutive wrestling matches using 76 youth wrestlers as subjects. For Match 1, win-loss and fun were the dominant predictors of postcompetition competitive A-state, accounting for 41% of the variance. Losing wrestlers were more anxious than were winners, and, independent of win-loss, wrestlers who had more fun during the match were less anxious than were wrestlers who had less fun. For Match 2, the findings were similar regarding win-loss and fun. Also, wrestlers who manifested higher competitive A-state following Match 1 were again more anxious after Match 2. Scanlan and Lewthwaite emphasized the importance of the finding that Match 1 win-loss was unrelated to Match 2 postcompetition competitive A-state. This finding indicates that the situational influence of win-loss on competitive A-state is acute and quickly replaced by subsequent outcomes. Similar to the earlier field studies using the SAIC, competitive A-trait was not a significant predictor of postcompetition competitive A-state.

Huband and McKelvie (1986) administered the CSAI to 21 high competitive and 21 low competitive A-trait collegiate athletes 24 hours before competition (baseline), 30 minutes before competition, immediately after competition, and 1 day after competition. Immediately after competition, competitive A-state in high competitive A-trait athletes declined but was still higher than their baseline measure and higher than that of the low competitive A-trait athletes. One day after competition, high competitive A-trait athletes' competitive A-state had declined to their baseline levels but still remained higher than that of the low competitive A-trait athletes. The low competitive A-trait athletes' competitive A-state fell significantly below their baseline measure the day after competition.

Although it is interesting to observe how differences in competitive A-trait influence competitive A-state after competition, it must be remembered that no situational factors were included in this analysis. The Scanlan and Passer (1977, 1978, 1979b) and Scanlan and Lewthwaite (1984) studies clearly demonstrate that success and failure account for the greatest amount of variance in A-state after competition. Thus, although competitive A-trait may influence postcompetition competitive A-state, the effects are minimal when compared to performance influences.

Postcompetition Expectancy

Another performance outcome examined in the literature is expectancy of future performance. In these studies, subjects were asked to assess how they feel they would perform in the future against the opponent they just competed against. Scanlan and Passer (1979a) examined the influence of game outcome and the intrapersonal factors of competitive A-trait, ability, and self-esteem on postcompetition expectancies of 192 female youth soccer players. Game outcome was the most significant predictor, as losers had lower postcompetition expectancies than did winners. Moreover, tying players had lower postcompetition expectancies than did winners. Neither competitive A-trait, soccer ability, nor self-esteem emerged as significant predictors of postcompetition performance expectancies.

A similar examination of predictors of postcompetition expectancies was conducted with 205 male youth soccer players (Scanlan & Passer, 1981). Again, competitive A-trait was not a significant predictor, but a significant interaction was found between game win-loss and self-esteem. Losing players with low self-esteem had low postcompetition expectancies, but losing players with high self-esteem had very positive expectancies. Winning players maintained high post-competition expectancies regardless of self-esteem level. These results suggest that high levels of self-esteem in children may offset some of the negative psychological effects of losing and maintain high levels of future performance expectancy.

It is not surprising that competitive A-trait is unrelated to postcompetition expectancies. As discussed earlier, these studies also indicated that competitive A-trait could not significantly predict precompetition expectancies (Scanlan & Passer, 1979a, 1981). Because expectancy represents confidence, or perceived ability to be successful, it seems logical that it is better predicted by ability and self-esteem. Thus, it is possible for children to feel threatened by competition and still believe that they can perform well.

Postcompetition Social Comparison Preferences

Scanlan (1977, 1978) and Scanlan and Ragan (1978) conducted a series of investigations examining how competitive A-trait affects subjects' preferences for future competition and opponents after they have performed in an experimental competitive situation. In the first study (Scanlan, 1977), 41 high competitive and 42 low competitive A-trait fifth- and sixth-grade boys were tested on the competitive motor maze used in the original SCAT laboratory validation studies (see chapter 4). A Competitive A-Trait × Success/Failure ANOVA indicated no differences in preference for future opponent, as all groups selected opponents of equal ability. However, differences between groups based on success/failure did emerge regarding whether subjects wanted their performance results made public. All the subjects who were highly successful on the task agreed to have their results made public, but only 54% of the subjects who were less successful, did so. Competitive A-trait was not a factor in these differences.

In the second study, Scanlan (1978) examined the competition and opponent preferences of 27 high competitive and 27 low competitive A-trait adult males after performing on a competitive ring-peg task. When asked whether they would prefer competitive or noncompetitive conditions on the task in the future, 81% of the low competitive and 74% of the high competitive A-trait subjects chose the competitive condition. When asked what type of opponent they would prefer to compete against in the future, 96% of the low competitive and 85% of the high competitive A-trait subjects preferred opponents of equal or greater ability. Thus, the responses of both competitive A-trait groups were similar for both groups, thus showing a strong preference for competitive conditions and a high level of social comparison. An interesting addition to this study would be to manipulate levels of success and failure to examine the interaction of competitive A-trait and performance on these social comparison preferences.

Scanlan and Ragan (1978) used SCAT and Mehrabian's (1968) MAT to measure the motives to avoid failure (Maf) and to achieve success (Mas), respectively. By choosing subjects who scored high and low on both inventories, Scanlan and Ragan dichotomized 24 subjects as high nACH (low SCAT, high MAT) and 24 subjects as low nACH (high SCAT, low MAT) to participate in the ring-peg task used in the previously discussed study. After competing on the task, more high than low nACH subjects preferred the evaluative competitive situation over the minimally evaluative noncompetitive situation. Also as predicted, more high than low nACH subjects selected opponents of equal or greater ability than they did opponents of less ability. Thus, high nACH subjects perceived less threat than did low nACH subjects by seeking out evaluative competition and attempting to maximize comparative appraisal information by preferring skilled opponents. It seems that using the MAT in conjunction with SCAT elicited more group differences in social comparison preferences than did using SCAT alone. Again, it would be interesting to examine the interacting influence of nACH and different situational outcomes on various social comparison preferences.

Additional Performance Outcomes

Cooley (1987) examined several postcompetition performance outcomes of 53 adult club tennis players participating in a weekend tournament. Using SCAT, the CSAI, and Spielberger et al.'s (1970) STAI as predictors, Cooley found that competitive A-trait as measured by SCAT was a significant predictor of perceived match outcome and perceived impact of tension on performance. Competitive A-trait accounted for 16% of the variance in each of the performance outcomes.

Causal attributions, or the perceived causes of performance, are examples of performance outcomes that have been of great interest in the achievement motivation literature. Scanlan (1977) and Biddle and Jamieson (1988) have examined the relationship between competitive A-trait and causal attributions. Consistent with attribution theory literature (Weiner, 1974, 1979), both studies found a significant relationship between success/failure and causal attributions. However, no relationships were indicated between competitive A-trait and causal attributions for performance. As with expectancy, it seems that causal attributions are most influenced by the situation and by intrapersonal factors such as self-confidence and self-esteem rather than by competitive A-trait.

INFLUENCE OF PERFORMANCE OUTCOMES ON COMPETITIVE A-TRAIT

The final link in the competitive anxiety model is Link 4, which represents the influence of performance outcomes on intrapersonal factors, particularly competitive A-trait. Over time and many competitive experiences, different performance outcomes (or consequences) influence personality. That is, an individual's level of competitive A-trait is based on the consequences of all of one's prior experiences in sport, such as whether one has succeeded or failed, whether one received positive or negative feedback, and whether the sport experience made one feel competent and worthy or incompetent and unworthy. Link 4 completes the cycle of reciprocal interactionism on which the competitive anxiety model is based.

Because this link represents a process that occurs over a period of time, no research directly addresses this link. Clearly, a longitudinal approach is needed to test this link by examining the influence of different performance outcomes, or consequences of sport participation, on competitive A-trait over time.

INTERVENTION

Several researchers have used SCAT in intervention situations with varying results. Smith (1980) discussed a case study of a highly skilled adolescent figure skater who completed a 3-week stress management program. After the treatment, the skater reported that the coping skills she learned were very successful in controlling the anxiety she experienced during competition. Smith indicated that the skater exhibited a large decrease in competitive A-trait after completing the treatment program. However, in an experimental study by Crocker et al. (1988), no differences emerged in competitive A-trait between the treatment group, which used Smith's (1980) stress management training program, and a control group.

Hellstedt (1987) conducted a psychological skills training program with 43 competitive skiers aged 12 to 18 over the course of a competitive season. SCAT was administered at the beginning and the end of the program. Hellstedt found that the skiers' competitive A-trait significantly decreased from pretest to posttest. Due to the lack of a control group, Hellstedt indicated that the decreases in competitive A-trait may be attributed to increases in skill and experience gained over the course of the season.

Lanning and Hisanaga (1983) investigated the effects of systematic relaxation training on the competitive A-trait and serving performance of 24 female volleyball players. High competitive A-trait players were randomly assigned to a control or a treatment group. Treatment consisted of seven 30-minute sessions of physical relaxation training over a 3-week period. The treatment group significantly decreased in competitive A-trait and increased serving efficiency from pretest to posttest. Also, these differences were sustained over a 2-week period. These results are suspect, however, as it is difficult to understand how a *physical* relaxation training program could significantly decrease an individual's tendency to perceive competition as threatening over a 3-week period. Lanning and Hisanaga did not report any changes in activity for the control group; thus, the Hawthorne effect could have accounted for the differences found for the treatment group.

Blais and Vallerand (1986) examined the effects of biofeedback training on high competitive A-trait boys as they competed in a bogus motor performance tournament. The biofeedback group was superior to the placebo group in reducing frontalis EMG both during rest periods and in competitive conditions. No differences were found in competitive A-trait between treatment and placebo groups on the posttest measure. The results are equivocal regarding the use of SCAT to measure change in competitive A-trait as the result of treatment. With the increasing interest in psychological skills training with athletes, it would be useful to develop a modified SCAT inventory to be used in applied intervention research.

COACHES' ABILITY TO PREDICT COMPETITIVE A-TRAIT AND A-STATE IN ATHLETES

Study 8 in the initial construction validation of SCAT (see chapter 4) examined coaches' ability to predict the competitive A-state levels of their athletes before competition (this study was later published by Martens and Simon, 1976a). The results indicate that coaches were not accurate predictors of their players' levels of competitive A-state $(r = .12$ between coaches' ratings and actual responses) and that SCAT was a much better predictor of competitive A-state $(r = .65)$.

A replication of this study by Martens, Rivkin, and Burton (1980) also found coaches to be poor predictors $(r = -.10)$ and SCAT to be a good predictor $(r = .53)$ of athletes' competitive A-state. However, there was much variability between individual coaches in their ability to predict athletes' competitive A-state, as the correlations ranged from $-.60$ to $.55$ for individual coaches. These results indicate that from an overall perspective coaches were not very good predictors of their athletes' A-state levels, yet at the same time some individual coaches appeared to be very accurate in aassessing their players' anxiety levels. Interestingly, athletes were much more accurate in predicting the competitive A-state levels of their coaches $(r = .51)$.

Hanson and Gould (1988) extended and replicated these two studies by asking coaches to predict the competitive A-state (CSAI) of their athletes as well as the competitive A-trait (SCAT) of their athletes. Hanson and Gould's procedures were different from those of the previous two studies, as they had the coaches complete the CSAI and SCAT as they thought their athletes would respond. In the previous studies, coaches rated their predicted anxiety responses of players on a Likert-type scale. Hanson and Gould also examined various characteristics about coaches that influenced their ability to predict athletes' anxiety and also attempted to identify how coaches assess anxiety in their athletes.

The correlation between coaches' assessment of their athletes' competitive A-trait and the athletes' actual competitive A-trait was .15, and this correlation accounted for only 6% of the total variance. These results indicate that overall there was not a strong relationship between coaches' estimates and their athletes' actual competitive A-trait levels. However, gender of the athlete was a factor in prediction, as coaches estimated female athletes' competitive A-trait much better $(r = .25)$ than they did male athletes' competitive A-trait $(r = -.02)$. The results also indicate that older, more experienced coaches were more accurate in predicting their athletes' competitive A-trait.

The correlation between coaches' assessment of their athletes' competitive A-state and the athletes' actual competitive A-state using the CSAI was .27 but accounted for only 7% of the total variance. Similar to previous studies, SCAT was a much better predictor of competitive A-state $(r = .70)$. Gender of athlete was also a factor in these analyses as coaches estimated female athletes' competitive A-state better $(r = .27)$ than they did male athletes' competitive A-state $(r = -.11)$. Also, the larger the size of the team, the less accurate were the coaches' predictions of athletes' competitive A-state. Finally, coaches rated changes in athletes' communication levels and behavior patterns as the most important cues to be used in assessing athletes' anxiety.

SUMMARY

This chapter has attempted to summarize and review the findings of all published research using SCAT to measure competitive A-trait. The review has been organized around a conceptual model of competitive anxiety expanded from Martens's (1977) original model. Clearly, the abundance of research using SCAT has supported many theoretical predictions in the model. However, in reviewing the research it became clear that many important questions remain. Thus, in chapter 7 broad conclusions based on the completed research are set forth, and possible future directions for competitive anxiety researchers suggested.

Chapter 7

SCAT: Conclusions, Problems, and Future Directions

The results discussed in chapter 6 indicate that SCAT has sparked an abundance of research in the area of competitive anxiety. Besides the empirical studies examined there and the doctoral dissertations summarized in Appendix B, competitive anxiety research using SCAT has been discussed in many sport psychology reviews (Bunker & Rotella, 1980; Gould & Petlichkoff, 1988; Martens, 1988; Martens, Gill, Simon, & Scanlan, 1975; Passer, 1982, 1984, 1988; Scanlan, 1984, 1986, 1988; Sonstroem, 1984) and textbooks (Carron, 1980; Cox, 1985; Cratty, 1983; Gill, 1986b; Iso-Ahola & Hatfield, 1986; Roberts, Spink, & Pemberton, 1986). Also, it is noteworthy that the conceptualization of competitive anxiety and psychometric development of SCAT has provided the impetus for the development of several other sport-specific psychological inventories (Ewing, 1981; Gill & Deeter, 1988; Vealey, 1986; Weiss, Bredemeier, & Shewchuk, 1985).

The purpose of this chapter is threefold. First, conclusions are set forth on the basis of the review of SCAT research reported in chapter 6. Second, both psychometric and theoretical problems that have arisen in the competitive anxiety research are discussed. Third, possible future directions for research using SCAT are outlined.

CONCLUSIONS DRAWN FROM RESEARCH USING SCAT

In this section, conclusions are drawn from the research that has used SCAT as a measure of competitive A-trait. Although a brief summary follows each stated conclusion, all the related studies are not discussed again here. Individual studies supporting each conclusion may be reviewed in chapter 6.

Psychometric Research

1. *Research supports the discriminating power, internal consistency, reliability, and content validity of SCAT as a measure of competitive A-trait.*

Weiner and Stewart (1984) defined a test as "a systematic procedure for measuring a representative sample of a person's behavior" (p. 2). A test, or psychological inventory, must be developed using systematic procedures to have confidence that the test score is an accurate and a representative indicator of the psychological construct that the test purports to measure. In the initial development of SCAT, the inventory underwent extensive and rigorous psychometric analyses to support the reliability and validity of SCAT as a measure of competitive A-trait (see Part I). Subsequent psychometric research supports the item discrimination ability, internal consistency, and reliability of SCAT.

2. *Research supports the concurrent, predictive, and construct validity of SCAT as a measure of competitive A-trait.*

Concurrent validity is supported by demonstrating significant relationships between the test and other personality measures obtained at the same time (Allen & Yen, 1979). Competitive A-trait as measured by SCAT has been shown to be positively related to the sport-specific dispositions of fear of failure, ineffective attentional focus, and cognitive and somatic anxiety as measured by a trait version of the CSAI-2. Conversely, competitive A-trait has been shown to be negatively related to the sport-specific dispositions of need for power and self-confidence. The research is equivocal regarding the relationship between competitive A-trait and perceived sport ability, but the findings suggest that as athletes move from youth sport into more highly structured situations, competitive A-trait and perceived ability are negatively related. With regard to general personality dispositions, competitive A-trait has demonstrated low positive relationships with general A-trait, test anxiety, external locus control, and sensitization to internal feelings of threat. Low negative relationships have been indicated between competitive A-trait and internal locus of control and self-esteem. These results are significant in that SCAT is related to other dispositions in the predicted directions and shows a stronger relationship with sport-specific measures than with general personality measures.

Although predictive validity was mentioned in this section to underscore its importance as part of the psychometric analysis of an inventory, the research supporting the predictive validity of SCAT is discussed later in this chapter. Also, it is important to realize that construct validity is inferred from the accumulation of evidence that supports theoretical predictions in the competitive anxiety model. Thus, the evidence for the construct validity of SCAT is not included in this section but may be inferred on the basis of the accumulated research that has supported different hypotheses regarding competitive A-trait. The findings discussed in the remainder of this chapter represent evidence for the construct validity of

SCAT and support the findings of the original construct validation research that were presented in chapter 4.

Individual Differences in Competitive A-Trait

3. *Research examining differences in competitive A-trait based on gender is equivocal, and these equivocal results may be explained by accounting for other intrapersonal factors and differences in socialization.*

Research has variously indicated that no differences exist in competitive A-trait based on gender, that females are higher in competitive A-trait than are males, and that males are higher in competitive A-trait than are females. Some evidence suggests that differences in competitive A-trait can be explained better by accounting for gender roles instead of gender per se. Specifically, regardless of gender, the feminine gender role is associated with higher levels of competitive A-trait and the masculine gender role with lower levels of competitive A-trait. Also, physical self-efficacy has been shown to be a contributing factor in gender and gender role differences in competitive A-trait. These findings suggest that differences in competitive A-trait may be a function not of biological sex but of differential socialization.

4. *Research examining differences in competitive A-trait based on age is equivocal.*

Research has variously indicated that no differences exist in competitive A-trait based on age, that older athletes are higher in competitive A-trait than are younger athletes, and that younger athletes are higher in competitive A-trait than are older athletes. The equivocal findings may be influenced by the age ranges and situational differences in the studies. Overall, it appears that very young athletes are lower in competitive A-trait than are older athletes because the young athletes have not yet been socialized to perceive competition as an intense, evaluative situation that threatens their self-esteem. However, once athletes (regardless of age) enter into more competitive, highly structured levels of sport, those that are younger and less experienced tend to manifest higher competitive A-trait than do older and more experienced athletes. Subsequent research needs to account for cognitive maturity levels of athletes and the structure, intensity, and importance of competition to further examine developmental changes in competitive A-trait.

5. *Overall, no relationship is indicated between competitive A-trait and ability, participation status, race, type of sport, and physiological capacity.*

Clearly, most of the studies investigating individual differences lack a theoretical focus. Later in this chapter, suggestions for future theoretical development and research are offered.

Perception of Threat

6. *High competitive A-trait individuals perceive greater threat in competitive situations than do low competitive A-trait individuals.*

The findings indicate that high competitive A-trait individuals worry more about making mistakes, not performing well, not playing up to their ability, improving on their last performance, participating in championship competition, being able to get mentally able to perform, and losing. Also, high competitive A-trait individuals expect to play less well; experience greater emotional upset, shame, and self-criticism after losing; have more trouble sleeping before competition; and feel that their nervousness more often hurts their performance than do low competitive A-trait individuals.

7. *Characteristics of competition that induce perception of threat are fear of failure, fear of evaluation, ego threat, outcome uncertainty, negative outcome certainty, external control, and perceived importance of sport.*

In addition to the specific behavioral differences in perceptions of threat found between high and low competitive A-trait individuals, researchers have attempted to identify the underlying characteristics of competition that high competitive A-trait individuals find threatening. Sources of threat have been found to emanate from both fear of failure and fear of evaluation, and SCAT is indicated as a significant predictor of these perceived sources of threat. Perceived threat also has been found to result from an external control/guilt source, but competitive A-trait was not related to this source of threat. Finally, outcome uncertainty, outcome certainty in a negative direction (losing), ego threat, and perceived importance of sport have been identified as sources of threat in sport competition.

8. *Situational factors and other intrapersonal factors mediate the influence of competitive A-trait on perception of threat.*

High competitive A-trait individuals predict higher anxiety for themselves before and during competition than do low competitive A-trait individuals, but these differences disappear in situations of low potential threat. Similarly, athletes' anxiety responses have been shown to vary with their perceptions of situational threat, with competitive A-trait accounting for almost half the anxiety response variance. Also, research indicates that gender may play a role in the perception of threat. Two studies have indicated that the relationship between competitive A-trait and perception of threat is more pronounced for males than for females. These findings suggest that gender socialization may cause males to value sport success more highly and thus to perceive more threat.

Predicting State Responses

The conclusions set forth in this section represent support for the predictive validity of SCAT. Predictive validity involves using test scores to predict future behavior (Allen & Yen, 1979). Thus, the findings discussed in this section demonstrate that SCAT, as a dispositional measure, can predict various state characteristics in advance. In this sense, SCAT enables reseachers to predict how individuals will respond before and during competition.

9. *SCAT is a significant predictor of A-state.*

SCAT as a measure of competitive A-trait has been shown to predict A-state significantly as measured by Spielberger et al.'s (1970) SAI and Spielberger's (1973) SAIC in precompetition and midcompetition. Supporting the interactional model, high competitive A-trait individuals manifest higher A-state than do low A-trait individuals, and these differences are more pronounced in competitive conditions than in noncompetitive (baseline) conditions and in failure conditions than in success conditions.

10. *SCAT is a significant predictor of competitive A-state.*

Martens, Burton, Rivkin, and Simon (1980) modified Spielberger's SAI and SAIC into the CSAI and CSAI-C by identifying items that were more sensitive to A-state changes in competitive situations. The SCAT-CSAI relationship was found to be stronger than the SCAT-SAI relationship because the CSAI measured *competitive* A-state. A meta-analysis using the validity generalization model indicated that the mean true validity (or correlation) between competitive A-trait and competitive A-state, with artifactual variance taken into account, was .61. Similar to previous findings, SCAT's ability to predict competitive A-state was found to increase under competitive conditions. True to competitive anxiety theory, both low and high competitive A-trait individuals increase in competitive A-state from noncompetition to competition conditions, but the increase is significantly greater for high competitive A-trait individuals.

11. *SCAT is a significant predictor of cognitive and somatic competitive A-state.*

As discussed in Part III, Martens, Burton, Vealey, Bump, and Smith (1982) modified the CSAI into the CSAI-2 to account for both cognitive and somatic manifestations of competitive A-state. In the original validation of the CSAI-2 (see Part III), SCAT was a significant predictor of both cognitive and somatic competitive A-state but demonstrated a stronger relationship with somatic competitive A-state. This was as predicted because most of the items in SCAT seem to tap somatic manifestations of anxiety. Although research supports significant relationships between competitive A-trait and somatic as well as cognitive competitive A-state, the stronger relationship between SCAT and somatic competitive A-state is not clearly supported. These equivocal findings indicate that situational factors must be accounted for in examining the relationship between competitive A-trait and multidimensional anxiety states.

12. *SCAT as a measure of competitive A-trait is not a significant predictor of precompetition performance expectancy.*

Ability and self-esteem, but not competitive A-trait, have been shown to predict precompetition performance expectancy significantly. Because expectancy is based on confidence in being successful, it seems logical that ability and self-esteem are better predictors. Thus, although high competitive A-trait individuals find competition threatening and respond with higher competitive A-state, they still expect to perform as well as do low competitive A-trait individuals. However, these findings need to be replicated, as significant relationships have been demonstrated between competitive A-trait and expectancy measured in baseline situations (i.e., expectancy about an upcoming tournament or season).

13. *The research is equivocal regarding the ability of SCAT to predict state self-confidence in competitive situations.*

Self-confidence has been measured in competitive situations using the SSCI (Vealey, 1986) and the self-confidence subscale of the CSAI-2. Although some significant findings have emerged, the relationship between competitive A-trait and state self-confidence is not firmly established.

14. *No relationship has been shown between SCAT and physiological measures of arousal.*

No relationship was indicated between competitive A-trait and heart rate (Cheatham & Rosentswieg, 1982). However, heart rate is but one physiological measure of arousal; thus, more research using multiple indicators of physiological arousal is needed to examine this relationship.

Predicting Motor Performance

15. *SCAT has significantly predicted performance in situations in which performance is based on complex motor skills or is qualitatively measured.*

State responses (in this case A-state) should theoretically be the best predictors of motor performance because they account for the interaction of intrapersonal and situational factors. However, in some cases, SCAT as a measure of competitive A-trait has emerged as a significant predictor of performance. High competitive A-trait individuals' utilization of muscular energy for performance has been demonstrated to be inhibited due to their perceived threat in competitive situations. This finding is significant in that performance is measured qualitatively in terms of efficiency of movement rather than quantitatively on the basis of performance outcome.

Also, performance prediction has been facilitated by computing a composite performance score based on several types of statistics and controlling for individual differences in competitive A-state responsiveness by using intraindividual measures. These intraindividual controls resulted in support for the arousal-performance inverted-U theory and in an especially pronounced effect for high competitive A-trait athletes. Finally, support for Oxendine's (1970) theory has been established by demonstrating that competitive A-trait is related to performance differently, depending on the type of sport.

However, the relationship between competitive A-trait and performance remains unclear. Significant findings have emerged for an overarm throwing task, basketball performance, golf performance, and team batting average. Nonsignificant findings have emerged for performance in a computerized dice game, golf putting, a flexed-arm hang-strength task, rugby performance, and marathon performance.

Performance Outcomes

Similar to the conclusion of the previous section, these in this section also support the predictive validity of SCAT. This research examined the influence of competitive A-trait and situational factors on the thoughts, feelings, and behaviors of individuals after they perform.

16. *Although competitive A-trait may influence postcompetition A-state, the effects are minimal when compared to performance influences.*

In studies using the SAIC as well as the CSAI/CSAIC, competitive outcome (win-loss) repeatedly emerged as the most significant predictor of postcompetition A-state. Losing athletes were higher in postcompetition A-state than were winning players. Also, the amount of fun experienced during competition significantly predicted postcompetition A-state of youth sport athletes. Independent of win-loss, athletes who had more fun during competition were less anxious than were athletes who experienced less fun.

17. *Competitive A-trait is unrelated to postcompetition expectancies.*

Competitive outcome has proven to be the most significant predictor of future performance expectancies measured after competition. Losing athletes manifested lower postcompetition expectancies than did winning athletes. Although competitive A-trait is not related to postcompetition expectancies, self-esteem has been shown to be an important factor in offsetting the negative psychological effects of losing. Losing players with high self-esteem demonstrated higher postcompetition expectancies than did losing players with low self-esteem.

18. *Differences in postcompetition social comparison preferences based on competitive A-trait emerge only when achievement motivation level is also considered.*

Differences in competitive A-trait measured by SCAT were shown to have no effect on preferences for future opponents (level of social comparison) or competitive versus noncompetitive conditions. However, by dichotomizing individuals as high and low nACH on the basis of SCAT and MAT scores, high nACH individuals were found to seek out evaluate competition and maximize social comparison by preferring skilled opponents more than did low nACH individuals.

19. *Competitive A-trait was found to be a significant predictor of perceived performance outcome and perceived impact of tension on performance.*

Cooley (1987) examined SCAT's ability to predict several postcompetition performance outcomes and found that competitive A-trait was a significant predictor of perceived match outcome and perceived impact of tension on performance.

20. *No relationship is indicated between competitive A-trait and causal attributions.*

Consistent with attribution theory (Weiner, 1974, 1979), the research indicates that success and failure were significant predictors of causal attributions for performance but that SCAT was unrelated to attributions.

Intervention

21. *The evidence indicates that SCAT can measure change in competitive A-trait as a result of treatment.*

Significant reductions in competitive A-trait have been demonstrated after a 3-week stress management program, a seasonal psychological skills training program, and a 3-week physical relaxation program.

Coaches' Ability to Predict the Anxiety of Athletes

22. *SCAT is a much better predictor of competitive A-state in athletes than are coaches.*

Overall, coaches were not accurate predictors of athletes' competitive A-state, but some individual coaches were quite accurate. Also, it was easier to predict the competitive A-state of females than that of males, and the larger the size of the team, the less accurate were the coaches' predictions of competitive A-state.

23. *Coaches are not accurate predictors of competitive A-trait in athletes.*

Although overall coaches are not indicated to be good predictors of their athletes' competitive A-trait, older coaches with more experience have been found to be more accurate in predicting the competitive A-trait of their athletes. Also, results indicate that coaches are better able to predict competitive A-trait in female than in male athletes.

International Use of SCAT

24. *Research with SCAT has been conducted internationally.*

Competitive anxiety research using SCAT has been conducted in the United States, Canada, Great Britain, Australia, Japan, France, Germany, Hungary,

Spain, and the Soviet Union. Some of this research has not been translated into English; thus, the results are not included in this review of the SCAT literature. Also, SCAT is perhaps translated and used in countries other than the ones mentioned here without our knowledge.

PROBLEMS IN SCAT RESEARCH

Although SCAT has provided an impetus for significant advances in competitive anxiety research, problems have arisen with respect to its use and interpretation. These problems may be categorized as either psychometric or theoretical.

Psychometric Problems

Psychometric problems refer to violation of the inventory's psychometric properties, which were established during its validation. Riddick (1984) violated the homogeneity and unidimensionality of the inventory by scoring items separately and comparing groups on the basis of each item instead of on a total score. Auvergne (1983) used selected items from SCAT to create a fear-of-failure scale for athletes. Again, this violated the homogeneity of SCAT and seems illogical, as it would have been easier and more appropriate to use SCAT (with its demonstrated reliability and validity) as a measure of sport-specific fear of failure. Researchers are urged to follow carefully the guidelines outlined in chapter 5 when using these inventories.

A problem was identified in conducting the validity generalization meta-analysis on the relationship between competitive A-trait and competitive A-state, as the reliabilities for SCAT and the CSAI were not reported in any of the samples. Although sample reliability is not a conventional inclusion in published articles, it seems that it would be a useful one. Reporting the reliability of each self-report measure used for that particular sample would provide subsequent researchers with valuable information about the reliability of the sample in that particular study. This seems particularly important if we wish to employ meta-analyses to gain greater statistical precision in our reviews.

Theoretical Problems

Theoretical problems refer to using SCAT in a way that is inappropriate on the basis of the theoretical conceptualization of competitive anxiety. The problem that occurs most frequently involves the timing of the administration of SCAT. SCAT is the operationalization of competitive A-trait, which is the "tendency to perceive competitive situations as threatening" (Martens, 1977, p. 23). Competitive A-trait, as a tendency or disposition, is how threatened an individual *generally* is by competitive situations. In responding to SCAT, individuals are asked to rate how they generally feel when competing in sport. Thus, it seems problematic when researchers administer SCAT in a competitive situation because the proximity of competition may confound the dispositional measure of competitive A-trait. Although SCAT's instructions emphasize completing the inventory as one generally feels, it seems likely that individuals will be influenced by how they feel at that moment due to the impending (or concluding) competitive situation. Researchers are urged to administer SCAT in a baseline, or noncompetitive, situation in which subjects can focus on their usual responses and not be affected by the saliency of a particular event.

The second problem involves the use of A-state inventories. In the initial validation of SCAT, Spielberger et al.'s (1970) SAI was used as a measure of A-state due to its careful development, extensive validation, and administration versatility. As reported in chapter 4, during the construct validation of SCAT an abbreviated version of the adult SAI was developed that was particularly sensitive to measuring A-states in competitive situations. The reliability and validity of this instrument, the CSAI, was independently documented in subsequent research (see Martens, Burton, Rivkin, & Simon, 1980). Recent theoretical conceptualization of anxiety as a multidimensional construct prompted the development and validation of the CSAI-2, which separately measures both cognitive and somatic components of A-state as well as state self-confidence. Each of these modifications represents a significant advance in the operationalization of A-state for sport psychology research. Although researchers certainly have the right to choose their own instruments, it seems important to keep up with theoretical advances in the operationalization of A-state. Thus, for studies in the area of competitive anxiety, the CSAI-2 would seem to be the most appropriate A-state inventory to use because it is based on current theory, which defines anxiety as a multidimensional construct. Use of the CSAI/CSAI-C is warranted in studies in which a less time-consuming measure or a children's version of A-state is needed. Certainly, there are different situations that require different A-state measures, but it seems important to use the most appropriate inventory for the particular situation.

The third theoretical problem identified in the literature involves mistakingly using the CSAI and calling it SCAT or vice versa. Again, the use of competitive anxiety measures (or any personality measures) should not involve haphazard selection. It is important to understand the theoretical framework on which the inventory is based and to understand clearly which inventory is being used.

The fourth problem identified in the SCAT research involves unsubstantiated conclusions regarding SCAT and competitive A-trait on the basis of one study. For example, the authors of one study concluded that SCAT was not a valid measure of competitive A-trait because the hypothesis of the study was not confirmed. It is important to view each study as one piece of evidence that either supports or does not support theoretical predictions, past research, or both.

FUTURE DIRECTIONS FOR SCAT RESEARCH

Because of the plethora of research that has been conducted using SCAT, it may appear that most of the important questions in competitive anxiety have been answered. However, after reviewing the research using SCAT, it becomes clear that many questions remain.

Individual Differences

As discussed previously, many researchers have examined individual differences in competitive A-trait based on age, gender, ability, and so on. For the most part, these studies are descriptive and atheoretical. It is not surprising that the results are equivocal, as there is no conceptual framework to provide theoretical understanding of why these differences in competitive A-trait might occur. Thus, future research is needed to develop theory to guide researchers in asking important questions and to provide them with a conceptual basis for interpreting the findings.

For example, theory is needed that addresses how competitive A-trait is developed in children. Harter's (1978) theoretical framework for the development of competence motivation and perceived competence is an excellent model. Harter's theory accounts for the multivariate antecedents and consequences that are involved in the complex process of developing perceived competence and competence motivation. Passer (1984) has offered a preliminary framework examining the antecedents of competitive A-trait that accounts for reinforcement and attributions from significant others, performance outcomes, causal attributions for performance, and expectancies. In particular, Passer advocates exploring the influence of children's histories of success and failure to understand better the development of competitive A-trait. Other needs in examining competitive A-trait from a developmental perspective include an accounting of the cognitive maturity levels of athletes and the influence of different competitive structures on children.

A theoretical examination of the developmental antecedents of competitive A-trait could also account for the equivocal findings regarding gender differences in competitive A-trait. The results strongly suggest that differential socialization, not biological sex, is responsible for differences between males and females in competitive A-trait. Thus, research in this area is needed to examine which socializing factors elicit the development of competitive A-trait in children.

Perception of Threat

Perception of threat has been identified as the key theoretical construct in the competitive anxiety model. Research has substantiated that situational and intrapersonal factors interact to influence perception of threat, but more research is needed to examine the underlying characteristics of perception of threat. Research discussed in this review (Fisher & Zwart, 1982; Gould et al., 1983b; Passer, 1983) and elsewhere (Endler, 1978; Kroll, 1979) has indicated several dimensions, or underlying charcteristics, of competition that high competitive A-trait individuals find threatening. Lewthwaite (1986) has developed a theoretical framework that proposes that threat is perceived when important or personally meaningful goals are believed to be endangered through participation in competitive sport. Additional theory and research is needed to clarify the underlying characteristics of perception of threat.

Predicting Performance, State Responses and Performance Outcomes

Significant advances in prediction will occur when significant advances in measurement and operationalization occur. The difficult questions in competitive anxiety research will be answered (or even asked) only when we account for the complex multidimensional and reciprocal nature of thoughts, feelings, and behaviors in sport. Many of the studies using SCAT have employed multivariate designs and statistics to account for the interacting influence of situational and intrapersonal factors on performance, state responses, and performance outcomes. More of this is needed in conjunction with theoretical development in the field.

Sonstroem and Bernardo (1982) provided an excellent example of using intraindividual analyses to facilitate prediction. Further research employing intraindividual measures of state responses and performance are encouraged to refine our understanding of the anxiety-performance relationship. Also, the use of alternative performance measures with an emphasis on qualitative assessment are encouraged to facilitate prediction. Weinberg's (1978) use of muscular energy as a qualitative performance measure is an example of this type of assessment. Finally, it is important to remember that anxiety (arousal) relates differently to performance, depending on the type of task. Although researchers may embrace the inverted-U hypothesis, differences in task characteristics influence the anxiety-performance relationship and must be accounted for in the research.

Psychometric Research

Although the evidence overwhelmingly supports SCAT as a reliable and valid measure of competitive A-trait, several research possibilities exist with respect to additional development of the scale. With the conceptualization of anxiety as multidimensional and the development of the CSAI-2, it would be useful to modify SCAT to account for both cognitive and somatic components of competitive A-trait.

Lewthwaite (1986) has suggested that the measurement of competitive A-trait should account for both the frequency (how often) and the intensity (how much) of competitive A-trait responses. Presently, SCAT accounts for only the frequency (hardly ever, sometimes, often) of competitive A-trait responses; thus, it may be useful to modify the response format to include a measure of intensity of competitive A-trait.

Finally, with the increasing interest in psychological skills training with athletes, sport psychologists are searching for inventories to be used in assessing the effectiveness of intervention programs. It may be useful to modify and expand the present SCAT inventory into one that could be used exclusively in applied settings. Particularly helpful would be subscales measuring different underlying components of competitive anxiety (e.g., fear of evaluation, fear of failure, etc.) as well as different ways in which anxiety is manifested (e.g., physical tension, negative self-talk, attentional narrowing, negative images, etc.).

SUMMARY

This chapter has attempted to provide a broad overview of the SCAT research that was reviewed in chapter 6. On the basis of the conclusions set forth, problems have been identified and future research directions outlined. It is the hope of the authors that this review will stimulate additional research in competitive anxiety. It is often said that by learning more you realize how much you do not know. That has been the realization of the authors in reviewing the SCAT research. Although a significant beginning in competitive anxiety reseach has been established, there is much that we do not know. We hope that, in 10 years, another review of the research using SCAT will demonstrate how far we have come.

Development and Validation of the Competitive State Anxiety Inventory–2

Rainer Martens, PhD
Human Kinetics Publishers

Damon Burton, PhD
University of Idaho

Robin S. Vealey, PhD
Miami University, Ohio

Linda A. Bump, PhD
Human Kinetics Publishers

Daniel E. Smith, PhD
State University of New York-Brockport

The heretofore unpublished procedures in developing the CSAI-2, first presented at a 1982 symposium of the North American Society for the Psychology of Sport and Physical Activity (NASPSPA), are presented in Part III. This part is authored separately by Martens, Burton, Vealey, Bump, and Smith to record the appropriate credit in the development of this scale. Chapter 8 presents a multidimensional theory of competitive A-state that is based on the distinction between cognitive and somatic competitive A-state constructs. Subsequent chapters describe the development, validation, and administration of the CSAI-2. Individuals who have read the unpublished paper reporting the development of the CSAI-2 will want to review the extensively revised section on the anxiety and performance relationship in chapter 10 because considerable additional evidence has been added. The scale, as well as norms for each subscale by age, gender, and certain sports, are presented in chapter 11.

Chapter 8

A Multidimensional Theory of Competitive State Anxiety

Beginning in the 1950s, anxiety researchers measured anxiety with general inventories such as the Taylor (1953) Manifest Anxiety Scale, the IPAT Anxiety Scale (Cattell, 1957), and the General Anxiety Scale (Sarason, et al., 1960). Results with these instruments led researchers to conclude that anxiety was too amorphous to be useful as a predictor of behavior. Indications were that anxiety was both acute and chronic, which led to a major conceptual advance best espoused by Spielberger (1966a). He is credited with articulating the distinction between momentary anxiety states (A-state) and more enduring anxiety traits (A-trait). This led Spielberger et al. (1970) to develop the STAI, a significant advance in measurement.

At about the same time, a number of researchers were finding that situation-specific anxiety scales predicted behavior better than did general anxiety inventories. For example, scales were developed to measure test anxiety (Sarason et al., 1960), social evaluation anxiety (Watson & Friend, 1969), and even anxieties about snakes, heights, and darkness (Mellstrom, Cicala, & Zuckerman, 1976). Within sport, Martens (1977) developed SCAT, a sport-specific A-trait inventory, and demonstrated that it predicted A-state in sport better than did Spielberger et al.'s (1970) SAI.

Early research with SCAT suggested that, although a sport-specific A-trait scale was needed, a sport-specific A-state scale would also be useful. Therefore, Martens, Burton, Rivkin, and Simon (1980) modified Spielberger et al.'s SAI by identifying 10 items from the 20-item scale that were most sensitive to changes in a competitive sport environment. This new scale was named the Competitive State Anxiety Inventory (CSAI) because it assesses sport-specific A-state.

Recent theory and research suggest that even with these conceptual developments anxiety may be a more useful construct with even greater conceptual specificity (Davidson, 1978). It is becoming increasingly evident that the prediction of behavior will not succumb to grand and parsimonious theoretical explanations but instead requires theoretical constructs of increasing specificity and hence instruments to measure them.

Endler (1978), for example, asserted that both A-trait and A-state were multidimensional and suggested five components of A-trait: interpersonal ego threat, physical danger, ambiguity, innocuousness, and social evaluation threat. He also cited the research of Sarason (1975a, 1975b) and Wine (1971) in support for a two-component model of A-state. These two components he labeled *cognitive-worry* and *emotional-arousal*. Actually, Liebert and Morris (1967) first introduced these two components in the test anxiety literature. More recently, Davidson and Schwartz (1976) and Borkovec (1976) have identified two similar components of anxiety that they have labeled *cognitive anxiety* and *somatic anxiety*. In fact, Morris, Davis, and Hutchings (1981), in a review of multidimensional conceptualizations of A-state, indicated that the cognitive-somatic distinction is essentially the same as the worry-emotionality distinction made by Liebert and Morris.

By whatever name, this conceptual distinction led to the construction of at least three inventories to measure cognitive and somatic anxiety. Liebert and Morris (1967) developed the Worry-Emotionality Inventory (WEI), which was later revised by Morris, Davis, and Hutchings (1981); Spielberger, Gonzalez, Taylor, Algaze, and Anton (1978) developed the Test Anxiety Inventory (TAI); and Schwartz, Davidson, and Goleman (1978) developed the Cognitive-Somatic Anxiety Questionnaire (CSAQ). The former is an A-state scale, and the latter two inventories measure A-trait. Thus, the cognitive-somatic distinction has been used for assessing both A-trait and A-state. However, because this chapter presents a multidimensional theory of competitive A-state, the remaining discussion about the cognitive-somatic anxiety distinction will focus on A-state, not A-trait.

The conceptual distinction between cognitive and somatic A-state and the subsequent development of instrumentation to tap these multidimensional components of anxiety initiated the reconceptualization of competitive anxiety and a modification of the CSAI to account for both components of A-state. The modification of the CSAI is discussed in chapters 9 and 10, and the remainder of this chapter focuses on the distinction between cognitive and somatic A-state and discusses why this distinction is important in understanding competitive anxiety.

COGNITIVE AND SOMATIC A-STATE DEFINED

Cognitive A-state is closely associated with worry, a mental process pervasive in our society. Morris, Davis, and Hutchings (1981) defined cognitive A-state as "negative expectations and cognitive concerns about oneself, the situation at hand, and potential consequences" (p. 541). In sport, cognitive A-state is most commonly manifested in negative expectations about performance and thus negative self-evaluation, both of which precipitate worry, disturbing visual images, or both.

Somatic A-state refers to the physiological and affective elements of the anxiety experience that develop directly from autonomic arousal. Somatic A-state is reflected in such responses as rapid heart rate, shortness of breath, clammy hands, butterflies in the stomach, and tense muscles.

SIGNIFICANCE OF
THE COGNITIVE-SOMATIC DISTINCTION

The value in measuring cognitive and somatic A-state rests separately with the conceptual arguments and empirical evidence that these two components are elicited by different antecedents and that they influence behavior differently (Davidson & Schwartz, 1976; Liebert & Morris, 1967). Thus, one person may respond to a stressor with primarily cognitive A-state and another with primarily somatic A-state, or the same person may experience primarily cognitive A-state in one situation and primarily somatic A-state in a different situation. Davidson and Schwartz (1976) offered the example of

> a person who is physically tired and somatically relaxed lies down, unable to fall asleep because his "mind is racing." This individual is manifesting cognitive symptoms of anxiety. Alternatively, somatic anxiety is characteristic of the person who complains of bodily tension and autonomic stress without accompanying cognitive symptoms. Often, beginning meditators report somatic aches and pains and diffuse muscle tension despite the presence of general "cognitive calmness." (Goleman, 1971, p. 402)

Although cognitive and somatic A-state are hypothesized to be conceptually independent, Morris, Davis, and Hutchings (1981) noted that they likely covary in stressful situations because these situations contain elements related to the arousal of each. Borkovec (1976) agreed, but for a different reason. He suggested that each component of anxiety may serve a conditional or a discriminative function for the other component.

For example, if powerful somatic responses have been conditioned to a particular stimulus, these responses may indicate to the person that there is reason to worry. An athlete may have acquired conditioned somatic responses to precontest events such as locker-room preparation, presence on the playing field, an audience in the stands, and precontest warm-up routines. The conditioned somatic responses may then trigger the athlete to begin worrying because he or she is feeling certain somatic symptoms of anxiety. On the other hand, cognitions in the form of negative self-talk and images of failure may trigger a specific pattern of somatic responses. Understanding how these components interact within an individual should help sport psychologists assist athletes in managing anxiety more effectively, and this requires that the cognitive and the somatic components of A-state be measured both reliably and validly.

INDEPENDENCE OF COGNITIVE
AND SOMATIC A-STATE

The original justification for revising the CSAI was based not only on these conceptual arguments but also on extensive scientific evidence that cognitive and somatic A-state are independent and thus warrant separate measurement.

Evidence Based on Correlations, Factor Analyses, and Item Analyses

Liebert and Morris (1967) were the first to investigate this relationship using their WEI. They hoped to demonstrate the theoretical independence of cognitive and somatic A-state by obtaining low to moderate correlations between these two components of anxiety. Unfortunately, they failed to obtain the evidence they sought, as correlations from six studies ranged from .55 to .76 (Deffenbacher, 1977, 1978, 1980; Morris & Liebert, 1970, 1973; Morris & Perez, 1972). Morris, Davis, and Hutchings (1981) revised the WEI and obtained a lower correlation of .48. In two other studies using the revised WEI, the correlations between cognitive and somatic A-state were .43 (Carden, 1979) and .41 (Parks, 1980). Schwartz et al. (1978), using the CSAQ (a trait scale), obtained a correlation of .42 between cognitive and somatic A-trait.

Even these latter correlations indicate modest dependence, but they have been interpreted by researchers in this area as evidence of relative independence. This interpretation appears to be warranted because most situations that are powerful stressors contain stimuli that elicit and maintain both anxiety components. This issue is discussed further in chapters 9 and 10.

Evidence for the independence of these two components also comes from factor analyzing and computing item analyses on the anxiety items commonly used in many general anxiety scales. Each of the studies doing so has found statistical support for two major subsets of anxiety items: cognitive and somatic (Barratt, 1972; Buss, 1962; Fenz & Epstein, 1967).

Evidence Based on Different Antecedents of Cognitive and Somatic A-State

Perhaps the most convincing evidence for the conceptual independence of cognitive and somatic A-state is found in the research identifying the different antecedents associated with these two components of anxiety (i.e., construct validity). When differential antecedents of cognitive and somatic A-state are tested for, experimental conditions must be established that elicit high levels of one component of A-state without elevating the other. Thus, if high arousal can be elicited without self-evaluation, then high levels of somatic A-state should be reported without accompanying increments in cognitive A-state. Similarly, different experimental conditions that are highly evaluative but not arousing should primarily elicit cognitive but not somatic A-state.

The extant research investigating cognitive versus somatic A-state has found some support for these predictions. Morris and Liebert (1973) reported that the threat of electric shock with no performance evaluation increased somatic A-state primarily and that failure feedback in the same setting predominantly increased cognitive A-state. Morris, Harris, and Rovins (1981) observed similar results in a social evaluation situation, and Morris, Brown, and Halbert (1977) observed peers exhibiting either cognitive or somatic A-state and found that cognitive and somatic A-state were elicited independently.

Two additional studies demonstrated that performance expectancies held by individuals before evaluation were highly correlated with cognitive but not somatic A-state (Liebert & Morris, 1967; Morris & Liebert, 1970). Moreover, research has confirmed that cognitive and somatic A-state follow different temporal patterns that correspond to predictions for these two components of anxiety. Four studies have shown that somatic A-state increased steadily until the start of an examination and then decreased significantly as the test progressed. Cognitive A-state changed before or during evaluation only when expectation of success was experimentally altered (Doctor & Altman, 1969; Morris & Engle, 1981; Morris & Fulmer, 1976; Smith & Morris, 1976).

However, the research evidence on the independence of cognitive and somatic anxiety is by no means unequivocal. Several studies have manipulated antecedent variables in ways similar to the procedures employed in the studies cited but have failed to obtain the hypothesized results (Deffenbacher & Dietz, 1978; Holroyd, 1978; Holroyd, Westbrook, Wolf, & Badhorn, 1978; Morris & Perez, 1972; Smith & Morris, 1976, 1977). What these studies suggest is that finding experimental conditions that elicit cognitive anxiety but not somatic anxiety or vice versa is difficult. As observed earlier, many situations offer cues that are salient to manifesting both cognitive and somatic anxiety.

Two other sources of evidence for the independence of cognitive and somatic A-state are found in

- the relationship between these anxiety components and performance and
- the research investigating the efficacy of various anxiety treatment methods for individuals who have predominantly cognitive or somatic anxiety.

These two topics have especially significant implications for sport psychologists.

Evidence Based on the Relationship Between Anxiety Components and Performance

Cognitive and somatic A-state should influence performance differently, depending on previous theorizing. Somatic A-state is likely to reach its peak at the onset of competition and to dissipate once the contest begins. Thus, somatic A-state should influence performance less than should cognitive A-state unless the somatic A-state becomes so great that attention is diverted from the task to these internal states or unless certain task demands (e.g., duration or complexity) become highly salient.

On the other hand, cognitive A-state is indicative of negative expectations about success in performing a task, and these expectations are known to have powerful effects on performance (Bandura, 1977; Feltz, Landers, & Raeder, 1979; Rosenthal, 1968; Weinberg, Gould, & Jackson, 1979). Thus, cognitive A-state should be more strongly related to performance than should somatic A-state. Wine (1971, 1980) has marshaled substantial evidence that the mechanism by which cognitive A-state inhibits performance is by disrupting attentional processes. When athletes are worried, they become preoccupied with their own self-evaluation and ruminate about possible failure rather than directing attention to the task at hand.

The research evidence examining the relationship between performance and cognitive-somatic components of A-state is limited, and none has employed sport populations. Morris, Davis, and Hutchings (1981), after reviewing the evidence, concluded that cognitive A-state is more consistently and strongly related to performance. In a set of studies using the motor skills of typing, Morris, Smith, Andrews, and Morris (1975) found that somatic A-state did not interfere with performance but that cognitive A-state did in one of three studies. Somatic A-state was significantly related to performance in several of the studies but always to a less significant degree than was cognitive A-state. Moreover, Deffenbacher (1977) found a complex interaction between cognitive and somatic A-state, suggesting that anxiety may become debilitating only when both components of anxiety are elevated to high levels. Thus, one of the challenges for future researchers is to untangle the possible cause-and-effect relationship between cognitive and somatic A-state as they influence performance.

Evidence Based on the "Matching Hypothesis" of Anxiety Reduction

Borkovec (1976) and Davidson and Schwartz (1976) have each described how cognitive and somatic anxiety reflect two independent systems of response to stressors. Thus, the treatment of anxiety may be more efficacious if the method of treatment is directed at the system most activated by the stressor, a process known as the "matching hypothesis." For example, relaxation therapies, systematic desensitization, implosive therapy, and biofeedback are expected to be better suited to reduce somatic anxiety. Rational emotive therapy, cognitive therapies, thought stopping, and expectancy manipulations should be more effective in reducing cognitive anxiety. However, anxiety-reduction methods directed at one system may indirectly facilitate relaxation through the other system because the systems do interact. Nevertheless, it is hypothesized that the more efficacious approach is to reduce anxiety with a method directed at the type of anxiety being experienced.

The evidence supporting the matching hypothesis is by no means unanimous, although the weight of the evidence tends to support it (Lehrer, Schoicket, Carrington & Woolfolk, 1980; Morris, Davis, and Hutchings, 1981; Ost, Jerremalm, & Johansson, 1981; Schwartz et al., 1978). Morris, Davis, and Hutchings (1981) suggested that cognitive anxiety is more resistant to change than is somatic anxiety and that it requires a more complex cognitive-oriented approach. Although several studies have found cognitive and somatic treatment methods equally effective in reducing cognitive A-state, those studies finding one method more effective used cognitive therapies (Cooley & Spiegler, 1980; Goldfried, Lineham, & Smith, 1978; Hahnloser, 1974; Kaplan, McCordick, & Twitchell, 1979).

Researchers have also examined the relationship between the methods used to reduce cognitive and somatic A-state and subsequent performance, especially on intellectual tasks. Of the five studies in which performance improved, cognitive A-state was significantly reduced, but in four of the studies somatic A-state also was significantly reduced (Deffenbacher, Mathis, & Michaels, 1979; Deffenbacher, Michaels, Michaels, & Daley, 1980; Kirkland & Hollandsworth, 1980; Osarchuk, 1976; Thompson, Griebstein, & Kuhlenschmidt, 1980). However, cognitive A-state accounted for more performance variance than did somatic A-state in each of these studies, although both anxiety components together accounted for less than 10% of the total variance. Interestingly, this finding may be more indicative of the problems associated with measuring performance accurately than with the hypothesis being tested.

SUMMARY

Despite some equivocality, the accumulated evidence clearly supports the value of distinguishing between cognitive and somatic A-state. This distinction has significance for sport psychology in helping us better understand the relationship between anxiety and performance and in the treatment of high A-state.

Currently, many sport psychologists are using progressive relaxation or desensitization therapies to help highly anxious athletes. These techniques may be appropriate if athletes are primarily experiencing somatic anxiety, but if the athlete is experiencing cognitive anxiety, then a cognitive-based relaxation procedure may be more efficacious. Only with sport-specific research and the instrumentation that is needed to conduct this research will answers to these conjectures be gained.

Recognizing and measuring cognitive and somatic A-state within the sport context may also help untangle the relationship between anxiety and sport performance. The past research on the relationship between anxiety and motor performance is equivocal, although evidence does support the inverted-U hypothesis (Martens, 1974; Yerkes & Dodson, 1908). However, it is not at all clear why performance deteriorates when athletes reach high levels of A-state. Some evidence suggests that the increased muscular tension (somatic A-state) causes the deterioration (Weinberg, 1978), but other evidence suggests that it is self-rumination, or turning attention inward rather than on the task (i.e., cognitive A-state), that causes the deterioration (Wine, 1980). Then too it will become necessary to unravel what most likely is the complex cause-and-effect relationship between cognitive and somatic A-state and performance.

Chapter 9

Development of the CSAI-2

The CSAI was revised to develop a sport-specific inventory that measured the cognitive and somatic components of A-state. In this chapter, the development of the CSAI-2 is described.

DEVELOPMENT AND ANALYSIS OF FORM A

The CSAI-2 was originally constructed to include subscales to measure not only cognitive and somatic A-state but also fear of physical harm and generalized anxiety. Initially, a pool of 102 items was generated, and items were selected to measure one of these four types of A-state. Items were obtained (a) from the original CSAI, (b) by modifying items from other cognitive-somatic A-state inventories (Liebert and Morris, 1967; Schwartz et al., 1978) to make them sport-specific, and (c) by composing them especially for the new inventory.

Three judges rated the 102 items for syntax, clarity, and face validity on the basis of the protocol earlier used for SCAT. Poor items were eliminated and a few items reworded on the basis of these ratings. The remaining 79 items became known as Form A of the CSAI-2.

Form A was given to 106 university football players who completed the scale approximately 1 hour before competition and to 56 undergraduate physical education students who completed the inventory on the basis of a hypothetical competitive situation. Their responses were analyzed by computing item analyses, item-to-subscale correlations, factor analyses, and discriminant analyses. A composite of all these analyses was used to select the more appropriate items for retention in the CSAI-2 item pool on the basis of standard test construction evaluation criteria (Magnusson, 1966).

Item Analyses

The item analyses were computed using the method for differences between extreme groups. The athletes from the upper 27% and the lower 27% of the total score distribution were separated. The proportion of individuals at each extreme who answered the item consistent with their total test score classification was compared with the proportion of individuals who answered the item opposite their total test score. An item analysis coefficient of .40 for both the upper and the lower total test score classifications was required for item inclusion. Using both coefficients as criteria for item acceptance ensured that the scale discriminated at both the low and the high extremes.

Item-to-Subscale Correlations

Item-to-subscale correlations also were used to select items due to the need for homogeneity among subscale items. An item was accepted for inclusion in the hypothesized subscale if the correlation coefficient was at least .50 and the item did not have a higher correlation coefficient with another subscale.

Factor Analyses

Factor analyses were used in conjunction with the item-to-subscale correlations to select items and verify hypothesized factors. Data for Form A were subjected to two types of factor analytic techniques: (a) principal components analysis and (b) the principal factor method with iterations (Nie, Hull, Jenkins, Steinbrenner, & Bent, 1975). Eigenvalue cutoffs greater than 1.00 were employed for factor extraction, and the obtained simple factor structures were then rotated using both varimax and oblique rotations. Principal components factor analysis generated factors congruent to those hypothesized for cognitive A-state, somatic A-state, and fear of physical harm but failed to substantiate the generalized anxiety factor. Iterative factor analysis confirmed the same three factors, but the analysis revealed an unexpected finding with the cognitive A-state subscale. Under iterative factor analytic procedures, cognitive A-state split into separate components. One factor consisted of positively worded items and was labeled *state self-confidence*, and the other factor retained the negatively worded items and was labeled *cognitive A-state*.

   This serendipitous finding seems significant for several reasons. To derive the most parsimonious factor solution, principal components factor analysis assumes that common factors account for all behavioral variance without any contribution from unique factors, whereas iterative factor analysis assumes that both common and unique factors are needed to account for behavioral variance accurately. When these two factor analytic approaches result in conflicting factor structures, researchers can empirically determine which technique is most appropriate by looking at final communality values following iteration. If most communalities equal one, principal components factor structures closely correspond to underlying factors, supporting the assumption that common factors can adequately account for all behavioral variance. However, if communalities are consistently less than one, then iterative factor analytic procedures are more appropriate because common factors have accounted for only a portion of the behavioral variance. Because all final communalities for Form A and all subsequent versions of the CSAI-2 were less than one, iterative factor analytic procedures were deemed more appropriate than were principal components analyses, and the derived iterative factor structures consistently demonstrated that athletes clearly had different perspectives about cognitive A-state and state self-confidence items. These findings suggest that cognitive A-state and state self-confidence represent the opposite ends of a cognitive evaluation continuum, state self-confidence being viewed as the absence of cognitive A-state, or conversely, cognitive A-state being the lack of state self-confidence. This notion is congruent with current cognitive theories of anxiety and self-confidence (Bandura, 1977; Ellis, 1969; Meichenbaum, 1977; Wine, 1971).

Nevertheless, these factor analyses, as well as a number of subsequent analyses, consistently demonstrated that subjects did not respond to cognitive A-state and state self-confidence items in a directly reciprocal manner. Although the general pattern of the relationship between cognitive A-state and state self-confidence was consistently inverse as hypothesized, the magnitude of the correlations varied dramatically with different samples and situational factors. Indeed, in the original iterative factor analyses, the state self-confidence factor accounted for over 62% of the total variance, whereas the cognitive A-state factor accounted for less than 13% (somatic A-state and fear of physical harm accounted for 17% and 8% of the variance, respectively). Anecdotal evidence and subsequent research suggested that these different response patterns may be due to the greater social desirability and other demand characteristics inherent in self-report measurement of cognitive anxiety that are less evident in the measurement of state self-confidence. Pragmatically, regardless of the underlying causes, these consistent differences in response patterns suggested that separate measurement of cognitive A-state and state self-confidence was warranted to provide a truer picture of precompetitive perceptions of challenge, threat, or both.

Discriminant Analyses

Discriminant analyses were employed as the final selection criteria to ensure that items discriminated between individuals high and low on each total subscale score. An item was accepted for inclusion in the hypothesized subscale if the absolute value of its discriminant function coefficient was at least one half the magnitude of the discriminant function coefficient with the largest weight (Tatsuoka, 1971).

FORM B

The composite picture of each item derived through these four separate statistical analyses led to the elimination of less discriminating items, reducing Form A from 79 to 36 items. This new form, labeled Form B, included a 12-item cognitive A-state subscale, a 12-item somatic A-state subscale, a 10-item state self-confidence subscale, and a two-item fear-of-physical-harm subscale.

The next step was to recalculate item analyses, item-to-subscale correlations, factor analyses, and discriminant analyses for the responses of the same 162 athletes on the 36-item Form B. The most significant finding of these reanalyses was the failure of the fear-of-physical-harm items to discriminate between athletes high and low in this type of anxiety. Neither of the two fear-of-physical-harm items received responses higher than a 2 on the 4-point scale, suggesting that athletes either have little fear of physical harm or are unwilling to admit such fear. Therefore, the fear-of-physical-harm subscale was eliminated from further versions of the scale.

Analyses of Form B demonstrated three stable subscales: cognitive A-state, somatic A-state, and state self-confidence. Because the state self-confidence subscale had not been originally hypothesized as a component of the CSAI-2, eliminating nondiscriminating items from each of the three subscales reduced the state self-confidence subscale to only seven items. Thus, six additional self-confidence items and six additional control items were constructed and included in the inventory to make all three subscales of comparable length.

At the same time, it was thought that Rotter's (1966) internal-external control construct may comprise an important component of state self-confidence, so 12 internal-external control items were composed and added to the item pool. Thus, a total of 24 items were added to, and 8 items deleted from, the 36-item Form B to construct a new 52-item CSAI-2, which was labeled Form C. Form C included four subscales: a 14-item cognitive A-state subscale, an 11-item somatic A-state subscale, a 13-item state self-confidence subscale, and a 12-item internal-external control subscale (along with two previously omitted items from the original CSAI that the researchers had a hunch were worth retaining).

FORM C

This form of the CSAI-2 was administered to 80 male and female athletes who participated in collegiate swimming and track and field, high school wrestling, and road racing. Form C was completed within 1 hour of competition by all athletes, and responses were again analyzed using item analyses, item-to-subscale correlations, factor analyses, and discriminant analyses. Principal components and iterative factor analyses with orthogonal and oblique rotations confirmed three of the four hypothesized subscales. Definite factors emerged for cognitive A-state, somatic A-state, and state self-confidence, but the internal-external control items failed to surface as a recognizable factor when any of the four combinations of factor analytic techniques was used. Several internal-external control items factored into other subscales, but seven items failed to achieve factor loadings greater than .30 on any factor. Moreover, doubt was cast on the cognitive nature of the way that Rotter (1966) operationalized internal-external control or its link with state self-confidence when more internal-external control items factored into the somatic A-state factor than into either the cognitive A-state or the state self-confidence factor. Because internal-external control items seemed to be generally unrelated to any of the three CSAI-2 subscales, the internal-external control subscale was deleted from subsequent versions of the inventory.

Because only 9 somatic A-state items had both upper and lower item analysis coefficients exceeding the criterion value of .40, the cognitive A-state and state self-confidence subscales were also pared to a similar length by selecting the 9 most discriminating items for each subscale. The final result of this selection process was a new 27-item CSAI-2, comprised of three 9-item subscales measuring cognitive A-state, somatic A-state, and state self-confidence. This version of the CSAI-2 was labeled Form D.

FORM D

All analyses were again recalculated for the same sample of 80 male and female athletes, using only the 27 items chosen for Form D. Results demonstrated the stability of these three subscales but suggested that one remaining cognitive A-state item was weak in discriminating highly anxious athletes. This item ("I'm afraid I might panic".) was eliminated from the subscale and a new item substituted ("I'm concerned that I should have prepared better for this competition".).

It was judged that Form D was sufficiently promising to investigate its reliability and concurrent validity. Table 9.1 summaries the statistical attributes of

Table 9.1   Summary Statistics for Item Selection of the CSAI-2 (Form D)

| Subscale | Mean item analysis coefficient | | Item to subscale | Mean discriminant function |
	Low	High	mean r	coefficient
CSAI-cog	.77	.54	.68	3.56
CSAI-som	.67	.56	.67	0.98
CSAI-sc	.68	.66	.78	4.92

each of these subscales. Hereafter, as in the table, reference to the three sub-scales will be abbreviated CSAI-cog for cognitive A-state, CSAI-som for somatic A-state, and CSAI-sc for state self-confidence.

RELIABILITY

Test-retest reliability is inappropriate for state scales, so the only method of estimating reliability for the CSAI-2 was by examining the internal consistency of the scale (Kerlinger, 1973). Internal consistency measures the degree to which items in the same subscale are homogeneous. Cronbach's alpha coefficient was computed to assess the internal consistency of the CSAI-2 on three samples using data collected in conjunction with concurrent validation. Separate alpha coefficients were computed for the three CSAI-2 subscales for each sample. Sample 1 was comprised of 35 male college track athletes and 22 elite high school wrestlers. Sample 2 consisted of 40 elite male high school wrestlers and women collegiate volleyball players. Sample 3 contained 54 elite high school wrestlers. As shown in Table 9.2, alpha coefficients ranged from .79 to .90, demonstrating a sufficiently high degree of internal consistency for each of the CSAI-2 subscales.

Table 9.2   Internal Consistency of CSAI-2 Subscales (Form D)

Sample	N	CSAI-cog	CSAI-som	CSAI-sc
1	57	.79	.82	.88
2	40	.83	.82	.87
3	54	.81	.83	.90

CONCURRENT VALIDITY

The American Psychological Association's (1974) *Standards for Educational and Psychological Tests* recommends that self-report inventories be first validated by demonstrating concurrent validity with previously validated scales. Thus, concurrent validity is inferred when a new inventory is congruent with or divergent from theoretically predicted relationships using previously validated scales.

The concurrent validity of the CSAI-2 was examined by investigating the relationships between each of the CSAI-2 subscales and eight selected A-state and A-trait inventories. The same three samples of athletes that were used to evaluate the CSAI-2's internal consistency also were tested for part of the new inventory's concurrent validation. Athletes in all samples completed SCAT and a second A-trait inventory and the CSAI-2 and a second A-state inventory within 1 hour of when they actually competed.

A-Trait Inventories

The four A-trait inventories used to determine the concurrent validity of the CSAI-2 (see Table 9.3) were

- SCAT (Martens, 1977),
- the TAI (Spielberger et al., 1970),
- the Achievement Anxiety Test (AAT) modified for competition (AAT-C) (Alpert & Haber, 1960), and
- the Internal-External Control Scale (I-E Control) (Rotter, 1966).

Table 9.3   Correlations of Trait Scales With the CSAI-2 (Form D)

Scale	N	CSAI-cog	CSAI-som	CSAI-sc
SCAT	151	.45	.62	−.55
TAI	54	.50	.37	−.46
AAT-C-debilitating	40	.35	.06	−.34
AAT-C-facilitating	40	−.22	.04	.33
I-E Control	57	.09	.11	−.17

Note. Correlational values represent the mean r of three samples.

SCAT

This test was expected to have the highest relationship with the subscales of the CSAI-2 because SCAT is a sport-specific A-trait scale. A content analysis of SCAT suggested that it is comprised of four somatic A-state items, two cognitive A-state items, one state self-confidence item, and three items that were not classifiable. Thus, it was expected that SCAT would correlate more highly with CSAI-som than with CSAI-cog or CSAI-sc.

Each of these predictions was supported (see Table 9.3). Of particular note, SCAT correlated negatively with CSAI-sc, supporting the assertion that cognitive A-state and state self-confidence are at opposite ends of the same cognitive evaluation continuum.

TAI

The original CSAI was a short form of Spielberger et al.'s (1970) SAI, which is similar to the TAI in item content and format. Thus, due to this common root, the relationship between the TAI and the subscales of the CSAI-2 were expected to be the next highest in magnitude. The correlations shown in Table 9.3 support these predictions.

AAT-C

The AAT measures both facilitating and debilitating components of achievement anxiety. It was modified for use in this concurrent validation process by inserting such words as *competition* and *sports* in appropriate places to make the scale appropriate for athletes to complete. Inspection of the AAT-C items, as modified for sport, suggests that its two subscales are highly congruent with cognitive A-state and state self-confidence, although some items bring in related topics (e.g., control) that appear to be less related to the CSAI-2. Thus, it was predicted that the relationship between the facilitating and the debilitating subscales of the AAT-C and CSAI-cog and CSAI-sc would be similar in magnitude to those of the TAI. The correlation of the AAT-C subscales with CSAI-som was expected to be lower than it was for the other two subscales of the CSAI-2. Cognitive A-state should be positively related to debilitating anxiety and negatively related to facilitating anxiety, whereas the opposite trend was expected for state self-confidence. As shown in Table 9.3, these predictions were generally supported, although the overall magnitude of these relationships was somewhat lower than it was with the TAI.

I-E Control

I-E Control was expected to have the weakest overall relationships with the subscales of the CSAI-2 because previous attempts to include control items in the CSAI-2 had failed. Control would appear to be more closely related to self-confidence, so the stronger relationship was expected between I-E Control and CSAI-sc. These predictions were moderately confirmed (see Table 9.3).

A-State Inventories

Concurrent validation continued by examining the relationship between the subscales of the CSAI-2 and each of the following A-state inventories:

- The revised WEI (Morris, Davis, & Hutchings, 1981)
- The CSAQ (Schwartz et al., 1978)
- The SAI (Spielberger et al., 1970)
- The Affect Adjective Checklist (AACL) (Zuckerman, 1960)

The revised WEI and Sample 2 of the SAI, along with the CSAI-2, were completed by 49 male golfers competing in the Western Junior National Golf Championships. The other state scales were completed by the same samples of athletes who completed the A-trait scales.

WEI

A moderately high positive correlation coefficient was predicted between WEI-worry and CSAI-cog and between WEI-emotionality and CSAI-som. A moderately high negative correlation coefficient was expected between WEI-worry and CSAI-sc. These results were affirmed. In addition, the correlations between nonmatching scales (WEI-worry and CSAI-som and WEI-emotionality and CSAI-cog) were lower, although the correlation coefficient between WEI-emotionality and CSAI-cog was quite high.

In general the correlation coefficients shown in Table 9.4 followed the expected pattern, although the relationship was somewhat greater than was expected; that is, these high correlation coefficients suggest that a sport-specific inventory is not substantially different from the more general WEI.

Table 9.4   Correlations of State Scales With the CSAI-2 (Form D)

Scale	N	CSAI-cog	CSAI-som	CSAI-sc
WEI-worry	49	.74	.37	−.62
WEI-emotionality	49	.57	.82	−.40
CSAQ-cog	54	.69	.48	−.57
CSAQ-som	54	.47	.75	−.46
SAI (Sample 1)	57	.65	.78	−.66
SAI (Sample 2)	49	.66	.69	−.77
AACL	40	−.63	−.66	.66

CSAQ

The CSAQ was constructed to be an A-trait scale but was used in this investigation as an A-state scale. Because the items in the questionnaire were written in appropriate form for an A-state scale, it was necessary only to change the instructions when administering the questionnaire, asking athletes to complete the inventory according to how they felt at the moment rather than how they generally felt. This adjustment resulted in the CSAQ being conceptually quite similar to the CSAI-2, and some CSAI-2 items were adapted from the CSAQ. Thus, CSAQ-cog was expected to correlate quite highly with CSAI-cog, and CSAQ-som was expected to correlate quite highly with CSAI-som. CSAQ-cog was expected to correlate substantially less well with CSAI-som as was CSAQ-som with CSAI-cog. Due to the cognitive nature of self-confidence, CSAI-sc was expected to demonstrate a moderately strong negative correlation with CSAQ-cog and a lower negative correlation with CSAQ-som.

The correlation coefficients shown in Table 9.4 confirm these predictions, although the matched components (CSAQ-cog with CSAI-cog and CSAQ-som with CSAI-som) were even higher than was expected. In general, however, these correlations provide good convergent validity, and the lower correlations among the unmatched components provide reasonable discriminant validity for the CSAI-2.

SAI

The SAI (Spielberger et al., 1970) was hypothesized to relate moderately strongly with all three CSAI-2 subscales because several items from the SAI were retained in the final version of the CSAI-2. More items were retained in CSAI-som, so a higher correlation was predicted for this scale; the fewest items were retained in CSAI-sc, which was expected to correlate most weakly with the SAI. Results shown in Table 9.4 partially support these predictions.

AACL

The AACL (Zuckerman, 1960) is a general A-state scale comprised of single-word adjectives describing feelings about evaluative situations. Individuals check only those adjectives that describe their feelings at that moment. Such a scoring system seems to be less sensitive to the subtleties of A-state than does the Likert format used by the other A-state inventories, so the AACL was expected to have weaker relationships with CSAI-2 subscales. As shown in Table 9.4, the results are consistent with these predictions, although somewhat higher coefficients were obtained than were expected.

Conclusions Regarding Concurrent Validity

Although further concurrent validation may be appropriate, the evidence presented here firmly supports the concurrent validity of the CSAI-2. The coefficients presented in Tables 9.3 and 9.4 are highly congruent with hypothesized relationships among the CSAI-2 subscales and scales of related constructs.

INDEPENDENCE OF THE CSAI-2 SUBSCALES

As explained in chapter 8, cognitive and somatic A-state are theorized to be conceptually independent but are acknowledged to be interrelated in many stressful situations. The evidence for the independence of the CSAI-2 subscales is summarized in Table 9.5 for eight samples. All these coefficients reflect the relationship among the three subscales in precompetitive situations (within 1 hour of the contest). The correlations between CSAI-cog and CSAI-som vary from .30 to .67 with a mean correlation coefficient of .55. The reasons for these fluctuations are unknown but are thought to reside in differences in the sports sampled and the situations to which subjects responded.

Table 9.5 Mean Intercorrelations Among CSAI-2 Subscales for Form D

Sample	N	CSAI-cog with CSAI-som	CSAI-cog with CSAI-sc	CSAI-som with CSAI-sc
College track and field and high school wrestlers	57	.49	−.57	−.54
High school wrestlers and college volleyball players	40	.53	−.62	−.60
High school wrestlers	54	.66	−.74	−.67
University gymnasts	42	.56	−.62	−.59
University basketball players	84	.30	−.36	−.42
High school wrestlers	45	.60	−.63	−.68
University swimmers	34	.67	−.87	−.59
Age-group swimmers	55	.56	−.46	−.44
Mean r		.546	−.609	−.566

In general, these correlations were somewhat higher than the .42 coefficient reported by Schwartz et al. (1978) using the CSAQ but are more consistent with the higher coefficients reported by Deffenbacher (1980) among those studies using the WEI (Liebert & Morris, 1967). Perhaps the lower correlations obtained with the CSAQ can be attributed to it being a trait inventory, measuring general tendencies to become cognitively or somatically anxious, whereas the WEI and the CSAI-2 are state scales, measuring momentary anxiety responses. Another possibility is that competitive sport elicits both cognitive and somatic A-state in somewhat similar degrees, producing a moderately high relationship.

Another means of examining the independence of CSAI-cog and CSAI-som is to determine how many individuals are very high on one component and very low on the other. The results of such an analysis of all subjects ($N = 436$) who have completed the CSAI-2 is reported in Table 9.6. High and low A-state was arbitrarily defined as obtaining a score in the upper or the lower 25% of that subscale distribution.

Only a small percentage of athletes tended to fall at the opposite extremes of the two subscales. Only 8% of the athletes were high somatic–low cognitive anxious, and 6% were low somatic–high cognitive anxious. These results concur with the previous findings that for most athletes the two forms of A-state are moderately related.

Although the number of athletes who scored at the opposite extremes was not large, the matching hypothesis may have the greatest relevance for these individuals. Using a cognitive anxiety–reduction method with high somatic–low cognitive anxious athletes or a somatic anxiety–reduction technique with high cognitive–low somatic anxious athletes would be expected to be less efficacious than would

Table 9.6　The Number and Percentage of Athletes With Extreme Scores on the CSAI-2 (Form D)

	CSAI-som			
	Low		High	
CSAI-cog	*N*	%	*N*	%
Low	146	33	36	8
High	26	6	68	16

a more congruent strategy. Research is needed on this question and on the anxiety-reduction methods that are more effective with athletes who are high in both cognitive and somatic anxiety. Perhaps methods such as Meichenbaum's (1977) stress inoculation procedure, which combines both cognitive and somatic techniques, will be more effective for this latter group of athletes.

SOCIAL DESIRABILITY
AND THE DEVELOPMENT OF FORM E

Paper-and-pencil questionnaires are susceptible to individuals distorting their responses to present themselves in a socially desirable way. The susceptibility of the CSAI-2 to social desirability biases was examined for 59 high school male and female softball players and track-and-field athletes. These subjects completed the CSAI-2 and the Marlowe-Crowne Social Desirability Scale (Crowne & Marlowe, 1960) before a practice session and the CSAI-2 again 30 minutes before competition. Results from this study revealed that CSAI-cog was correlated significantly with social desirability ($r = .30$; $p < .01$) as was CSAI-som ($r = -.29$, $p < .02$). CSAI-sc did not correlate significantly with social desirability ($r = .17$, $p > .10$).

The social desirability problem was a serious limitation of the CSAI-2 and needed to be corrected. Morris, Davis, and Hutchings (1981) reported that the word *worry* appeared to be reactive to the subjects they tested when developing the revised WEI. Thus, following their suggestion, the word *worry* was replaced with *concern* in all items of the CSAI-cog subscale in which it appeared. This version of the CSAI-2 was labeled Form E.

With only this change, the CSAI-2 was given to another sample of 55 16- to 18-year-old competitive swimmers. Each swimmer completed the CSAI-2 and a short form of the Marlowe-Crowne Social Desirability Scale (Reynolds, 1982) just prior to swimming in a local Amateur Athletic Union meet. These changes seemed to eliminate the social desirability problem for CSAI-cog ($r = .16$, p

= n.s.), but CSAI-som and social desirability were even more strongly and significantly related in this sample ($r = .46, p < .01$) than they were in the previous sample.

Although the changes had made CSAI-cog less sensitive to social desirability distortion, the results indicated that CSAI-som was even more affected by this type of bias. Thus, a set of so-called anti–social desirability instructions were developed. Two groups of women softball players were administered the CSAI-2 and the short-form of the Marlowe-Crowne Social Desirability Scale moments before a tournament game. One group ($n = 31$) received the anti–social desirability instructions and the other group ($n = 36$) the normal instructions. An ANOVA revealed that no significant differences were obtained for CSAI-cog or CSAI-sc, but the CSAI-som scores did differ significantly between the two groups, $F(1, 65) = 4.92, p < .03$. The group receiving the anti–social desirability instruction admitted to higher somatic anxiety ($M = 20.42$) than did the regular instruction group ($M = 17.42$).

In addition, the correlations between social desirability and the three CSAI-2 subscales indicated that the anti–social desirability instructions were effective: $r = .08$ for CSAI-cog, $r = .01$ for CSAI-som, and $r = .09$ for CSAI-sc. Thus, the use of the anti–social desirability instructions is recommended (instructions are given in chapter 11).

Because social desirability research had prompted the development of Form E with reworded CSAI-cog items and new administration instructions, the independence of the CSAI-cog and CSAI-som subscales was further evaluated on the basis of data from the five additional samples completing Form E. These coefficients for the intercorrelations among the three subscales of Form E of the CSAI-2 are shown in Table 9.7 and reveal somewhat lower values, suggesting that the modifications from Form D to Form E improved the subscales' independence, particularly between CSAI-cog and CSAI-som. Thus, Form E was accepted as

Table 9.7 Mean Intercorrelations Among CSAI-2 Subscales for Form E

Sample	N	CSAI-cog with CSAI-som	CSAI-cog with CSAI-sc	CSAI-som with CSAI-sc
Sports festival gymnasts	40	.54	−.56	−.51
Sports festival swimmers	69	.52	−.55	−.53
Sports festival field hockey players	41	.45	−.38	−.51
Junior golfers	49	.48	−.60	−.39
Women softball players	67	.60	−.31	−.39
Mean r		.518	−.480	−.466

the final form of the CSAI-2 on the basis of the initial psychometric analyses. All references to the CSAI-2 hereafter refer to Form E.

SUMMARY

The development of the CSAI-2 as a sport-specific measure of multidimensional A-state followed a systematic psychometric process. In the development of Form A, items representing cognitive A-state, somatic A-state, fear of physical harm, and generalized anxiety were generated and analyzed for content validity by expert judges. Items were selected for inclusion on the basis of item analyses, item-to-subscale correlations, factor analyses, and discriminant analyses. The most significant finding from the analyses on Form A was the serendipitous emergence of a state self-confidence subscale. Form A was modified into Form B to include subscales of cognitive A-state, somatic A-state, state self-confidence, and fear of physical harm. However, the analyses on Form B indicated that the fear-of-physical-harm subscale was not a significant discriminator of anxiety in sport situations. Thus, the cognitive A-state, somatic A-state, and state self-confidence subscales were retained in Form C, and an internal-external control subscale was added. Internal-external control failed to surface as a recognizable subscale in the Form C analyses; thus, the inventory was modified into Form D, which contained nine-item subscales of cognitive A-state, somatic A-state, and state self-confidence. Evidence for the reliability and concurrent validity of Form D for the independence of the subscales was accumulated and was consistent with the theoretical literature. Form D was found to be susceptible to social desirability response bias and was modified into Form E to lessen this bias. The scale modifications and the use of anti–social desirability instructions in administering the CSAI-2 reduced the response bias to an acceptable level and also improved the subscales' independence. Form E was accepted as the final form of the CSAI-2 to be used in the subsequent construct validation research.

Chapter 10

Construct Validation of the CSAI-2

The final and most important phase in the development of the CSAI-2 was its construct validation. Construct validity is determined by an accumulation of evidence that the operational definitions of the new constructs (sport-specific cognitive A-state, somatic A-state, and state self-confidence) are related to other constructs as predicted by theory. The model for construct validation of the CSAI-2 is shown in Figure 10.1 and is an extension of the model used by Martens (1977) in the development of SCAT (see Figure 4.1).

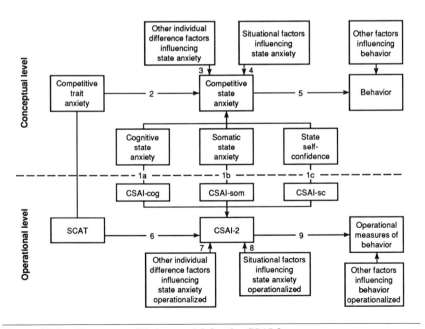

Figure 10.1. Construct validation model for the CSAI-2.

In Figure 10.1, the theoretical constructs and their relationships are shown above the broken line and the relevant operational definitions of these constructs and their relationships below the broken line. The construct validity of the CSAI-2 is determined by examining Links 1a, 1b, and 1c. This cannot be done directly, so it is done by examining the influence of the three competitive A-state constructs on various behaviors as shown by Link 5. Also, it can be done by investigating those factors that are predicted to influence these competitive A-state constructs (Links 2, 3, and 4).

In other words, if evidence can be marshaled that at the operational level Links 6, 7, 8, and 9 are supported, then the validity of Links 1a, 1b, and 1c is established. The evidence presented in chapter 9 for the concurrent validity of the CSAI-2 (Links 6 and 7) is therefore partial support for the construct validity of the inventory. The purpose of the next four studies was to continue investigating the construct validity of the CSAI-2 by the further study of Links 2, 3, 4, and 5 as operationally defined by Links 6, 7, 8, and 9.

STUDY 1: VARIABLES INFLUENCING COMPETITIVE A-STATE

The purpose of this study was to examine how the situational factor of sport type (Link 4) and individual difference variables of competitive A-trait (Link 2), skill level, and gender (Link 3) relate to the three components of the CSAI-2.

Sport Type

Three comparisons among different types of sports were made to determine their influence on competitive A-state. The first was made between individual and team sports. Research has indicated that individual sport participants manifest greater A-state than do team sport participants (Griffin, 1972; Simon & Martens, 1979). Individual sports are expected to create higher competitive A-state than are team sports because the threat of evaluation is maximized; that is, the diffusion of responsibility for performance errors is minimized (Scanlan, 1975). Thus, it was expected that athletes in individual sports would report higher cognitive A-state and lower state self-confidence than would athletes in team sports. Somatic A-state was expected not to differ between individual and team sport participants.

The second sport-type comparison was made between subjectively and objectively scored sports. Subjectively scored sports are those for which the score is derived from the evaluation of judges. Objectively scored sports are those in which the scoring is determined by the achievement of an objective standard and are influenced, if at all, only minimally by judges or officials. Due to the increased uncertainty and lack of control over the outcome of an athlete's performance, subjectively scored sports are hypothesized to be higher in cognitive A-state and lower in state self-confidence than are objectively scored sports. No difference in somatic A-state was predicted between participants in subjectively and objectively scored sports.

The third comparison was made between contact and noncontact sports. Simon and Martens (1979) reported that contact sports elicited higher A-state than did noncontact sports. Thus, it was expected that higher cognitive A-state and lower state self-confidence would be demonstrated in contact sports due to the increased threat arising from personal confrontation. It was also speculated that athletes in contact sports would have a greater probability of having acquired conditioned somatic A-state responses (Borkovec, 1976) than would athletes in noncontact sports. Thus, higher somatic A-state was predicted for contact sport participants than it was for noncontact sport participants.

Individual Differences

Next, predictions were made for the three individual difference variables. Competitive A-trait was expected to demonstrate a moderately strong relationship with both cognitive and somatic A-state. Based on the evidence already reported in chapter 9, where concurrent validity was discussed, it was expected that the relationship between competitive A-trait and somatic A-state would be stronger than the relationship between competitive A-trait and cognitive A-state or state self-confidence.

The individual difference variable of skill level and its relationship to anxiety has been the subject of some research. For example, experienced sport parachutists demonstrated lower physiological arousal and fear estimates than did novice jumpers immediately before and during the activity (Fenz & Epstein, 1967; Fenz & Jones, 1972). This finding has been supported by other researchers for gymnasts (Mahoney & Avener, 1977), racquetball players (Meyers, Cooke, Cullen, & Liles, 1979), and wrestlers (Highlen & Bennett, 1979). Fenz (1975) has suggested that inexperienced and less skilled athletes tend to focus more on internal fears, whereas the more skilled performers exhibit an external task orientation. This finding is consistent with the evidence reviewed by Wine (1980) for cognitive tasks. In addition, it has been suggested that more skilled athletes possess better coping skills to deal with anxiety than do less skilled athletes. Thus, it was hypothesized that more skilled athletes will show less cognitive and somatic A-state and greater state self-confidence before competition than will less skilled athletes.

The final individual difference variable studied was the gender of the athlete. Martens (1977) reported that females were slightly higher in competitive A-trait than were males. Considering this fact, along with the general trend that females have had less experience in sport, it was hypothesized that females would report higher levels of cognitive and somatic A-state and less state self-confidence than would their male counterparts.

Method

To test these hypotheses regarding how individual difference and situational variables influence cognitive A-state, somatic A-state, and state self-confidence, subjects were selected and procedures designed.

Subjects

The subjects were 185 male and 92 female college athletes from a variety of sports. All subjects competed in regular-season, intercollegiate competition and participated in the study as volunteers with the approval of their coaches.

The categorization of sports and the number of participants are listed in Table 10.1. The categorization was based on task characteristics of each sport. For example, gymnastics qualified as individual, subjectively scored, and noncontact. Sports either were or were not placed into categories to maximize control over confounding variables. For example, the contact-noncontact comparison became one of individual sports. The team sports of basketball and volleyball were not placed into the noncontact category so that individual and team differences could be controlled and to assure that any differences found could be attributed to the contact-noncontact distinction.

Table 10.1 Categorization of Sports With Number and Gender of Each Sample for Study 1

Sport type	N	Sport	n of samples by gender	
			Male	Female
Team	96	Basketball	41	43
		Volleyball	. . .	12
Individual	111	Gymnastics	22	20
		Swimming	18	16
		Track	35	. . .
Subjective	42	Gymnastics	22	20
Objective	69	Swimming	18	16
		Track	35	. . .
Contact	77	Wrestling	77	. . .
Noncontact	77	Gymnastics	22	20
		Track	35	. . .

Note. Total N = 277 (92 females, 185 males).

Two additional samples were tested to assess differences between groups differing in skill level. The high-skill athletes were participants in the 1982 National Sports Festival, an annual event sponsored by the U.S. Olympic Committee to groom athletes for Olympic competition. This high-skill group ($N = 167$) consisted of 40 gymnasts, 86 swimmers, and 41 field hockey players whose mean age was 17.14 years. Forty of the athletes were male and 127 female. The low-skill group included 104 high school athletes participating in wrestling ($n = 45$), track and field ($n = 34$), and softball ($n = 25$). Seventy-nine were males and 25 females, and the mean age was 16.94 years. The inclusion of team and individual sport types in both groups and the similarity in age between groups served to control sport-type and maturational differences, which could possibly confound the comparison between the high- and the low-skill groups.

Procedures

Subjects were administered SCAT (Martens, 1977) during a noncompetitive situation to assess competitive A-trait. Two days to 1 week later, the CSAI-2 was administered approximately 1 hour before the competitive event.

Results of Study 1

Initial t tests were computed between genders and each sport-type comparison to determine whether there were any significant differences in competitive A-trait, but none were found. Correlation coefficients (see Table 10.2) indicated that the dependent variables were significantly related. Significant correlations also were obtained between SCAT and the three CSAI-2 subscales. As expected, SCAT was related negatively to CSAI-sc and positively to CSAI-cog and CSAI-som. The higher correlation between SCAT and CSAI-som supported previous concurrent validity findings, suggesting that SCAT is more of a somatic A-trait inventory than a it is a cognitive A-trait scale. Moreover, the significant correlations among the CSAI-2 subscales indicated that multivariate procedures were appropriate for analyzing group differences.

Table 10.2 Correlations of Dependent Variables and SCAT for Study 1

CSAI-2 subscale	SCAT	CSAI-cog	CSAI-som
CSAI-cog	.40	. . .	. . .
CSAI-som	.60	.51	. . .
CSAI-sc	−.51	−.59	−.58

The means and standard deviations for each comparison among the three sub-scales of the CSAI-2 are given in Table 10.3. The individual-team and subjective-objective sport-type comparisons were analyzed using two 2 × 2 (Sport Type × Gender) multivariate analyses of variance MANOVAs, using the CSAI-2 subscales as dependent variables. Gender was not an independent variable in the contact-noncontact comparison because no females participated in the contact sport group.

Table 10.3 Means and Standard Deviations for All Comparisons in Study 1

Category	CSAI-cog		CSAI-som		CSAI-sc	
	M	SD	M	SD	M	SD
Team	13.92	3.99	15.55	4.58	27.64	4.79
Individual	15.43	4.62	17.34	4.27	25.08	5.72
Subjective	16.74	4.69	18.19	4.04	23.61	5.26
Objective	14.64	4.42	16.83	4.36	25.96	5.84
Contact	17.83	4.49	19.60	5.11	22.28	4.88
Noncontact	15.83	4.66	17.31	3.95	25.10	5.38
High SCAT	18.86	5.01	22.39	4.35	20.28	2.72
Low SCAT	15.47	3.78	15.13	2.64	25.33	5.35
High skilled	17.23	6.05	15.38	5.46	23.80	7.55
Low skilled	23.63	4.86	18.76	4.12	17.99	4.50

The MANOVA for competitive A-trait differences was performed on one sample of wrestlers ($N = 77$) in which the top 25% were designated high and the bottom 25% low in competitive A-trait. Better control over confounding variables such as sport type and gender were obtained by testing athletes from only one sport. MANOVA was also used to assess differences between high- and low-skilled athletes on the three CSAI-2 subscales. Follow-up stepwise discriminant analyses were performed for all comparisons to assess the relative contribution of each CSAI-2 subscale to the differences between groups.

Individual-Team Comparison

A significant multivariate main effect for sport type was obtained, $F(3, 201) = 5.16$, $p < .002$. Post hoc univariate ANOVAs on each CSAI-2 subscale were computed, as was a discriminant analysis. The results indicated that

- individual sport athletes ($M = 15.43$) displayed significantly higher CSAI-cog, $F(1, 203) = 7.00$, $p < .009$, than did team sport athletes ($M = 13.92$);

- individual sport athletes (M = 17.34) were significantly higher in CSAI-som, $F(1, 203)$ = 9.54, $p < .003$, than were team sport athletes (M = 15.55); and
- individual sport athletes (M = 25.08) were significantly lower in CSAI-sc, $F(1, 203)$ = 12.70, $p < .001$, than were team sport athletes (M = 27.64).

The standardized discriminant function coefficients indicated that CSAI-sc (0.59) was the most discriminating variable between individual and team sports, followed by CSAI-som (-0.42) and CSAI-cog (-0.22).

A significant multivariate main effect also was obtained for gender, $F(3, 201)$ = 10.01, $p < .001$. The post hoc univariate ANOVA revealed that

- females (M = 16.25) demonstrated significantly higher CSAI-cog, $F(1, 203)$ = 20.85, $p < .001$, than did males (M = 13.49);
- females (M = 18.01) demonstrated significantly higher CSAI-som, $F(1, 203)$ = 18.12, $p < .001$, than did males (M = 15.40); and
- females (M = 24.58) were significantly lower in CSAI-sc, $F(1, 203)$ = 18.32, $p < .001$, than were males (M = 27.76).

The discriminant analysis indicated that CSAI-cog, (-0.52) was the most discriminating variable between the genders, followed by CSAI-som (-0.44) and CSAI-sc (-0.30).

Subjective-Objective Comparison

The multivariate analysis revealed no main effect, $F(3, 105)$ = 2.08, $p > .10$. The univariate analyses, however, suggested some trends in the data worth noting although the overall F was not significant.

- Athletes in subjectively scored sports (M = 16.74) were significantly higher in CSAI-cog, $F(1, 107)$ = 5.77, $p < .02$, than were those in objectively scored sports (M = 14.64).
- Athletes in subjectively scored sports (M) = 18.19) did not differ significantly from athletes in objectively-scored sports (M = 16.83) on CSAI-som.
- Athletes in subjectively scored sports (M = 23.61) were also significantly lower in CSAI-sc, $F(1, 107)$ = 4.75, $p < .03$, than were athletes in objectively scored sports (M = 25.96).

The post hoc standardized discriminant function coefficients showed CSAI-cog (-0.65) to be substantially more discriminating than CSAI-sc (0.37) and CSAI-som (-0.09).

The multivariate main effect for gender was significant, $F(3, 105)$ = 4.84, $p < .004$. Univariate ANOVAs indicated that

- females (M = 17.29) were significantly higher in CSAI-cog, $F(1, 107)$ = 7.60, $p < .007$, than were males (M = 14.66);

- females ($M = 19.88$) were significantly higher in CSAI-som, $F(1, 107) = 14.01$, $p < .001$, than were males ($M = 16.51$); and
- females ($M = 22.80$) scored significantly lower in CSAI-sc, $F(1, 107) = 6.03$, $p < .02$, than did males ($M = 25.71$).

The discriminant analysis indicated that CSAI-som (-0.84) was by far the most discriminating variable, with CSAI-cog (-0.29) and CSAI-sc (0.04) making less meaningful contributions.

Contact-Noncontact Comparison

The multivariate main effect for sport type was significant, $F(3, 142) = 4.33$, $p < .006$. The univariate analyses showed that

- contact sport athletes ($M = 17.83$) manifested greater CSAI-cog, $F(1, 144) = 4.14$, $p < .05$, than did noncontact athletes ($M = 15.83$);
- contact sport athletes ($M = 19.60$) were significantly higher in CSAI-som, $F(1, 144) = 9.21$, $p < .003$, than were noncontact sport athletes ($M = 17.31$); and
- contact sport athletes ($M = 22.28$) were significantly lower in CSAI-sc, $F(1, 144) = 10.86$, $p < .002$, than were noncontact sport athletes ($M = 25.10$).

The follow-up discriminant analysis showed that CSAI-sc (0.71) and CSAI-som (-0.53) were more discriminating between contact and noncontact sport athletes than was CSAI-cog (0.16).

Trait Anxiety

The multivariate ANOVA for competitive A-trait proved highly significant, $F(3, 47) = 15.99$, $p < .001$. The univariate F tests revealed that

- high A-trait athletes ($M = 18.86$) exhibited higher CSAI-cog, $F(1, 49) = 7.02$, $p < .02$, than did low A-trait athletes ($M = 15.47$);
- high A-trait athletes ($M = 22.39$) responded with significantly greater CSAI-som, $F(1, 49) = 35.92$, $p < .001$, than did low A-trait athletes ($M = 15.13$); and
- high A-trait athletes ($M = 20.28$) showed significantly less CSAI-sc, $F(1, 49) = 20.07$, $p < .001$, than did low A-trait athletes ($M = 25.33$).

The standardized discriminant function coefficients revealed that CSAI-som (-0.85) and CSAI-sc (0.58) were more discriminating than was CSAI-cog (0.22) between high and low competitive A-trait groups.

High- Versus Low-Skilled Athletes

The multivariate analysis of A-state responses between high- and low-skilled athletes was highly significant, $F(3, 267) = 54.44$, $p < .001$. The univariate tests indicated that

- low skilled athletes ($M = 23.63$) were significantly higher in CSAI-cog, $F(1, 269) = 83.08$, $p < .001$, before competition than were high-skilled athletes ($M = 17.23$);
- low-skilled athletes ($M = 18.76$) were significantly higher in CSAI-som, $F(1, 269) = 29.44$, $p < .001$, than were high-skilled athletes ($M = 15.38$); and
- low-skilled athletes ($M = 17.99$) were significantly lower in CSAI-sc, $F(1, 269) = 50.39$, $p < .001$, than were high-skilled athletes ($M = 23.80$).

The standardized discriminant function coefficients showed that CSAI-sc (0.71) and CSAI-cog (-0.66) were substantially better discriminators than was CSAI-som (-0.34) in differentiating between high- and low-skilled athletes.

Discussion of Study 1

The results of this study indicate that each of the CSAI-2 components were significantly influenced by competitive A-trait, gender, skill levels of athletes, and the type of sport. Moreover, these results closely conformed to hypothesized differences for cognitive A-state and state self-confidence, although, somewhat unexpectedly, individual sport athletes were significantly higher in somatic A-state than were team sport athletes.

It had been hypothesized that somatic A-state would not change in situations in which the differences between the groups being compared were due primarily to cognitive factors. For example, the difference between individual and team sports was thought to be primarily cognitive (i.e., evaluation of performance). The results indicated, however, that although cognitive A-state and state self-confidence differed as expected, somatic A-state increased significantly whenever cognitive A-state increased and state self-confidence decreased. Although these findings are consistent with predictions that competitive situations elicit both cognitive and somatic A-state, an alternative explanation is that the physiological arousal demands of the specific sports tested confounded the individual-team comparison. Volleyball and basketball, the team sports used in this comparison, seem to demand moderate arousal levels for optimal performance, whereas performers in individual sports such as gymnastics, swimming, and track and field would seem to find somewhat higher arousal levels necessary for optimal performance. Thus, the significant differences in somatic anxiety between individual and team sport athletes in this investigation may simply reflect the differential arousal demands of the sports chosen for comparison rather than meaningful differences between these sport types.

Although these findings add to the construct validity of the three components of the CSAI-2 in that each subscale was significantly different in the expected direction, they do not provide conclusive evidence that cognitive and somatic A-state are independent systems. However, these results should not be interpreted as evidence refuting the independence of these two anxiety components. Instead, the results indicate that for those sport situations compared, both cognitive and somatic A-state were affected in much the same way. It remains the task of another study to determine the independence of cognitive and somatic A-state.

STUDY 2: CHANGES IN COMPETITIVE A-STATE AS THE TIME TO COMPETE NEARS

The purpose of this study was to investigate the independence of A-state components to ascertain whether there is any justification for the development of a sport-specific A-state scale that measures both cognitive and somatic components. As described in chapter 8, to determine the independence of the cognitive and somatic components of A-state, conditions must be created in which high levels of one component are elicited without elevation of the other.

In Study 1, both components of competitive A-state differed in the same way, providing no evidence that these components are independent. All comparisons made in Study 1, however, consisted of A-state responses obtained within 1 hour of competition, suggesting that this precompetitive situation may contain stimuli evoking both cognitive and somatic A-state. The question arises: Do other times during the competitive process evoke different levels of cognitive as compared to somatic A-state?

The basis for Study 2 was derived from observations of Morris, Davis, and Hutchings (1981) with test-anxious students and the authors' observations of anxiety in sport. They stated that somatic anxiety is "typically of shorter duration and . . . consist[s] primarily of initially nonevaluative cues—the stimulus setting of the classroom, the instructor passing out tests, student conversation about the test—which should lose their salience as attention is turned to the test itself" (p. 542). They support this observation with evidence that somatic A-state significantly decreased once testing began (e.g., Doctor & Altman, 1969; Morris & Engle, 1981; Smith & Morris, 1976). However, cognitive A-state did not decrease significantly throughout testing unless the students' performance expectancies changed (Morris & Fulmer, 1976).

Similar speculations of changes in cognitive and somatic A-state may be made in competitive sport. However, testing these notions during a significant sport contest is nearly impossible. Changes in cognitive and somatic A-state may also be expected over several days before competition and may be more easily tested.

It appears understandable that athletes respond with both cognitive and somatic A-state immediately before competition, as Study 1 showed. However, several days before competition, athletes sometimes reported that they worried about the forthcoming event but did not experience significant increases in somatic anxiety. Thus, it was hypothesized that somatic A-state would be considerably lower several days before competition than would cognitive A-state and that somatic A-state would tend to increase rapidly once athletes were actually present at the competitive site. On the other hand, unless the athletes' evaluations of performance expectancy changed during the period assessed, cognitive A-state should remain relatively constant. Moreover, because one of the most commonly used precompetition anxiety management strategies is simply diverting one's attention to more pleasant topics, cognitive A-state often remains unchanged until individuals begin the evaluation process (Wine, 1980).

Support of these predictions would provide evidence of the independence of cognitive and somatic A-state and thus the construct validity of the CSAI-2. Using Figure 10.1 for reference, this study investigated Link 4 by testing the pattern of cognitive and somatic A-state responses at Link 8 to determine the construct validity of the CSAI-2 subscales (Links 1a, 1b, and 1c). The study involved two separate samples of high school wrestlers and elite gymnasts.

Method for the Wrestling Sample

The initial study was conducted with high school wrestlers ($N = 45$) from four teams who were participating in their conference tournament. The CSAI-2 was administered to each wrestler during the following times before competition:

1. 48 to 64 hours
2. 20 to 24 hours
3. 2 hours
4. 1 hour
5. 15 to 20 minutes

CSAI-2 scores for Times 1 and 2 were taken before practice sessions. Time 3 was shortly after the teams arrived at the tournament facility (about 8:00 a.m.). Time 4 occurred when wrestlers warmed up on the mats, and Time 5 was during the match immediately preceding the wrestler's next bout.

Results for the Wrestling Sample

A repeated measures multivariate analysis of variance (MANOVA) was computed to determine whether significant differences existed among the five precompetition scores on the three subscales of the CSAI-2. A significant main effect for time was obtained, $F(12, 660) = 3.09$, $p < .0003$, and was followed with separate univariate F tests on each component of the CSAI-2. The CSAI-som analysis was highly significant, $F(4, 220) = 6.98$, $p < .0001$, but neither the CSAI-cog, $F(4, 220) = 0.90$, $p > .46$, nor the CSAI-sc, $F(4, 220) = 0.55$, $p > .70$, analysis reached significance. These results are graphically illustrated in Figure 10.2, and the means and standard deviations for CSAI-2 components at each time period are given in Table 10.4. The post hoc discriminant analysis supported the univariate analyses, namely, that CSAI-som (-1.26) was the most discriminating variable, followed by CSAI-cog (0.80) and CSAI-sc (-0.07).

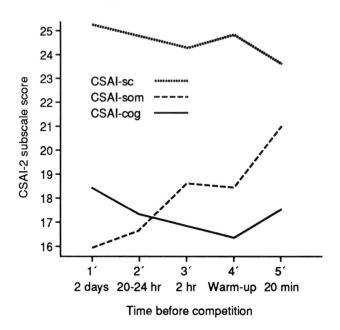

Figure 10.2. Changes in CSAI-2 scores over time for Study 2 (wrestling sample).

Table 10.4 Means and Standard Deviations for the CSAI-2 in Study 2 (Wrestling Sample)

Subscale	Time before the competitive event									
	1		2		3		4		5	
	M	SD	M	SD	M	SD	M	SD	M	SD
CSAI-cog	18.29	4.9	17.20	4.8	16.84	4.8	16.49	4.8	17.16	5.3
CSAI-som	16.13	5.0	16.60	5.5	18.42	5.6	18.27	5.5	21.89	6.9
CSAI-sc	25.16	4.8	24.84	5.4	24.33	5.2	24.98	6.0	23.67	5.8

Post hoc analysis of CSAI-som data using pairwise comparisons for the five time periods revealed the only significant difference to be between Times 4 and 5. The initial spurt in somatic A-state experienced by the wrestlers 2 hours before the competition, just after they arrived at the contest site, was not significant. Although somatic A-state remained about the same through the warm-up, it increased significantly when wrestlers were waiting for the preceding match to conclude so they could begin wrestling.

In contrast, cognitive A-state was higher than was somatic A-state 2 to 3 days before the competition and then decreased as time to compete neared, with a small increase moments before the bout was to begin. However, the cognitive A-state changes over time were not significant and thus should be interpreted as essentially the same over the five times they were measured. State self-confidence followed a similar unchanging pattern, although a slight decrease in state self-confidence at Time 5 is worth noting. It should be noted also that the relative levels of both somatic and cognitive A-state reported by the wrestlers were not high.

The results of this study provided clear support for the construct validity of the CSAI-2 and revealed meaningful differences in the pattern of cognitive and somatic A-state. Thus, it was deemed appropriate to replicate this study with a second sample.

Method for the Gymnastics Sample

Gymnasts ($N = 40$) from the U.S. men's, women's, and rhythmic national gymnastics teams were subjects for the replication as they competed in the National Sports Festival in Indianapolis in July 1982. The CSAI-2 was administered to each gymnast at the following times before competition:

1. 4 days
2. 24 hours
3. 2 hours
4. 5 minutes

Among the wrestlers, cognitive A-state and state self-confidence remained unchanged during the 2- to 3-day period in which CSAI-2 scores were obtained. Thus, among the gymnasts the initial CSAI-2 score was obtained 4 days before competition to determine whether cognitive A-state and state self-confidence remained constant over this longer time period. It should be noted, though, that the gymnasts were already at the competitive site practicing when the CSAI-2 was administered at Times 1 and 2. Time 3 was when the teams arrived at the facility immediately before warming up for their first competitive event. Time 4 was taken between the end of the warm-up and the start of their first competitive routine.

Results for the Gymnastics Sample

The repeated measures MANOVA was significant, $F(9, 468) = 2.53, p < .008$. The univariate ANOVAs once again showed CSAI-som to be significant, $F(32, 156) = 8.57, p < .0001$, but both CSAI-cog, $F(3, 156) = 0.96, p > .41$, and CSAI-sc, $F(3, 156) = 0.59, p > .62$, to be nonsignificant. These results are illustrated in Figure 10.3, and the means and standard deviations of CSAI-2 subscales at each time period are given in Table 10.5. The discriminant analysis yielded coefficients of -1.12 for CSAI-som, 0.71 for CSAI-cog, and -0.05 for CSAI-sc.

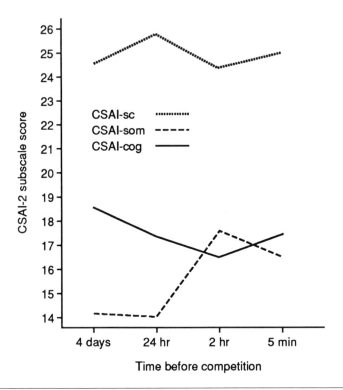

Figure 10.3.   Changes in CSAI-2 scores over time for Study 2 (gymnastics sample).

Table 10.5   Means and Standard Deviations for the CSAI-2 in Study 2 (Gymnastics Sample)

	Time before the competitive event							
	1		2		3		4	
Subscale	M	SD	M	SD	M	SD	M	SD
CSAI-cog	18.28	4.7	17.15	4.4	16.5	4.8	17.1	5.3
CSAI-som	14.08	3.3	13.85	3.5	17.53	4.2	16.8	4.9
CSAI-sc	24.35	5.4	25.75	5.7	24.25	5.8	24.83	5.7

The results of the gymnasts were remarkably similar to those of the wrestlers. The post hoc univariate pairwise comparisons indicated that Time 2 was significantly different from Times 3 and 4. Looking at Figure 10.3, it can be seen that somatic A-state remained low and unchanged until the gymnasts arrived at the competition site just prior to competition, but then somatic A-state increased dramatically. However, somatic A-state did not increase further but decreased slightly immediately before the gymnasts were to compete. The somatic A-state scores 2 hours before the beginning of the contest were similar for wrestlers and gymnasts, but the wrestlers experienced considerably higher somatic A-state moments before the contest was to begin, presumably reflecting differences in the arousal demands of the two sports.

The pattern and absolute values of the cognitive A-state scores is almost identical between the two samples. Cognitive A-state did not significantly change over the time periods sampled in both studies but tended to decrease from as early as 4 days before competition to 2 hours before competition and then increased slightly moments before competition. The state self-confidence scores, although fluctuating slightly, remained relatively unchanged over time.

Discussion of Study 2

Both the wrestlers and the gymnasts provide support for the hypothesis that somatic A-state is lower than is cognitive A-state several days before competition, but somatic A-state increases rapidly once athletes are at the competition site just prior to competition. This increase in somatic A-state may possibly be the result of what Borkovec (1976) has called *conditioned anxiety,* especially because cognitive A-state did not follow the same pattern of increases, but remained essentially unchanged. The unchanging pattern of cognitive A-state was hypothesized because expectancies about the outcome were thought to remain unaltered throughout the time period sampled. These results provide support for the independence of the cognitive and the somatic A-state systems and thus the construct validity of the CSAI-2.

STUDY 3: THE RELATIONSHIP BETWEEN PERFORMANCE AND THE CSAI-2 SUBSCALES

In chapter 8, the hypothesis was put forth that performance is more likely to have a higher relationship with cognitive A-state and state self-confidence than with somatic A-state, a prediction henceforth referred to as the *anxiety-performance hypothesis.* The primary purpose of Study 3 was to investigate this hypothesis. In reference to Figure 10.1, this study investigated Link 5 by testing Link 9 to examine indirectly the construct validity of Links 1a, 1b, and 1c. A secondary purpose of the study was to extend Study 2 by looking at how the CSAI-2 scores changed not only before but also during the contest.

Method

Forty-nine male golfers who competed in the 1983 Western Junior National Golf Tournament were the subjects in this study. They ranged in age from 16 to 19. The CSAI-2 was completed three times by each golfer:

1. Noncompetition: 1 to 2 days before the tournament began.
2. Precompetition: Within 1 hour of teeing off and in most cases within a few minutes of teeing off.
3. Midcompetition: Completed immediately after the first round of 18 holes. When they completed the CSAI-2 at this time, however, the golfers were asked to describe their emotional state retrospectively after having completed the first 9 holes. In other words, they were asked to recall their emotions at the "turn" rather than how they felt at that moment at the conclusion of the round. This procedure had to be used because tournament officials would not permit the investigators to obtain CSAI-2 responses from golfers after the first 9 holes.

Two performance scores were recorded for each golfer. The score for the first 9 holes was labeled Score 1 and the score for the second 9 holes Score 2. All data were collected for the first 18-hole round of the tournament only.

Results of Study 3

The means and standard deviations for the CSAI-2 scores for each of the three time periods are given in Table 10.6. A repeated measures ANOVA was computed for each of the three CSAI-2 subscales to assess changes in A-state and state self-confidence before and during competition. All three were significant: CSAI-cog, $F(2, 96) = 9.95$, $p < .0001$; CSAI-som, $F(2, 96) = 5.05$, $p < .008$; and CSAI-sc, $F(2, 96) = 14.15$, $p < .00001$.

Post hoc comparisons indicated that noncompetition and precompetition CSAI-cog were each significantly lower than midcompetition CSAI-cog, but noncompetition CSAI-cog was not significantly different from precompetition CSAI-cog.

Table 10.6   Means and Standard Deviations for CSAI-2 Scores in Study 3

Subscale	Noncompetition		Precompetition		Midcompetition	
	M	SD	M	SD	M	SD
CSAI-cog	18.71	5.08	17.51	4.89	20.29	6.42
CSAI-som	14.27	3.93	15.69	4.33	14.06	4.88
CSAI-sc	26.18	5.13	25.80	4.63	22.59	6.61

Precompetition CSAI-som was significantly higher than noncompetition and mid-competition CSAI-som, but noncompetition and midcompetition CSAI-som were not significantly different from each other. Noncompetition CSAI-sc was significantly higher than midcompetition CSAI-sc but not significantly higher than precompetition CSAI-sc. Precompetition CSAI-sc was significantly higher than midcompetition CSAI-sc.

Similar to the results in Study 2, cognitive A-state did not significantly change from noncompetition to precompetition, but once the golfers had played the first nine holes, their cognitive A-state increased significantly. This is consistent with Morris, Davis, and Hutching's (1981) hypothesis that cognitive anxiety does not change unless performance expectancy changes. The completion of the first nine holes, of course, gave the golfers information for changing their performance expectancies. These findings indicate that the golfers as a group not only increased their cognitive A-state but also significantly lowered their state self-confidence.

The somatic A-state scores were the highest at precompetition and then significantly dropped at midcompetition. This finding also is highly consistent with the results of Study 2 and provides another bit of evidence for the independence of cognitive and somatic A-state. At midcompetition, when the golfers were able to assess their performance on the first nine holes and reflect on how they may perform for the round, their cognitive A-state increased and their somatic A-state decreased.

The correlation coefficients between each of the CSAI-2 subscales and each of the two performance scores are given in Table 10.7. The noncompetition and precompetition CSAI-2 subscale scores were not significantly correlated

Table 10.7   Correlation Coefficients Between CSAI-2 Subscales and Performance Scores in Study 3

Variable	Score 1		Score 2	
	r	p	r	p
Noncompetition				
CSAI-cog	.14	.17	.34	.009
CSAI-som	.04	.39	.34	.009
CSAI-sc	−.20	.08	−.10	.26
Precompetition				
CSAI-cog	.13	.19	.27	.03
CSAI-som	.21	.08	.26	.03
CSAI-sc	−.06	.35	−.15	.16
Midcompetition				
CSAI-cog	.41	.002	.29	.02
CSAI-som	.21	.07	.34	.009
CSAI-sc	−.48	.001	−.30	.02

with Performance Score 1. The noncompetition and precompetition CSAI-cog and CSAI-som scores, however, were significantly correlated with Performance Score 2. These correlations are not high but are noteworthy, given that anxiety is only one of many factors influencing performance.

What is perplexing about these results, however, is that the coefficients were significant not for Score 1, which was temporally closer to the golfers' performance, but for Score 2. These are inexplicable findings. Rather than precompetition CSAI-2 scores correlating with performance, the midcompetition scores on all three CSAI-2 subscales correlated significantly with both Performance Scores 1 and 2. The only correlation between the CSAI-2 subscale and performance that was not significant at midcompetition was that for somatic A-state. The other trend worth noting in Table 10.7 is that state self-confidence correlated significantly with performance only for the midcompetition measure.

Separate multiple regression analyses were computed for the three time periods with the three CSAI-2 subscales as the predictor variables and each performance score as the criterion variable. The results, summarized in Table 10.8, are even more perplexing. The noncompetition regression analysis did not significantly predict Performance Score 1 but did significantly predict Performance Score 2. The precompetition regression analysis, containing state scores taken closer to the performance, were not significant for Performance Scores 1 and 2. Interestingly, the midcompetition regression analysis better predicted Performance Score 1 than it did Performance Score 2.

Discussion of Study 3

Although these analyses do not permit any cause-and-effect inferences, the pattern of results suggests that an immediately preceding performance may have greater influence on anxiety states than anxiety states have on performance. This hypothesis merits further attention.

STUDY 4: THE RELATIONSHIP BETWEEN CSAI-2 SUBSCALES AND A MORE SENSITIVE INTRAINDIVIDUAL PERFORMANCE MEASURE

Although Study 3 did not provide construct validity evidence that CSAI-2 components correlated with performance in a theoretically consistent pattern, these findings may be more the result of weak performance measures than of conceptual limitations of the CSAI-2.

It was speculated that the performance measure employed in Study 3 may have lacked the precision necessary to assess accurately the subtle influence of anxiety on performance. A score for a round of golf allows only between-subjects (i.e.,

Table 10.8   Stepwise Multiple Regression Analyses for Non-, Pre-, and Midcompetition on Each Performance Score in Study 3

Time period and performance score	Variable entered	Multiple R	R^2	F	p
Noncompetition on Performance Score 1	CSAI-sc	.20	.04	2.05	.16
	CSAI-som	.21	.05	1.09	.35
	CSAI-cog	.22	.05	.77	.52
Noncompetition on Performance Score 2	CSAI-som	.34	.12	6.33	.02
	CSAI-cog	.39	.15	4.04	.02
	CSAI-sc	.42	.17	3.15	.03
Precompetition on Performance Score 1	CSAI-som	.21	.04	2.13	.15
	CSAI-cog	.21	.04	1.07	.35
	CSAI-sc	.22	.05	.74	.53
Precompetition on Performance Score 2	CSAI-cog	.27	.07	3.79	.06
	CSAI-som	.31	.10	2.47	.10
	CSAI-sc	.31	.10	1.65	.19
Midcompetition on Performance Score 1	CSAI-sc	.48	.23	13.86	.001
	CSAI-cog	.50	.25	7.74	.001
	CSAI-som	.51	.26	5.18	.004
Midcompetition on Performance Score 2	CSAI-som	.34	.11	5.97	.02
	CSAI-sc	.38	.14	3.80	.03
	CSAI-cog	.38	.14	2.51	.07

interindividual) rather than more precise within-subjects (i.e., intraindividual) comparisons. The major limitation of interindividual performance measures is that they make it impossible to determine whether differences among competitors' scores on a particular round of golf are the result of mediating factors (e.g., anxiety) or simply of differences in skill level. Consequently, interindividual performance measures make virtually impossible qualitative inference about whether posting a score of 72 is good or bad for a particular athlete.

Intraindividual performance measures afford such qualitative precision because they can account for differences in skill level by evaluating current performance on the basis of comparison to average or best previous performance. Thus, a more sensitive intraindividual performance measure would be to compare (a) a golfer's score today to his or her season average (i.e., handicap), (b) a basketball player's free throw performance in a particular game to his or her season free throw percentage, or (c) a sprinter's 100-yd-dash time in this race to his or her best previous performance (i.e., personal record). The ability of intraindividual performance measures to control for differences in skill level provides a greater level of measurement sensitivity that can more accurately "tease out" the exact influence of anxiety on performance. For example, although the impact of elevated levels of anxiety may not be sufficient to change the outcome of a contest or a competitor's place in a race, it can cut several tenths of a second off a 100-yd-dash time or can add several strokes to a golfer's score.

The failure of Study 3 to employ this type of intraindividual performance measure suggests that further research using improved performance methodology is warranted. Therefore, Burton's (1988) primary purpose for conducting Study 4 was to test the anxiety-performance hypothesis by using a more sensitive intraindividual measure of performance. In terms of Figure 10.1, this study again investigated Link 5 by testing Link 9 to examine indirectly the construct validity of Links 1a, 1b, and 1c.

Testing the Inverted-U Relationship

Another important issue assessed in this investigation was the nature of relationships among CSAI-2 subscales and performance across a series of competitions representing at least three distinct levels of objective threat. Previous researchers have demonstrated an inverted-U relationship between unidimensional measures of A-state and performance, suggesting that athletes perform best when anxiety is moderate and that performance deteriorates when anxiety increases or decreases from this optimal level (e.g., Klavora, 1978; Sonstroem & Bernardo, 1982; Weinberg & Genuchi, 1980). However, adoption of multidimensional anxiety theory suggests that somewhat different predictions may be made for the relationships among multiple measures of CSAI-2 subscale scores and performance. On the basis of the nature of cognitive A-state, somatic A-state, and state self-confidence and their patterns of change over time, multidimensional anxiety theory predicts that cognitively based measures such as cognitive A-state and state self-confidence will demonstrate linear relationships with performance, whereas an inverted-U relationship is hypothesized between physiologically based somatic A-state and performance (e.g., Morris, Davis, and Hutchings, 1981).

Specifically, three predictions can be inferred from multidimensional anxiety theory. First, because cognitive anxiety misdirects attention from task-relevant cues to task-irrelevant self- or social evaluation cues (e.g., Wine, 1980), performance should decrease linearly with increases in cognitive A-state. Second, previous researchers have found that state self-confidence increases as positive expectations of success increase (e.g., Morris & Fulmer, 1976). Because previous research has demonstrated the significant impact that expectancies can have on performance (e.g., Bandura, 1977; Feltz, 1982; Feltz et al., 1979; Rosenthal, 1968; Weinberg, Gould, & Jackson, 1979), performance should increase linearly with increases in state self-confidence. Finally, previous research that has consistently found an inverted-U relationship between anxiety or arousal and performance has often measured arousal with predominantly physiological indices (e.g., Klavora, 1978; Landers & Boutcher, 1986; Sonstroem & Bernardo, 1982). Therefore, physiologically based somatic A-state should demonstrate an inverted-U relationship with performance.

Therefore, a secondary purpose of this study was to test predictions about the nature of relationships between multiple measurements of the CSAI-2 components and performance. Three specific hypotheses were derived:

- Cognitive A-state was predicted to show a negative linear relationship with performance.
- A positive linear relationship was predicted between state self-confidence and performance.
- Somatic A-state was predicted to demonstrate an inverted-U relationship with performance.

In terms of Figure 10.1, the construct validity of Links 1a, 1b, and 1c was indirectly examined by testing operational Link 9 to investigate theoretical Link 5 further.

Impact of Task Variables on the Relationship Between Somatic A-State and Performance

In Study 1 the unexpected finding that individual sport athletes reported higher somatic A-state than did team sport athletes prompted speculation that this difference may have been due to the differential physiological arousal demands of the sports tested. This hypothesis that task variables may mediate the relationship between somatic A-state and performance is provocative and warrants further study. Although no empirical research has previously investigated the influence of task variables on the relationship between somatic A-state and performance, somatic A-state's basic pattern of change suggests that it should influence competition of short duration more than it should ongoing performance of longer duration. Additionally, the related arousal-performance literature has widely acknowledged for some time that task variables mediate the relationship between arousal and performance (e.g., Landers & Boutcher, 1986; Martens, 1974). In fact, Landers and Boutcher have recently identified task complexity as a critical variable mediating the relationship between arousal and performance. Thus, on the basis of somatic A-state's characteristic pattern of change and of previous arousal-performance research, two task variables have been hypothesized to influence significantly the relationship between somatic A-state and performance. These variables are

- task duration and
- task complexity.

Because somatic A-state is believed to be classically conditioned to environmental cues associated with the onset of competition, it was hypothesized that somatic A-state should exert a greater impact on task performance of short (e.g., sprint races) than of long (e.g., distance races) duration. Moreover, competitors in long-distance events have more time to dissipate somatic manifestations during the events, thus further lessening the impact of somatic A-state on performance.

It was also hypothesized that performance in discontinuous tasks that involve a series of separate, relatively short duration performances with sufficient intervals between trials to elicit somatic A-state change patterns similar to those occurring at the start of competition (e.g., diving, gymnastics, ski jumping, and golf) should be more influenced by somatic A-state levels than should performance in more continuous tasks (e.g., basketball, volleyball, tennis, and racquetball) that allow somatic A-state to return to stable levels as players become involved in the activity. Nevertheless, Feltz's (1982) self-efficacy research has suggested clearly that somatic A-state should affect the first performance of a discontinuous task more directly and strongly than it should subsequent performances, which are most influenced by expectations derived from immediately previous performance.

Landers and Boutcher (1986) have recently used task complexity as the basis for a model to determine the optimal level of arousal for different sports and sport tasks. They suggested that task complexity is comprised of three primary factors: (a) decision characteristics, (b) perceptual characteristics, and (c) motor response characteristics. They concluded that the greater the overall task complexity, the lower the arousal level that is optimal for best performance. According to this model, archery, golf, and field-goal kicking are examples of high-complexity activities, and football blocking and running 200 to 400 m are typical low-complexity tasks. Due to the similarity between physiological components of arousal and somatic anxiety, this model may be valuable in predicting the impact of task complexity on the relationship between somatic A-state and performance.

Although Landers and Boutcher (1986) suggested that under- or overarousal can inhibit performance at all complexity levels of their model, it can be easily inferred from research on the inverted-U relationship that tasks high in complexity have a narrower optimal arousal range. Therefore, performance on high-complexity tasks should be greatly impaired by excessive somatic A-state because it slows or inhibits perceptual processing, decision making, response production, or all these (Broadhurst, 1957). Moreover, performance on low-complexity tasks should also be impaired by inadequately low levels of somatic A-state, which prevent adequate mobilization of energy stores for maximal strength, speed, or endurance performance (Oxendine, 1970).

Landers and Boutcher (1986) did not directly categorize endurance events in their model, but these events clearly fit the low-complexity criteria of this model. Nevertheless, no hypothesis was made for expected relationships between somatic A-state and endurance performance because different predictions are derived on the basis of the task duration and the task complexity characteristics of these events.

Therefore, the final purpose of this investigation was to evaluate the influence of task duration and task complexity on the relationship between somatic A-state and swimming performance. Two specific hypotheses were made. First, a stronger relationship was predicted between somatic A-state and performance for swimming events of short duration (e.g., 50- and 100-m freestyle) than for events of moderate (e.g., 200 to 400 m) and long (e.g., 800 to 1,500 m) duration. Second, a stronger relationship was predicted between somatic A-state and performance for swimming events high (e.g., 100- and 200-m breaststroke) and low in complexity (e.g., 50-, 100-, 800-, and 1,500-m freestyle) than for events of moderate complexity (e.g., other technical events and 200- to 400-m freestyle). According to Figure 10.1, the impact of the situational factor of event type (Link 4) on CSAI-som (Link 1b) was investigated by testing operational Link 8.

Method

To test these hypotheses regarding the relationship of performance on different types of tasks with the CSAI-2 components, subjects were selected and procedures designed to facilitate a more precise, intraindividual measure of performance.

Sample

This investigation included two samples of swimmers. Sample 1 consisted of 15 male and 13 female collegiate swimmers from a Big 10 swim team who ranged in age from 18 to 23 years. Each swimmer completed the CSAI-2 during three separate meets throughout the swim season, including (a) an early-season invitational meet, (b) a midseason conference dual meet, and (c) the Big 10 championships.

Sample 2 was comprised of 39 female and 31 male swimmers with a mean age of 17.4 years who were chosen to compete at the 1982 National Sports Festival in Indianapolis. Each swimmer completed the CSAI-2 twice, once following a practice session 2 days before the competition and again within 1 hour before his or her most important race of the meet.

Performance Measure

Because swimming is a conditioning rather than a technique sport, performance often fluctuates drastically from one competition to the next, depending on where the athlete is in the training cycle. Therefore, previous best performance is generally deemed a more appropriate intraindividual performance measure than is average performance (Costill, 1985). Performance scores for Samples 1 and 2 were calculated according to an identical formula by subtracting each swimmer's personal record in that event from his or her time in this competition and then dividing these deviation scores by an adjustment factor designed to convert all performance to 50-yd (or 50-m) increments to facilitate comparison across races of different distances.

Results of Study 4

Overall, the results supported several of the hypotheses in the study and provided evidence that the anxiety-performance relationship may be better understood by accounting for the multidimensionality of competitive A-state.

Testing the Inverted-U Hypothesis

To test for an inverted-U relationship among CSAI-2 subscale scores and performance for swimmers in Sample 1, techniques advocated by Sonstroem and Bernardo (1982) were employed. Initially, each swimmer's three scores for each CSAI-2 subscale were reordered so that the swimmer's lowest score on each subscale was always first, the middle score always second, and the highest score always third (see Table 10.9). Sonstroem and Bernardo justified this manipulation because it did not matter which meet created the most or the least A-state or state self-confidence but only that swimmers demonstrated distinct differences among the three levels of anxiety and self-confidence.

Table 10.9   Means and Standard Deviations for Reordered CSAI-2 Subscale Scores for Sample 1

Ranking	N	CSAI-cog		CSAI-som		CSAI-sc	
		M	SD	M	SD	M	SD
Low	27	11.4	3.3	14.0	3.2	22.4	5.4
Moderate	27	13.4	3.7	15.6	3.5	26.0	5.7
High	27	16.3	4.4	18.1	4.1	28.9	5.5

Repeated measures ANOVA techniques with orthogonal post hoc comparisons demonstrated the effectiveness of this manipulation by revealing significant differences between each of the three levels of cognitive A-state, somatic A-state, and state self-confidence, thus satisfying McGrath's (1970b) precondition for testing the inverted-U relationship. CSAI-2 and performance data were then standardized according to procedures suggested by Sonstroem and Bernardo (1982) to negate between-subject response variation. Means and standard deviations were calculated for each swimmer's three cognitive A-state, somatic A-state, state self-confidence, and performance scores, and intraindividual standard scores were computed for each CSAI-2 subscale and performance. Separate polynomial trend analyses were then employed to test for linear or curvilinear relationships among standardized CSAI-2 subscale scores and both standardized and unstandardized swimming performance.

Inspection of Figure 10.4 reveals that these data generally confirmed theoretical predictions. As predicted, these results demonstrated a significant

- negative linear trend between CSAI-cog and performance ($t = 3.87$, $p < .0002$),
- positive linear trend between CSAI-sc and performance ($t = -4.93$, $p < .0001$), and
- no linear trend for CSAI-som and performance ($t = 0.05$, $p > .96$).

However, somatic anxiety did exhibit the predicted curvilinear trend with performance ($t = 2.03$, $p < .05$).

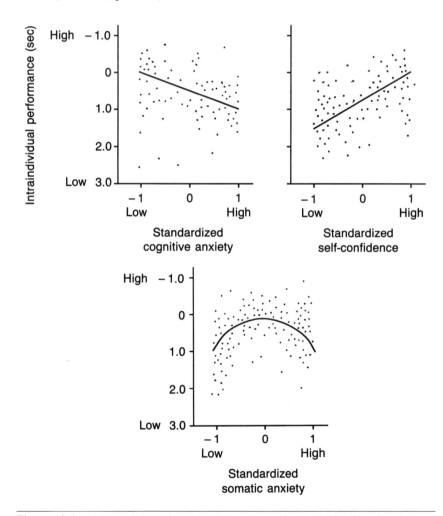

Figure 10.4. Polynomial trend analyses between standardized CSAI-2 subscale scores and intraindividual performance for Sample 1. *Note.* From "Do Anxious Swimmers Swim Slower? Reexamining the Elusive Anxiety-Performance Relationship" by D. Burton, 1988, *Journal of Sport & Exercise Psychology,* **10**(1), p. 56. Copyright 1988 by Human Kinetics Publishers. Reprinted by permission.

Testing the Anxiety-Performance Hypothesis

Means and standard deviations for CSAI-2 subscales and performance scores of Sample 1 swimmers for three selected meets are given in Table 10.10. The correlation coefficients among the CSAI-2 subscales and performance shown in Table 10.11 are highly congruent with the anxiety-performance hypothesis. Overall, CSAI-cog and CSAI-sc were significantly related to performance in each of the three meets, whereas CSAI-som was significantly correlated with performance only for the midseason meet. However, CSAI-cog was still more strongly related to midseason performance than was CSAI-som.

Finally, these data also are consistent with the prediction that anxious swimmers swim slower. Although these correlational data do not allow cause-and-effect inference, the positive correlations between performance and both CSAI-cog and CSAI-som shown in Table 10.11 are consistent with the hypothesized debilitating effect of anxiety on performance (i.e., performance times increased). The inverse relationship between CSAI-sc and performance confirms predictions about the facilitating impact of self-confidence on performance.

Table 10.10 Means and Standard Deviations for CSAI-2 and Performance Scores in Three Swim Meets for Sample 1

		CSAI-cog		CSAI-som		CSAI-sc		Performance	
Meet	N	M	SD	M	SD	M	SD	M	SD
Early season	18	15.3	4.8	17.7	5.7	24.2	7.6	1.34	.95
Midseason	20	13.4	5.1	14.7	4.1	26.1	6.6	.07	.90
Big 10	24	14.8	4.9	18.1	4.2	24.2	6.1	.32	.39

Note. Six subjects were eliminated from analyses of the early-season meet and four subjects from analyses of the midseason meet due to missing data.

Table 10.11 Correlation Coefficients Among CSAI-2 Subscales and Performance in Three Swim Meets for Sample 1

		CSAI-cog		CSAI-som		CSAI-sc	
Meet	N	r	p	r	p	r	p
Early season	18	.40	.05*	.17	.25	−.46	.03*
Midseason	20	.68	.001***	.61	.002**	−.41	.04*
Big 10	24	.39	.03*	.32	.07	−.39	.03*

Note. From "Do Anxious Swimmers Swim Slower? Reexamining the Elusive Anxiety-Performance Relationship" by D. Burton, 1988, *Journal of Sport & Exercise Psychology,* **10**(1), p. 52. Copyright 1988 by Human Kinetics Publishers. Reprinted by permission.
*p < .05.   **p < .01.   ***p < .001.

Separate multiple regression analyses were computed for each of the three meets in Sample 1 with the three CSAI-2 subscales as the predictor variables and performance as the criterion variable. The results summarized in Table 10.12 reveal that derived regression equations significantly predicted performance for all three meets, although only a single variable, CSAI-sc, was a significant predictor of performance for the early-season and Big 10 meets. CSAI-som entered the regression equation last in the midseason and Big 10 meets, and, although it did enter ahead of CSAI-cog in the early-season meet, its contribution to the regression equation was minimal.

Table 10.12   Stepwise Multiple Regression Analyses Predicting Swimming Performance From Precompetition CSAI-2 Subscales for Sample 1 in Three Meets

Variable entered	Multiple R	R^2	F	p
Performance in early-season meet				
CSAI-sc	.46	.21	4.23	.05*
CSAI-som	.49	.24	2.35	.13
CSAI-cog	.50	.25	1.54	.25
Performance in midseason meet				
CSAI-cog	.68	.46	15.13	.001***
CSAI-sc	.74	.54	10.13	.001***
CSAI-som	.75	.57	6.93	.003**
Performance in Big 10 meet				
CSAI-sc	.39	.16	4.04	.05*
CSAI-cog	.41	.17	2.15	.14
CSAI-som	.42	.18	1.43	.26

Note. From "Do Anxious Swimmers Swim Slower? Reexamining the Elusive Anxiety-Performance Relationship" by D. Burton, 1988, *Journal of Sport & Exercise Psychology,* **10**(1), p. 53. Copyright 1988 by Human Kinetics Publishers. Reprinted by permission.
*$p < .05$.   **$p < .01$.   ***$p < .001$.

Means and standard deviations for CSAI-2 subscales and performance scores of Sample 2 swimmers for all National Sports Festival events are provided in the first line of Table 10.13. The correlation coefficients among CSAI-2 subscales and performance for all the events shown in the first line of Table 10.14 are again consistent with theoretical predictions. CSAI-cog, but not CSAI-som, was significantly correlated with performance. Moreover, multiple regression analysis for all events using the CSAI-2 subscales as predictor variables and performance as the criterion variable confirmed that CSAI-cog was the only significant predictor of performance, but it accounted for only 7% of the variance in performance scores (see Table 10.15). Overall, data from Samples 1 and 2 provide strong support for the hypothesis that CSAI-cog will demonstrate a stronger and more consistent relationship with performance than will CSAI-som.

Table 10.13   Means and Standard Deviations for CSAI-2 Subscales and Swimming Performance for Nine Types of Events for Sample 2 at the National Sports Festival

Types of events	N	CSAI-cog M	CSAI-cog SD	CSAI-som M	CSAI-som SD	CSAI-sc M	CSAI-sc SD	Performance M	Performance SD
All events	70	18.1	4.4	16.6	4.0	24.0	5.4	.32	.45
50-m freestyle	5	17.2	4.1	16.2	6.2	23.2	4.7	.26	.57
50- and 100-m freestyle	10	17.2	3.8	16.6	4.6	23.0	3.6	.38	.47
All 50- and 100-m events	26	17.4	3.3	15.8	4.0	24.5	4.7	.28	.42
All 50- to 200-m events	55	17.6	4.0	16.4	4.1	24.4	5.0	.31	.47
All technical events	44	17.6	4.1	16.3	3.8	24.8	5.0	.26	.45
100- to 200-m breaststroke	10	20.2	3.4	17.1	4.9	24.0	5.7	.15	.27
All 400- to 1,500-m events	15	19.9	5.4	17.4	3.6	22.7	6.7	.33	.40
800- and 1,500-m freestyle	5	18.0	2.3	17.4	3.2	25.8	3.7	.19	.53

Note. Higher scores indicate greater cognitive and somatic A-state and state self-confidence, whereas lower times indicate better performance (a negative performance time indicates the establishment of a new personal record).

Table 10.14   Correlation Coefficients Among CSAI-2 Subscales and Swimming Performance for Nine Types of Events for Sample 2 at the National Sports Festival

Event	N	CSAI-cog r	CSAI-cog p	CSAI-som r	CSAI-som p	CSAI-sc r	CSAI-sc p
All events	70	.26	.02*	.07	.27	−.17	.08
50-m freestyle	5	.90	.02*	.79	.05*	−.42	.24
50- and 100-m freestyle	10	.66	.02*	.49	.07	−.21	.29
All 50- and 100-m events	26	.21	.15	.09	.33	−.02	.47
All 50- to 200-m events	55	.14	.16	.02	.46	−.07	.30
All technical events	44	.01	.49	−.04	.40	.05	.37
100- and 200-m breaststroke	10	.71	.01**	.61	.03*	−.42	.11
All 400- to 1,500-m events	15	.69	.002**	.36	.09	−.50	.03*
800- and 1,500-m freestyle	5	−.70	.09	−.78	.05*	.61	.14

Note. Higher scores indicate greater cognitive and somatic A-state and state self-confidence, whereas lower times indicate better performance. From ''Do Anxious Swimmers Swim Slower? Reexamining the Elusive Anxiety-Performance Relationship'' by D. Burton, 1988, *Journal of Sport & Exercise Psychology,* **10**(1), p. 54. Copyright 1988 by Human Kinetics Publishers. Reprinted by permission.

*p < .05   **p < .01.

Table 10.15   Stepwise Multiple Regression Analyses Predicting Swimming Performance From Precompetition CSAI-2 Subscales for Sample 2

Variable entered	Multiple R	R^2	F	p
All events				
CSAI-cog	.26	.07	4.85	.03*
CSAI-som	.27	.07	2.59	.08
CSAI-sc	.27	.08	1.79	.16
50-m freestyle				
CSAI-cog	.90	.80	12.11	.04*
CSAI-som	.93	.87	6.61	.13
CSAI-sc	.94	.89	2.72	.41
50- and 100-m freestyle				
CSAI-cog	.66	.44	6.27	.04*
CSAI-som	.68	.46	2.99	.11
CSAI-sc	.68	.46	1.72	.26
All 50- and 100-m events				
CSAI-cog	.21	.05	1.13	.30
CSAI-sc	.22	.05	0.56	.58
CSAI-som	.22	.05	0.36	.78
All 50-, 100-, and 200-m events				
CSAI-cog	.14	.02	1.03	.32
CSAI-som	.15	.02	0.61	.54
CSAI-sc	.16	.02	0.42	.74
All technical events				
CSAI-sc	.05	.01	0.11	.74
CSAI-som	.06	.01	0.07	.93
CSAI-cog	.06	.01	0.06	.98
100- and 200-m breaststroke				
CSAI-cog	.71	.51	8.24	.02*
CSAI-som	.77	.60	5.15	.04*
CSAI-sc	.78	.61	3.11	.11
All 400-, 800-, and 1,500-m events				
CSAI-cog	.69	.48	11.91	.004**
CSAI-som	.69	.48	5.53	.02*
CSAI-sc	.69	.48	3.38	.06
800- and 1,500-m freestyle				
CSAI-som	.78	.60	4.58	.12
CSAI-cog	.92	.84	5.22	.16
CSAI-sc	.99	.99	109.62	.009**
CSAI-som	.99	.99	80.12	.08

Note. In the stepwise regression analysis for 800- and 1,500-m freestyle events, CSAI-som was the single variable that maximized R^2. However, at Step 2 the best two-variable solution that maximized R^2 was created when CSAI-cog entered the equation and CSAI-sc replaced CSAI-som.
*$p < .05$.   **$p < .01$.

Impact of Task Characteristics on the Relationship Between CSAI-som and Performance

Means and standard deviations for CSAI-2 subscales and performance scores for eight categories of swimming events that systematically varied task duration and complexity are also shown in Table 10.13. Correlation coefficients among CSAI-2 subscales and performance for these eight categories of events shown in Table 10.14 reveal an interesting pattern of results that is generally consistent with predictions.

Task duration results were equivocal. For the five swimmers whose most important race was the 50-m freestyle, CSAI-som was significantly related to performance as predicted, although CSAI-cog still demonstrated a stronger relationship with performance and was the only variable that contributed significantly to the regression equation (see Tables 10.14 & 10.15). Even when this category was expanded to include the 100-m freestyle, the relationship between CSAI-som and performance approached significance, suggesting that somatic anxiety regulation is indeed an important mediator of sprint freestyle performance.

As expected, the relationship between CSAI-som and the performance deteriorated sharply as distance increased, but only up to a point. Surprisingly, for distance events over 400 m, and particularly for those 800 m and longer, the strength of the relationship increased again, approaching significance for events 400 m and longer and achieving significance for the category including the two longest distance freestyle events. In fact, for the 800- and 1,500-m freestyle events, CSAI-som was the only variable significantly related to performance.

Task complexity results were generally congruent with predictions. CSAI-som correlated significantly with performance for high-complexity (e.g., breaststroke) and low-complexity (e.g., sprint and distance freestyle) events, but not for moderate-complexity ones (see Tables 10.13 through 10.15). Interestingly, in the technical breaststroke events, both CSAI-cog and CSAI-som were significantly related to performance, but CSAI-cog again correlated more strongly with performance than did CSAI-som. Regression analyses also suggested that CSAI-som was a better predictor of performance in sprint and distance events than it was in middle-distance or moderate-complexity technical events. However, CSAI-cog was consistently a better predictor of performance than was CSAI-som, which made a significant contribution only to prediction efficiency for the breaststroke events.

One particularly noteworthy finding was that the direction of the relationship between somatic A-state and performance was different for sprint and distance freestyle events. In sprint races, correlations suggested that swimmers who performed better tended to keep somatic A-state under control more than did sprinters who performed more poorly, whereas in distance events swimmers whose times closely approached their personal records tended to get themselves more physiologically aroused than did swimmers who posted poorer times.

Another interesting finding was the failure to find differences in somatic A-state levels between high- and low-complexity events. Landers and Boutcher's (1986) task complexity model suggests that competitors in low-complexity events such as sprints and distance freestyle races can tolerate higher levels of optimal arousal than can competitors in high-complexity events such as the breaststroke. Nevertheless, the somatic A-state means for these different categories of events were not consistent with this prediction. Not only were there no differences between the somatic A-state means for these three categories of events, but, inexplicably, the somatic A-state means for the two breaststroke events were almost as large as those for the distance freestyle events and somewhat larger than those for sprint freestyle events (see Table 10.13).

Discussion of Study 4

The correlational and multiple regression analyses assessing the relationship among CSAI-2 subscales and performance were strikingly consistent in their demonstration of a significant relationship between anxiety and performance. Apparently, the more conceptually explicit measure of competitive A-state afforded by the CSAI-2 and the more sensitive intraindividual performance measure employed in this investigation were beneficial refinements in the search to verify the intuitive link between anxiety and performance. Moreover, the highly consistent support for the anxiety-performance hypothesis reaffirms results previously obtained in academic testing situations that cognitive worry more directly impairs performance than does somatic arousal and greatly strengthens the construct validity of the CSAI-2.

The consistent support of the polynomial trend analyses for the predicted (a) inverted-U relationship between somatic A-state and performance, (b) negative linear relationship between cognitive A-state and performance, and (c) positive linear relationship between state self-confidence and performance further strengthens the construct validity of the CSAI-2. Moreover, these data also confirm the previous prediction that, for swimming, employing an intraindividual performance measure based on best previous performance is indeed more appropriate than is using a measure based on average performance.

The findings testing the impact of task demands on the relationships between somatic A-state and performance supported not only predictions that differential task demands may be responsible for individual sport athletes reporting higher somatic A-state than did team sport athletes in Study 1 but also the construct validity of the CSAI-2.

Two related findings concerning the impact of task demands on the relationship between somatic A-state and performance are especially provocative. First, the unexpected finding of a significant relationship between somatic A-state and distance freestyle performance supports task complexity rather than task duration predictions. Apparently, success in distance freestyle events requires mobilization of energy resources, and distance swimmers who are unable to "get up" for a race because of inappropriate training or poor mental preparation may not be able to mobilize sufficient energy resources to maintain a strong pace. Although previous research has not directly assessed arousal demands of short- versus long-duration events, these data are generally congruent with Morgan's (1978) "iceberg profile" data with marathoners that showed that elite runners scored higher on the *vigor* and lower on the *fatigue* subscales of the Profile of Mood States (POMS) than did subelite runners.

Second, these data also suggest that sprint and distance freestyle performers apparently have different types of somatic A-state problems. Sprinters tended to get too physiologically aroused, whereas distance freestylers suffered more from problems of underarousal. Although somatic A-state levels for sprinters did not significantly differ from those of distance swimmers, trends were for distance swimmers to have higher somatic A-state levels than had sprinters.

In interpreting these results, sprint data are consistent with the hypothesis that excessive somatic A-state diverts attention away from the task at hand and promotes worry, negative rumination, and fear of failure, all of which limit performance (e.g., Wine, 1980). Two explanations, one physical and the other psychological, seem to describe why distance swimmers have trouble getting sufficiently aroused. First, swimmers may have "tapered" poorly, either getting too little rest to maximize energy reserves or resting so long that the so-called training effect began to diminish (Costill, 1985). Second, distance swimmers may have done a poor job of psyching up for the race, thus failing to mobilize available energy resources effectively. Weinberg, Gould, and Jackson (1979, 1980, 1981) have documented that mental psych-up strategies have a significant impact on performance and that such strategies may be particularly important in endurance events.

Although these data do not permit any cause-and-effect inferences, the pattern of results suggests that distance performers may benefit from sport psychology techniques designed to help them psych up for their events, whereas sprinters and breaststrokers may benefit most from techniques to help them relax and lower their somatic A-state levels.

In conclusion, although Study 3 failed to confirm theoretical predictions about the relationship between CSAI-2 components and performance, data from Study 4 using a more sensitive intraindividual performance measure demonstrated expected relationships, thus supporting the construct validity of the CSAI-2.

SUMMARY

Evidence supporting the construct validity of the CSAI-2 as a measure of sport-specific A-state, somatic A-state, and state self-confidence is provided through a systematic progression of research studies. Study 1 supported hypothesized relationships between the CSAI-2 components and various individual difference and situational factors. Study 2 provided support for the hypothesized independence of the CSAI-2 components by demonstrating differential changes in the components based on the proximity of competition. Study 3 examined the relationship between the CSAI-2 components and performance yet found equivocal results.

To study the relationship between CSAI-2 components and sport performance more precisely, Study 4 extended Study 3 by utilizing intraindividual performance measures. The results of Study 4 provided evidence that the relationship between anxiety and performance is influenced by the multidimensionality of A-state as well as by task complexity and duration.

Chapter 11

Using the CSAI-2 and CSAI-2 Norms

The CSAI-2 is an A-state inventory designed to measure existing states of cognitive A-state, somatic A-state, and state self-confidence in competitive situations. The CSAI-2 was constructed primarily as a research tool, and the usefulness of the inventory as a diagnostic instrument for clinical purposes has not been established.

ADMINISTRATION OF THE CSAI-2

The CSAI-2 normally takes less than 5 minutes to complete and should be administered no more than 1 hour and ideally as close as possible before competition. When administering the CSAI-2 it is recommended that the title on the form given to subjects be the Illinois Self-Evaluation Questionnaire (or the state of your choosing). This technique may help reduce response bias to the inventory. In addition, the anti–social desirability instructions found on page 176 should be committed to memory and orally communicated with conviction to the respondents. Social desirability can further be reduced by not having subjects put their names on their questionnaires. If possible, subjects can respond anonymously, or, if identification is needed to match questionnaires from the same subject, numbers or code names can be employed.

Before allowing subjects to begin completing the CSAI-2, make sure that the instructions are completely understood and particularly that responses should be based on how the respondent feels at the moment. The examiner should answer questions by reiterating or clarifying the instructions. Do not offer any information regarding the purpose of the inventory. Be sure to instruct the respondent to answer all items.

THE INVENTORY

Form E of the CSAI-2 is presented on page 177. Researchers are invited to use the scale without written permission from the authors or publisher, but the scale cannot be represented in another publication without permission of the publisher.

Anti–Social Desirability Instructions

The effects of highly competitive sports can be powerful and very different among athletes. The inventory you are about to complete measures how you feel about this competition at the moment you are responding. Please complete the inventory as honestly as you can. Sometimes athletes feel they should not admit to any nervousness, anxiety, or worry they experience before competition because this is undesirable. Actually, these feelings are quite common, and to help us understand them we want you to share your feelings with us candidly. If you are worried about the competition or have butterflies or other feelings that you know are signs of anxiety, please indicate these feelings accurately on the inventory. Equally, if you feel calm and relaxed, indicate those feelings as accurately as you can. Your answers will not be shared with anyone. We will be looking only at group responses.

SCORING THE CSAI-2

The CSAI-2 is scored by computing a separate total for each of the three subscales, with scores ranging from a low of 9 to a high of 36. The higher the score, the greater the cognitive or somatic A-state or the greater the state self-confidence. No total score for the inventory is computed.

The cognitive A-state subscale is scored by totaling the responses for the following 9 items: 1, 4, 7, 10, 13, 16, 19, 22, and 25. The somatic A-state subscale is scored by adding the responses to the following 9 items: 2, 5, 8, 11, 14R, 17, 20, 23, and 26. Scoring for item 14 must be reversed in calculating the score for the somatic A-state subscale as indicated below:

$$1 = 4$$
$$2 = 3$$
$$3 = 2$$
$$4 = 1$$

The Competitive State Anxiety Inventory-2 (CSAI-2) appears on the facing page.

Illinois Self-Evaluation Questionnaire

Name: _____ Sex: M F Date: _____

Directions: A number of statements that athletes have used to describe their feelings before competition are given below. Read each statement and then circle the appropriate number to the right of the statement to indicate *how you feel right now*—at this moment. There are no right or wrong answers. Do *not* spend too much time on any one statement, but choose the answer which describes your feelings *right now*.

	Not At All	Somewhat	Moderately So	Very Much So
1. I am concerned about this competition	1	2	3	4
2. I feel nervous	1	2	3	4
3. I feel at ease	1	2	3	4
4. I have self-doubts	1	2	3	4
5. I feel jittery	1	2	3	4
6. I feel comfortable	1	2	3	4
7. I am concerned that I may not do as well in this competition as I could	1	2	3	4
8. My body feels tense	1	2	3	4
9. I feel self-confident	1	2	3	4
10. I am concerned about losing	1	2	3	4
11. I feel tense in my stomach	1	2	3	4
12. I feel secure	1	2	3	4
13. I am concerned about choking under pressure	1	2	3	4
14. My body feels relaxed	1	2	3	4
15. I'm confident I can meet the challenge	1	2	3	4
16. I'm concerned about performing poorly	1	2	3	4
17. My heart is racing	1	2	3	4
18. I'm confident about performing well	1	2	3	4
19. I'm concerned about reaching my goal	1	2	3	4
20. I feel my stomach sinking	1	2	3	4
21. I feel mentally relaxed	1	2	3	4
22. I'm concerned that others will be disappointed with my performance	1	2	3	4
23. My hands are clammy	1	2	3	4
24. I'm confident because I mentally picture myself reaching my goal	1	2	3	4
25. I'm concerned I won't be able to concentrate	1	2	3	4
26. My body feels tight	1	2	3	4
27. I'm confident of coming through under pressure	1	2	3	4

The state self-confidence subscale is scored by adding the following items: 3, 6, 9, 12, 15, 18, 21, 24, and 27.

Inventories that are missing no more than one response per subscale can still be scored, but any inventory in which two or more items from any one subscale are omitted should be invalidated. To obtain subscale scores when an item has been omitted, compute the mean item score for the eight answered items, multiply this value by 9, and then round the product to the nearest whole number.

CSAI-2 NORMS

Normative information for each of the three subscales of the CSAI-2 is provided for male and female high school, college, and elite athletes (see Table 11.1 and Tables 11.4-11.9) as well as for the sports of basketball, cycling, golf, swimming, track and field, and wrestling (see Tables 11.2, 11.3, and 11.10-11.15). Over half the data used in computation of these norms were obtained from colleagues who have conducted independent competitive anxiety research with such sports as golf (Krane & Williams, 1987), gymnastics (Krane & Williams, 1987), shooting (Gould et al., 1987; Weiss, 1988), track and field (Krane & Williams, 1986), volleyball (Gould et al., 1984), and wrestling (Gould & Weinberg, 1985; Gould et al., 1984) as well as data from the sport psychology data bank of the U.S. Olympic Training Center.

Percentile ranks and standard scores are provided for each norm group. The percentile rank of an individual's score indicates the percentage of individuals in the norm group who scored lower on each CSAI-2 subscale. Thus, a percentile rank of 63 indicates that 63% of the respondents in the norm group had lower scores on that CSAI-2 subscale.

Standard scores are also provided because percentile ranks represent measurement on an ordinal scale only, whereas standard scores are expressed on an interval scale. A standard score is simply the deviation of a raw score from the mean expressed in standard deviation units:

$$z = \frac{x - M}{s}$$

where z = a standard score, x = a specified raw score, M = the mean, and s = the standard deviation of the raw-score distribution. The z scores were transformed by setting the mean to 50 and the standard deviation to 10. Thus, the transformed z is

$$z = 50 + 10z$$

This transformation is linear in contrast to an area transformation, which is used to obtain a normalized standard score. The normalized standard score permits reference to a standard distribution (the normal curve) and direct conversion to percentiles. If the norm group closely approximates a normal distribution, then both the unnormalized and the normalized standard scores will be the same. Both standard scores were computed, and for all norm groups the two standard scores were identical for the first two places.

The interpretation of the standard scores is based on standard deviation units. A standard score of 60 indicates a score of 1 standard deviation above the mean of the distribution. A score of 35 represents a score 1-1/2 standard deviations below the mean.

A summary of the test statistics for male and female high school, college, and elite athletes is presented in Table 11.1, and summary test statistics for each of the six sports and the composition of each sport group by competitive level in Tables 11.2 and 11.3. It is interesting to note the trend for cognitive A-state to decrease from high school to college but then increase for elite athletes. State self-confidence demonstrated the opposite pattern, and both trends seem slightly stronger for females than for males. Finally, females on the average were also higher in cognitive A-state and lower in state self-confidence than were males for both groups.

Table 11.1 Summary of Test Statistics for Norm Samples by Competitive Level and Gender

Sample	N	CSAI-cog		CSAI-som		CSAI-sc	
		M	SD	M	SD	M	SD
High school							
Male	284	18.48	5.35	17.70	5.53	24.73	5.52
Female	309	21.61	6.47	18.92	5.97	22.50	5.51
College							
Male	158	17.68	4.84	17.68	4.86	25.37	5.15
Female	220	18.40	5.99	16.85	4.94	24.67	5.90
Elite							
Male	161	19.29	4.80	16.29	4.65	26.21	4.81
Female	102	20.11	5.42	17.98	5.20	24.56	5.33

Table 11.2 Summary of Test Statistics for Norm Samples by Sport

Sport	N	CSAI-cog		CSAI-som		CSAI-sc	
		M	SD	M	SD	M	SD
Basketball	181	20.92	6.11	18.57	6.02	24.64	5.42
Cycling	102	20.51	5.29	18.89	5.01	25.28	4.99

(cont.)

Table 11.2 (Continued)

Sport	N	CSAI-cog		CSAI-som		CSAI-sc	
		M	SD	M	SD	M	SD
Golf	113	16.97	5.45	15.31	3.91	26.27	5.50
Swimming	109	16.50	4.99	16.85	4.11	24.68	5.68
Track and field	259	20.34	5.76	18.73	5.68	22.88	5.79
Wrestling	140	17.74	5.25	19.90	5.49	23.51	5.80

Table 11.3 Summary of Competitive Levels Comprising Sport Samples

Sport	N	High school	College	Elite
Basketball	181	111	70	. . .
Cycling	102	. . .	. . .	102
Golf	113	49	64	. . .
Swimming	109	. . .	38	71
Track and field	235	124	104	31
Wrestling	140	103	37	. . .

Table 11.4 CSAI-2 Norms for Male High School Athletes

Raw score	Standard score (percentile)		
	CSAI-cog	CSAI-som	CSAI-sc
36	828 (99)	831 (99)	704 (99)
35	809 (99)	813 (99)	686 (96)
34	790 (99)	795 (99)	668 (94)
33	771 (99)	777 (98)	650 (91)
32	753 (99)	758 (98)	632 (87)
31	734 (98)	740 (97)	614 (83)
30	715 (98)	722 (96)	596 (79)
29	697 (96)	704 (95)	577 (76)
28	678 (95)	686 (94)	559 (71)
27	659 (93)	668 (93)	541 (66)
26	641 (89)	650 (92)	523 (60)
25	622 (86)	632 (89)	505 (52)
24	603 (83)	614 (85)	487 (46)

Raw score	Standard score (percentile)		
	CSAI-cog	CSAI-som	CSAI-sc
23	585 (80)	596 (82)	469 (39)
22	566 (75)	578 (79)	450 (34)
21	547 (68)	560 (75)	432 (28)
20	529 (61)	542 (71)	414 (22)
19	510 (55)	524 (63)	396 (17)
18	491 (48)	505 (55)	378 (12)
17	472 (40)	487 (49)	360 (7)
16	454 (34)	469 (42)	342 (3)
15	435 (28)	451 (35)	324 (2)
14	416 (23)	433 (27)	305 (1)
13	398 (18)	415 (21)	287 (0)
12	379 (12)	397 (16)	269 (0)
11	360 (7)	379 (10)	251 (0)
10	342 (4)	361 (5)	233 (0)
9	323 (1)	343 (1)	215 (0)

Table 11.5   CSAI-2 Norms for Female High School Athletes

Raw score	Standard score (percentile)		
	CSAI-cog	CSAI-som	CSAI-sc
36	723 (99)	786 (99)	744 (99)
35	707 (98)	770 (99)	726 (98)
34	692 (96)	753 (99)	708 (97)
33	676 (94)	736 (99)	690 (96)
32	661 (92)	719 (98)	672 (94)
31	645 (89)	703 (98)	654 (92)
30	630 (87)	686 (97)	636 (89)
29	614 (84)	669 (94)	618 (86)
28	599 (80)	652 (91)	600 (83)
27	583 (76)	636 (89)	582 (78)
26	568 (73)	619 (86)	563 (73)
25	552 (70)	602 (83)	545 (67)
24	537 (65)	585 (79)	527 (61)
23	521 (60)	568 (73)	509 (55)
22	506 (55)	552 (67)	491 (48)
21	491 (49)	535 (61)	473 (41)
20	475 (44)	518 (57)	455 (35)
19	460 (39)	501 (51)	437 (28)

(cont.)

Table 11.5   (Continued)

Raw score	Standard score (percentile)		
	CSAI-cog	CSAI-som	CSAI-sc
18	444 (33)	485 (46)	418 (21)
17	429 (26)	468 (41)	400 (14)
16	413 (20)	451 (35)	382 (11)
15	398 (16)	434 (30)	364 (8)
14	382 (11)	418 (24)	346 (5)
13	367 (8)	401 (18)	328 (3)
12	351 (5)	384 (14)	310 (2)
11	336 (3)	367 (10)	292 (1)
10	320 (1)	351 (6)	274 (0)
9	305 (0)	334 (1)	256 (0)

Table 11.6   CSAI-2 Norms for Male College Athletes

Raw score	Standard score (percentile)		
	CSAI-cog	CSAI-som	CSAI-sc
36	879 (99)	879 (99)	706 (98)
35	858 (99)	858 (99)	687 (96)
34	837 (99)	837 (99)	667 (94)
33	817 (99)	817 (99)	648 (90)
32	796 (99)	796 (99)	629 (87)
31	775 (99)	774 (98)	609 (83)
30	755 (98)	754 (97)	590 (80)
29	734 (97)	733 (96)	570 (75)
28	713 (96)	713 (96)	551 (68)
27	693 (95)	692 (95)	532 (62)
26	672 (93)	671 (94)	512 (55)
25	651 (91)	651 (92)	493 (47)
24	631 (91)	630 (90)	473 (39)
23	610 (88)	610 (88)	454 (33)
22	589 (83)	589 (84)	435 (27)
21	569 (77)	568 (79)	415 (22)
20	548 (69)	548 (71)	396 (17)
19	527 (61)	527 (61)	376 (12)
18	507 (54)	507 (52)	357 (8)
17	486 (46)	486 (45)	338 (4)
16	465 (37)	465 (37)	318 (1)
15	445 (29)	445 (31)	299 (1)

	Standard score (percentile)		
Raw score	CSAI-cog	CSAI-som	CSAI-sc
14	424 (23)	424 (26)	279 (1)
13	403 (17)	404 (19)	260 (1)
12	383 (12)	383 (12)	240 (1)
11	362 (10)	363 (7)	221 (0)
10	341 (5)	342 (3)	202 (0)
9	321 (1)	321 (0)	182 (0)

Table 11.7   CSAI-2 Norms for Female College Athletes

	Standard score (percentile)		
Raw score	CSAI-cog	CSAI-som	CSAI-sc
36	794 (99)	888 (99)	692 (97)
35	777 (99)	867 (99)	675 (95)
34	761 (98)	847 (99)	658 (93)
33	744 (98)	827 (99)	641 (90)
32	727 (98)	807 (99)	624 (87)
31	710 (97)	786 (99)	607 (82)
30	694 (96)	766 (98)	590 (77)
29	677 (94)	746 (97)	573 (74)
28	660 (91)	726 (95)	556 (70)
27	644 (89)	706 (94)	540 (64)
26	627 (87)	685 (93)	523 (57)
25	610 (84)	665 (92)	506 (51)
24	594 (81)	645 (91)	489 (46)
23	577 (77)	625 (88)	472 (40)
22	560 (73)	604 (84)	455 (35)
21	543 (68)	584 (80)	438 (31)
20	527 (62)	564 (76)	421 (26)
19	510 (57)	544 (72)	404 (21)
18	493 (50)	523 (66)	387 (15)
17	477 (44)	503 (58)	370 (9)
16	460 (39)	483 (49)	353 (6)
15	443 (32)	463 (39)	336 (3)
14	427 (27)	442 (31)	319 (1)
13	410 (22)	422 (25)	302 (1)
12	393 (16)	402 (16)	285 (0)
11	377 (10)	382 (7)	268 (0)
10	360 (6)	361 (3)	251 (0)
9	343 (2)	341 (1)	234 (0)

Table 11.8 CSAI-2 Norms for Male Elite Athletes

| Raw score | Standard score (percentile) | | |
	CSAI-cog	CSAI-som	CSAI-sc
36	848 (99)	925 (99)	704 (98)
35	828 (99)	903 (99)	683 (96)
34	807 (99)	881 (99)	662 (95)
33	786 (98)	860 (99)	641 (91)
32	765 (98)	838 (99)	620 (86)
31	744 (97)	816 (99)	600 (81)
30	723 (97)	795 (99)	579 (76)
29	702 (96)	773 (98)	558 (70)
28	682 (95)	751 (98)	537 (65)
27	661 (93)	730 (97)	516 (56)
26	640 (90)	709 (96)	496 (46)
25	619 (87)	687 (95)	475 (39)
24	598 (82)	666 (93)	454 (33)
23	577 (77)	644 (91)	433 (25)
22	556 (73)	623 (86)	412 (19)
21	536 (66)	601 (80)	392 (13)
20	515 (60)	580 (74)	371 (8)
19	494 (53)	558 (70)	350 (6)
18	473 (44)	537 (67)	329 (5)
17	452 (33)	515 (61)	308 (3)
16	431 (24)	494 (55)	287 (3)
15	410 (18)	472 (47)	267 (2)
14	390 (12)	451 (38)	246 (2)
13	369 (8)	429 (28)	225 (1)
12	348 (5)	408 (17)	204 (0)
11	327 (2)	386 (10)	183 (0)
10	306 (0)	365 (6)	162 (0)
9	285 (0)	343 (2)	141 (0)

Table 11.9 CSAI-2 Norms for Female Elite Athletes

| Raw score | Standard score (percentile) | | |
	CSAI-cog	CSAI-som	CSAI-sc
36	793 (99)	846 (99)	715 (98)
35	775 (99)	827 (99)	696 (97)
34	756 (99)	808 (99)	677 (95)
33	738 (98)	789 (99)	659 (94)
32	719 (95)	769 (99)	640 (93)

	Standard score (percentile)		
Raw score	CSAI-cog	CSAI-som	CSAI-sc
31	701 (93)	750 (98)	621 (90)
30	682 (93)	731 (98)	602 (85)
29	664 (92)	712 (97)	583 (80)
28	645 (91)	693 (97)	565 (72)
27	627 (90)	673 (95)	546 (64)
26	609 (87)	654 (91)	527 (57)
25	590 (83)	635 (87)	508 (50)
24	572 (76)	616 (85)	490 (43)
23	553 (70)	596 (83)	471 (35)
22	535 (65)	577 (79)	452 (31)
21	516 (60)	558 (73)	433 (26)
20	498 (53)	539 (65)	414 (20)
19	480 (44)	520 (58)	396 (16)
18	461 (37)	500 (51)	377 (12)
17	443 (32)	481 (44)	358 (9)
16	424 (25)	462 (39)	339 (6)
15	406 (18)	443 (32)	320 (5)
14	387 (14)	424 (24)	302 (3)
13	369 (8)	404 (17)	283 (2)
12	351 (4)	385 (12)	265 (1)
11	332 (1)	366 (9)	246 (0)
10	314 (0)	347 (6)	227 (0)
9	295 (0)	327 (2)	209 (0)

Table 11.10   CSAI-2 Norms for Basketball

	Standard score (percentile)		
Raw score	CSAI-cog	CSAI-som	CSAI-sc
36	747 (99)	790 (99)	709 (99)
35	730 (99)	773 (98)	691 (97)
34	714 (98)	756 (98)	673 (94)
33	698 (98)	740 (98)	654 (91)
32	681 (95)	723 (98)	636 (89)
31	665 (93)	706 (97)	617 (85)
30	649 (91)	690 (96)	599 (80)
29	632 (89)	673 (94)	580 (75)
28	616 (85)	657 (92)	562 (70)

(cont.)

Table 11.10   (Continued)

Raw score	Standard score (percentile)		
	CSAI-cog	CSAI-som	CSAI-sc
27	600 (81)	640 (91)	543 (66)
26	583 (76)	623 (88)	525 (59)
25	567 (72)	607 (84)	507 (53)
24	550 (68)	590 (81)	488 (48)
23	534 (64)	574 (76)	470 (42)
22	518 (59)	557 (70)	451 (34)
21	501 (51)	540 (65)	433 (26)
20	485 (44)	524 (60)	414 (21)
19	469 (39)	507 (53)	396 (16)
18	452 (35)	490 (47)	378 (11)
17	436 (31)	474 (42)	359 (7)
16	420 (26)	457 (36)	341 (4)
15	403 (20)	441 (29)	322 (2)
14	387 (15)	424 (24)	304 (2)
13	370 (11)	407 (21)	285 (1)
12	354 (7)	391 (17)	267 (1)
11	338 (2)	374 (12)	249 (0)
10	321 (0)	358 (8)	230 (0)
9	305 (0)	341 (3)	211 (0)

Table 11.11   CSAI-2 Norms for Cycling

Raw score	Standard score (percentile)		
	CSAI-cog	CSAI-som	CSAI-sc
36	793 (99)	842 (99)	715 (98)
35	774 (99)	822 (99)	695 (97)
34	755 (99)	802 (99)	675 (96)
33	736 (97)	782 (99)	655 (94)
32	717 (95)	762 (99)	634 (91)
31	698 (94)	742 (98)	614 (87)
30	679 (93)	722 (98)	594 (81)
29	661 (92)	702 (97)	574 (73)
28	642 (91)	682 (96)	554 (67)
27	623 (89)	662 (93)	534 (62)
26	604 (85)	642 (88)	514 (53)
25	585 (81)	622 (85)	494 (46)
24	566 (73)	602 (83)	474 (41)

Raw score	Standard score (percentile)		
	CSAI-cog	CSAI-som	CSAI-sc
23	547 (66)	582 (79)	454 (34)
22	528 (61)	562 (72)	434 (26)
21	509 (56)	542 (65)	414 (19)
20	490 (51)	522 (58)	394 (14)
19	471 (46)	502 (52)	374 (11)
18	453 (40)	482 (46)	354 (8)
17	434 (31)	462 (39)	334 (4)
16	415 (20)	442 (34)	314 (2)
15	396 (12)	422 (27)	294 (1)
14	377 (9)	402 (19)	274 (1)
13	358 (5)	382 (12)	254 (1)
12	339 (2)	362 (6)	234 (0)
11	320 (0)	342 (2)	214 (0)
10	301 (0)	322 (0)	194 (0)
9	282 (0)	302 (0)	174 (0)

Table 11.12   CSAI-2 Norms for Golf

Raw score	Standard score (percentile)		
	CSAI-cog	CSAI-som	CSAI-sc
36	849 (99)	1029 (99)	677 (95)
35	831 (99)	1003 (99)	659 (91)
34	812 (99)	978 (99)	641 (89)
33	794 (99)	952 (99)	622 (85)
32	776 (99)	927 (99)	604 (80)
31	757 (99)	901 (99)	586 (75)
30	739 (98)	876 (99)	568 (73)
29	721 (96)	850 (99)	550 (71)
28	702 (93)	825 (99)	531 (65)
27	684 (92)	799 (99)	513 (58)
26	666 (91)	774 (98)	495 (49)
25	647 (89)	748 (97)	477 (41)
24	629 (87)	723 (96)	459 (34)
23	611 (85)	697 (95)	440 (28)
22	592 (82)	671 (94)	422 (22)
21	574 (79)	646 (92)	404 (18)
20	556 (72)	620 (89)	386 (14)

(cont.)

Table 11.12   (Continued)

Raw score	Standard score (percentile)		
	CSAI-cog	CSAI-som	CSAI-sc
19	537 (66)	594 (84)	368 (11)
18	519 (60)	569 (76)	349 (7)
17	500 (54)	543 (68)	331 (3)
16	482 (47)	518 (60)	313 (2)
15	464 (40)	492 (50)	295 (1)
14	445 (34)	466 (41)	277 (0)
13	427 (29)	441 (32)	259 (0)
12	409 (21)	415 (21)	241 (0)
11	390 (14)	390 (11)	222 (0)
10	372 (7)	364 (6)	204 (0)
9	354 (2)	338 (2)	186 (0)

Table 11.13   CSAI-2 Norms for Swimming

Raw score	Standard score (percentile)		
	CSAI-cog	CSAI-som	CSAI-sc
36	891 (99)	966 (99)	700 (98)
35	871 (99)	942 (99)	682 (96)
34	851 (99)	917 (99)	664 (94)
33	831 (99)	893 (99)	647 (91)
32	811 (99)	869 (99)	629 (89)
31	791 (98)	844 (99)	612 (84)
30	771 (98)	820 (99)	594 (78)
29	751 (98)	796 (99)	576 (74)
28	731 (97)	771 (99)	559 (69)
27	711 (97)	747 (98)	541 (64)
26	691 (96)	722 (97)	523 (58)
25	670 (94)	698 (96)	506 (52)
24	650 (93)	674 (95)	488 (46)
23	630 (91)	650 (93)	470 (39)
22	610 (86)	625 (89)	453 (34)
21	590 (81)	601 (83)	435 (29)
20	570 (75)	577 (75)	417 (22)
19	550 (67)	552 (69)	400 (17)
18	530 (59)	528 (62)	382 (13)
17	510 (52)	504 (53)	364 (10)
16	490 (48)	479 (44)	347 (7)
15	470 (44)	455 (35)	329 (4)

Raw score	Standard score (percentile)		
	CSAI-cog	CSAI-som	CSAI-sc
14	450 (36)	431 (27)	312 (3)
13	430 (28)	406 (20)	294 (1)
12	410 (22)	382 (11)	277 (0)
11	390 (15)	358 (6)	259 (0)
10	370 (10)	333 (3)	242 (0)
9	350 (3)	309 (1)	224 (0)

Table 11.14   CSAI-2 Norms for Track and Field

Raw score	Standard score (percentile)		
	CSAI-cog	CSAI-som	CSAI-sc
36	772 (99)	804 (99)	726 (99)
35	755 (99)	786 (99)	709 (97)
34	737 (98)	769 (99)	692 (96)
33	720 (97)	751 (99)	675 (94)
32	703 (96)	734 (98)	657 (91)
31	685 (94)	716 (97)	640 (89)
30	668 (92)	698 (96)	623 (87)
29	651 (90)	681 (95)	606 (84)
28	633 (89)	663 (93)	588 (80)
27	616 (86)	646 (91)	571 (75)
26	598 (83)	628 (89)	554 (70)
25	581 (79)	610 (85)	537 (64)
24	564 (74)	593 (80)	519 (57)
23	546 (69)	575 (75)	502 (51)
22	529 (63)	558 (69)	485 (44)
21	512 (57)	540 (64)	467 (39)
20	494 (50)	522 (59)	450 (34)
19	477 (44)	505 (53)	433 (29)
18	459 (38)	487 (47)	416 (23)
17	442 (30)	470 (41)	398 (16)
16	425 (22)	452 (36)	381 (11)
15	407 (17)	434 (30)	364 (8)
14	390 (14)	417 (23)	347 (5)
13	373 (10)	399 (17)	329 (2)
12	355 (6)	382 (12)	312 (1)
11	338 (4)	364 (8)	295 (0)
10	320 (1)	346 (5)	278 (0)
9	303 (0)	329 (1)	261 (0)

Table 11.15   CSAI-2 Norms for Wrestling

	Standard score (percentile)		
Raw score	CSAI-cog	CSAI-som	CSAI-sc
36	848 (99)	793 (99)	715 (98)
35	829 (99)	775 (99)	698 (96)
34	810 (99)	757 (98)	681 (94)
33	791 (99)	738 (97)	664 (92)
32	772 (99)	720 (96)	646 (89)
31	753 (98)	702 (95)	629 (85)
30	734 (98)	684 (94)	612 (82)
29	714 (97)	666 (92)	595 (79)
28	695 (95)	647 (90)	577 (75)
27	676 (94)	629 (87)	560 (71)
26	657 (92)	611 (85)	543 (67)
25	638 (90)	593 (82)	526 (62)
24	619 (89)	575 (77)	508 (57)
23	600 (86)	556 (74)	491 (52)
22	581 (79)	538 (70)	474 (46)
21	562 (70)	520 (64)	457 (41)
20	543 (65)	502 (56)	439 (32)
19	524 (59)	484 (46)	422 (25)
18	505 (51)	465 (36)	405 (19)
17	486 (44)	447 (29)	388 (12)
16	467 (37)	429 (23)	370 (6)
15	448 (32)	411 (18)	353 (3)
14	429 (26)	393 (14)	336 (1)
13	410 (21)	374 (10)	319 (1)
12	391 (17)	356 (7)	302 (1)
11	372 (12)	338 (3)	284 (1)
10	352 (7)	320 (2)	267 (0)
9	333 (3)	302 (1)	250 (0)

Competitive State Anxiety Inventory–2: Literature Review, Current Status, and Future Directions

Although the CSAI-2 scale was not formally published until now (as explained in the preface), 16 published studies have used the CSAI-2 and are reviewed in Part IV. This review focuses on the interrelationship between subscales, temporal changes in cognitive and somatic A-state, and the relationship between performance and competitive A-state. This part closes with conclusions, problems, and suggestions for future research on competitive A-state.

Chapter 12

Research Using the CSAI-2: Review and Analysis

In Part III, the original psychometric process followed in the development of the CSAI-2 was presented. This process is significant for two reasons. First, the operationalizaton of competitive state anxiety (A-state) was based on current theory and research that supports anxiety as a multidimensional construct containing a cognitive and a somatic component. Second, the instrument was subjected to a systematic, rigorous series of psychometric analyses. Surprisingly, these analyses produced not only separate cognitive and somatic A-state components but also a state self-confidence component. Thus, evidence was produced to support the reliability, content validity, concurrent validity, and construct validity of the CSAI-2 as a measure of sport-specific cognitive A-state, somatic A-state, and state self-confidence.

The development of the CSAI-2 represents a significant advance in the measurement of competitive anxiety, and the separation of competitive A-state into cognitive and somatic components may help to clarify some of the equivocal findings that have plagued anxiety research. It is hoped that the publication of this book will make the CSAI-2 more accessible and understandable to researchers in the field of sport psychology. To date, several research studies using the CSAI-2 have been published. A reference table of all published studies using the CSAI-2 is provided in Appendix C. Although other studies using the CSAI-2 have been presented at conferences, this review includes only published work.

Thus, the purpose of this chapter is to review all published articles using the CSAI-2 to examine whether research supports theoretical predictions and provides additional validity for the instrument as a multidimensional competitive A-state measure. The review is divided into five sections. First, the relationships between CSAI-2 components and other intrapersonal factors are discussed. Second, interrelationships between the CSAI-2 components are examined. Third, temporal changes in the CSAI-2 components based on the proximity of competition are examined. Fourth, antecedents of the CSAI-2 components are identified and discussed. Finally, the relationships between CSAI-2 components and motor performance are examined.

RELATIONSHIPS BETWEEN CSAI-2 COMPONENTS AND OTHER INTRAPERSONAL FACTORS

In this section, the relationships between various intrapersonal factors and the CSAI-2 components are examined. Specifically, the personality constructs of competitive A-trait, attentional style, and state self-confidence are examined with regard to their relationships to CSAI-2 components. Also, the relationships between physiological measures of arousal and CSAI-2 components are examined.

Competitive Trait Anxiety

Clearly, cognitive and somatic A-state have been shown to be strongly related to competitive trait anxiety (A-trait) as measured by SCAT. The positive relationships between somatic and cognitive A-state and competitive A-trait were established by Martens et al. (1982) in the original CSAI-2 validation research (see chapter 9). They emphasized that competitive A-trait's stronger relationship with somatic than with cognitive A-state was as predicted due to the somatic nature of SCAT items.

Subsequent research using SCAT as a predictor of CSAI-2 components has substantiated the predicted positive relationships between cognitive and somatic A-state and competitive A-trait (Albrecht & Feltz, 1987; Crocker et al., 1988; Gould et al., 1984; Karteroliotis & Gill, 1987; Maynard & Howe, 1987; see chapter 6). However, the research is equivocal whether competitive A-trait as measured by SCAT is related more strongly to cognitive or to somatic A-state. As discussed in chapter 6, it may be that different situational factors influence the relationships between the A-state components and competitive A-trait.

Although Martens et al. (1982) demonstrated a significant negative relationship between state self-confidence and competitive A-trait (see chapter 9), subsequent research is equivocal regarding this relationship (see chapter 6). However, it seems obvious that cognitive and somatic A-state are more strongly related to competitive A-trait than to state self-confidence.

Attentional Style

On the basis of Nideffer's (1976) theory of attentional style, Albrecht and Feltz (1987) hypothesized that increases in anxiety are associated with an internal attentional focus and reductions in attentional breadth. To measure attentional style, they developed a baseball and softball attentional-style inventory (B-TAIS) modeled after Nideffer's (1976) Test of Attentional and Interpersonal Style (TAIS). As part of the construct validation of their inventory, Albrecht and Feltz administered a trait version of the CSAI-2 (CTAI-2), SCAT, the TAIS, and the B-TAIS to 29 collegiate baseball and softball players. The predicted anxiety-attention relationships were not as clear with the CTAI-2 as with SCAT (this evidence for the construct validity of SCAT is discussed in chapter 6), but some significant findings emerged for the CTAI-2.

Both the TAIS and the B-TAIS subscales assessing the ability to effectively narrow attentional focus were positively correlated to state self-confidence and negatively related to cognitive and somatic A-state. Also confirmed were the predicted positive relationships between the TAIS subscales assessing the ability to broaden attention and state self-confidence effectively. Finally, cognitive A-state was positively related to both internal and external attentional overload and somatic A-state to internal attentional overload as predicted.

Self-Confidence

Vealey (1986) conceptualized sport confidence as the degree of certainty athletes possess about their ability to be successful in sport. She separated sport confidence into trait (SC-trait) and state (SC-state) components and developed and validated two inventories to measure these constructs. As part of the concurrent validity phase of her study, Vealey predicted that SC-trait and SC-state would be negatively related to cognitive and somatic A-state and positively related to state self-confidence as measured by the CSAI-2. Also, she predicted that CSAI-2 components would be more strongly related to the state measure of sport confidence than to the trait measure and that sport confidence would be more strongly related to cognitive than to somatic A-state. All predictions were confirmed. In particular, state self-confidence as measured by the CSAI-2 demonstrated a strong relationship with the other state self-confidence scale ($r = .69$) as well as with the trait self-confidence scale ($r = .48$).

Yan Lan and Gill (1984) investigated the relationship between CSAI-2 components and self-efficacy for 32 subjects performing both an easy and a difficult task. For the easy task, cognitive A-state was negatively related to three of the four self-efficacy questions (r range $= -.32$ to $-.49$), but somatic A-state and state self-confidence (surprisingly) were not significantly related to self-efficacy in this condition. For the difficult task, state self-confidence was positively related to self-efficacy questions (r range $= .53$ to $.66$), but the other two components were not related to self-efficacy. After a cognitive feedback manipulation designed to increase the self-efficacy of subjects was introduced, the CSAI-2 relationships between the components and self-efficacy showed a similar pattern yet stronger relationships. Although these results are equivocal, they demonstrate an initial link between self-efficacy and CSAI-2 components and suggest that situational factors and individual perceptions of the situation influence these relationships.

Physiological Arousal

Anxiety research has lacked consistent agreement between self-report measures and physiological measures. Supporting previous research, Yan Lan and Gill (1984) found no relationship between heart rate and CSAI-2 components. It is interesting that actual and perceived physiological arousal appear to be unrelated. Certainly, measurement error may confound this relationship because subjects may not admit to obvious physiological symptoms and the use of one physiological indicator may not be a valid measure of arousal or anxiety for all subjects. Landers and Boutcher (1986) advocated using multiple physiological measures as an index of heightened arousal. However, Karteroliotis and Gill (1987) found no significant relationships between somatic A-state and heart rate and two blood pressure measures using both absolute and change scores. Furthermore, in contrast to the self-report measures, which were significantly correlated, the physiological measures did not show consistent interrelationships. Clearly, an important area of future inquiry is the relationship between physiological manifestations of anxiety, perceived anxiety, and sport behavior.

INTERRELATIONSHIPS BETWEEN CSAI-2 COMPONENTS

The value in measuring cognitive and somatic A-state separately is based on the conceptual arguments and empirical evidence that these two anxiety components are elicited by different antecedents and that they influence behavior differently. Although cognitive and somatic A-state are theorized to be conceptually independent, researchers acknowledge that these components are likely to be interrelated in many stressful situations (Borkovec, 1976; Morris, Davis, & Hutchings, 1981). In this section, studies examining the correlations between CSAI-2 subscales are examined.

Meta-Analysis of Precompetitive CSAI-2 Interrelationships

In the original CSAI-2 validation studies (see chapter 9), Martens et al. (1982) found mean correlations of .55 for cognitive and somatic A-state, −.61 for cognitive A-state and self-confidence, and −.57 for somatic A-state and self-confidence over eight samples in precompetitive situations (see Table 9.5). Five subsequent studies have examined the interrelationships between CSAI-2 components (Barnes, Sime, Dienstbier, & Plake, 1986; Gould et al., 1984; Maynard

& Howe, 1987; McAuley, 1985; Taylor, 1987).[2] The correlations between the CSAI-2 subscales for these studies are depicted in Tables 12.1 through 12.3. In the Gould et al. and Maynard and Howe studies, the CSAI-2 was adminstered before two different competitive situations, so two correlations are reported for each of these studies.

Table 12.1 Correlations Between Cognitive and Somatic A-State

Study	r	N
Barnes, Sime, Dienstbier, & Plake (1986)	.21	14
Gould, Petlichkoff, & Weinberg (1984)	.50	37
Gould, Petlichkoff, & Weinberg (1984)	.61	37
Maynard & Howe (1987)	.67	22
Maynard & Howe (1987)	.73	22
McAuley (1985)	.17	7
Taylor (1987)	.44	26

Table 12.2 Correlations Between Somatic A-State and State Self-Confidence

Study	r	N
Barnes, Sime, Dienstbier, & Plake (1986)	−.43	14
Gould, Petlichkoff, & Weinberg (1984)	−.29	37
Gould, Petlichkoff, & Weinberg (1984)	−.50	37
Maynard & Howe (1987)	−.49	22
Maynard & Howe (1987)	−.51	22
McAuley (1985)	−.18	7
Taylor (1987)	−.35	26

---

[2]Crocker et al. (1988) reported interrelationships between CSAI-2 components, but these correlations were not included in the meta-analysis because they were published after the book had gone to press. These correlations were as follows: Pretreatment correlations were .72 for CSAI-cog and CSAI-som, −.82 for CSAI-cog and CSAI-sc, and −.61 for CSAI-som and CSAI-sc. Posttreatment correlations were .48 for CSAI-cog and CSAI-som, −.72 for CSAI-cog and CSAI-sc, and −.33 for CSAI-som and CSAI-sc.

Table 12.3   Correlations Between Cognitive A-State and State Self-Confidence

Study	r	N
Barnes, Sime, Dienstbier, & Plake (1986)	−.54	14
Gould, Petlichkoff, & Weinberg (1984)	−.48	37
Gould, Petlichkoff, & Weinberg (1984)	−.55	37
Maynard & Howe (1987)	−.38	22
Maynard & Howe (1987)	−.45	22
McAuley (1985)	−.31	7
Taylor (1987)	−.39	26

To examine with greater statistical precision the intercorrelations between sub-scales, a meta-analysis was conducted using procedures for cumulating correlations across studies described by Hunter et al., (1982). Included in the analyses were the eight studies from the original CSAI-2 validation research (see Table 9.5) and the five studies represented in Tables 12.1 through 12.3. Thus, 15 correlations were used in each of the analyses.

For the relationship between cognitive and somatic A-state, the mean correlation corrected for sample size was .52 with sampling error accounting for 76% of the total variance in the correlations. Because reliability information was not reported in any of the studies, measurement error was computed from the distribution of reliability coefficients reported in the original CSAI-2 validation research (see Table 9.2). After eliminating variance due to both sampling and estimated measurement errors, the mean true score correlation between cognitive and somatic A-state was .63 with a standard deviation of .07. Thus, the 95% confidence interval for this relationship was .49 to .77.

For the relationship between cognitive A-state and state self-confidence, the mean correlation corrected for sample size was −.54 with sampling error accounting for 64% of the total variance in correlations. After computing the distribution of true score correlations by eliminating measurement error, the mean true score correlation was −.64 with a standard deviation of .10. Thus, the 95% confidence interval for the correlation between cognitive A-state and state self-confidence was −.44 to −.84.

For the relationship between somatic A-state and state self-confidence, the mean correlation corrected for sample size was −.51 with over 75% of the variance accounted for by sampling error. After accounting for estimated measurement error, the mean true score correlation was −.60 with a standard deviation of .03. Thus, the 95% confidence interval for the correlation between somatic A-state and state self-confidence was −.54 to −.66.

The meta-analytic procedures control for differences in sample sizes and estimated measurement error to provide more precise information about the interrelationships of the CSAI-2 components. These analyses indicate moderately high interrelationships between the CSAI-2 components in precompetitive situations. As Morris, Davis, and Hutchings (1981) suggested, it is likely that the threatening precompetitive conditions aroused all three state manifestations; or, as Borkovec (1976) argued, the arousal of one component in the precompetitive situation may serve as a stimulus for the conditioned response of the other components.

CSAI-2 Interrelationships Based on the Proximity of Competition

Despite their theoretical independence, the CSAI-2 subscales were moderately correlated in precompetitive situations. Additional research has examined whether these interrelationships change based on the proximity of competition. Testing 37 collegiate wrestlers the night before competition, Gould et al. (1984) found interrelationships between cognitive and somatic A-state, $r = .44$; cognitive A-state and state self-confidence, $r = -.40$; and somatic A-state and state self-confidence, $r = -.40$. Gould et al. also administered the CSAI-2 to 63 high school volleyball players 1 week, 48 hours, 24 hours, 2 hours, and 20 minutes before competition. The results shown in Table 12.4 indicate that all correlations were significant in the predicted direction and that all remained moderately high. Karteroliotis and Gill (1987) measured baseline, precompetitive, midcompetitive, and postcompetitive responses on the CSAI-2 for 41 subjects competing on a pegboard task. Significant positive correlations between cognitive and somatic A-state were indicated for baseline (.50), precompetitive (.41), and midcompetitive

Table 12.4   Intercorrelations Between CSAI-2 Components Scores

	Intercorrelations*		
Time of assessment	CSAI-cog and CSAI-som	CSAI-cog and CSAI-sc	CSAI-som and CSAI-sc
1 wk	.41	−.52	−.35
48 h	.58	−.58	−.46
24 h	.46	−.57	−.39
2 h	.47	−.49	−.44
20 min	.50	−.55	−.46
M	.48	−.54	−.42

Note. From "Antecedents of, Temporal Changes in, and Relationships Between CSAI-2 Subcomponents" by D. Gould, L. Petlichkoff, and R.S. Weinberg, 1984, *Journal of Sport Psychology*, **6**, p. 299. Copyright 1984 by Human Kinetics Publishers. Adapted by permission.

*All correlations significant ($p < .05$).

(.59) measures. The postcompetitive measures of cognitive and somatic A-state were not related, and the relationship of the A-state components to state self-confidence was not reported. However, McAuley (1985) administered the CSAI-2 to 7 collegiate golfers immediately following their 18-hole rounds and found significant relationships between postcompetitive cognitive and somatic A-state (.22), cognitive A-state and state self-confidence (−.54), and somatic A-state and state self-confidence (−.39).

Conclusions Regarding CSAI-2 Interrelationships

Overall, the completed research indicates that the interrelationships between CSAI-2 components remain moderately high across all situations. However, correlational evidence does not provide information about the changes in each component that are based on the proximity of competition. To illustrate that the CSAI-2 components are independent and triggered by different antecedents, the pattern of change for the components must be charted over the course of several days before and after competition. Thus, one needs to examine changes in CSAI-2 components that are based on the proximity of competition.

TEMPORAL CHANGES IN CSAI-2 COMPONENTS

In the original CSAI-2 validation research, Martens et al. (1982; see also Part III) provided evidence for the construct validity of the CSAI-2 as a multidimensional anxiety measure by demonstrating different patterns of responses over time for cognitive A-state, somatic A-state, and state self-confidence. In two separate studies, Martens et al. demonstrated that cognitive A-state and state self-confidence remained relatively unchanged for days before competition and that somatic A-state rapidly increased as time to compete neared (see chapter 10).

The pattern of change in CSAI-2 components found by Martens et al. in the original validation research was substantiated by Gould et al. (1984). As discussed previously, Gould et al. administered the CSAI-2 to 63 high school volleyball players 1 week, 48 hours, 24 hours, 2 hours, and 20 minutes before competition. As predicted, only somatic A-state significantly increased as the time of competition approached, and cognitive A-state and state self-confidence remained stable over time (see Figure 12.1). Also, Gould et al. examined whether temporal changes in CSAI-2 components would differ according to the experience of the athletes. On the basis of the work of Fenz (1975) with experienced and novice parachutists, Gould et al. (1984) hypothesized that inexperienced athletes would demonstrate a linear increase in somatic A-state before competition and that experienced athletes would demonstrate an inverted-U pattern of somatic A-state responsiveness. Although no support was found for the hypothesis, the influence of individual differences and situational factors on the temporal changes in CSAI-2 components seems to be a provocative area for future research.

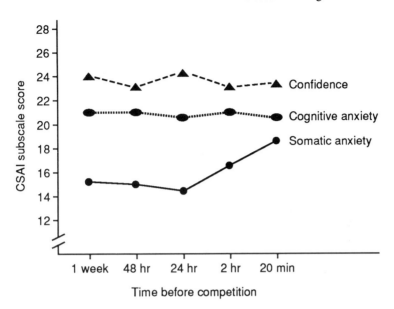

Figure 12.1. Temporal changes in CSAI-2 scores. *Note.* From "Anetecedents of, Temporal Changes in, and Relationships Between CSAI-2 Subcomponents" by D. Gould, L. Petlichkoff, and R.S. Weinberg, 1984, *Journal of Sport Psychology*, **6**, p. 299. Copyright 1984 by Human Kinetics Publishers. Adapted by permission.

A study conducted by Krane and Williams (1987) provides additional support for the mediating effect of intrapersonal and situational factors on the temporal patterns of CSAI-2 component responses. In this study, the CSAI-2 responses of high school gymnasts and collegiate golfers were measured 24 hours, 2 hours, and 10 minutes before a competitive event. Temporal changes in CSAI-2 components were different for the two samples. Cognitive A-state decreased for the golfers and increased for the gymnasts as time to compete neared. For somatic A-state, no differences emerged between samples on the 24-hour measure, but the gymnasts then increased as competition approached, whereas the golfers remained constant. For state self-confidence, the golfers increased and the gymnasts decreased as competition neared. These findings supported the predictions of Krane and Williams that subjectively scored sport athletes would be higher in cognitive and somatic A-state and lower in state self-confidence than would objectively scored sport athletes. However, an alternative interpretation is that high school athletes are higher in anxiety and lower in state self-confidence than are collegiate athletes. Also, a multivariate statistical design was not used to account for the interactions between the intercorrelated CSAI-2 subscale dependent variables.

Karteroliotis and Gill (1987) found similar patterns for cognitive and somatic A-state in baseline, precompetitive, midcompetitive, and postcompetitive CSAI-2 measures for subjects participating in a novel motor task. Both somatic and cognitive A-state increased from precompetition to midcompetition and then decreased from midcompetition to postcompetition. State self-confidence only significantly increased from midcompetition to postcompetition. Although these findings differed from theory and previous research, Karteroliotis and Gill admitted that individuals showed little ego involvement in the outcome of the contrived competitive situation and that tension levels normally observed in sport competition were not exhibited in this setting.

ANTECEDENTS OF CSAI-2 COMPONENTS

In the previous section, the independence of the CSAI-2 components was supported, as differential patterns of responses were noted for cognitive A-state, somatic A-state, and state self-confidence over time based on the proximity of competition. A critical question remains: What factors elicit the different A-state and self-confidence responses? To answer this question and to add further support for the independence of the CSAI-2 components, researchers have examined the potential antecedents of the CSAI-2 components.

Competitive A-Trait, Perceived Ability, Experience, and Previous Match Outcome

Gould et al. (1984) examined the ability of competitive A-trait, perceived ability, experience, and previous match outcome to predict CSAI-2 components for 37 collegiate wrestlers over two matches. Several patterns of findings were demonstrated. No single antecedent was strongly related to all the CSAI-2 components. As discussed in chapter 6, competitive A-trait was a significant predictor of cognitive A-state for both matches but predicted somatic A-state only in Match 1. Experience was the strongest predictor of cognitive A-state for both matches. Perceived ability predicted state self-confidence in Match 1 but was not related to cognitive and somatic A-state. Previous match outcome was not a significant predictor of any of the CSAI-2 components. Overall, the various antecedents predicted the CSAI-2 components in Match 1 better than those in Match 2.

The results indicate that various antecedents influence CSAI-2 components in different ways. Although the findings are not entirely in accord with the original predictions of Martens et al. (1982; see also chapter 9), it seems clear that the situational factors inherent in this study can account for the differential relationships between antecedents and CSAI-2 components. For example, contrary to the prediction of Martens et al., competitive A-trait was found to be a better predictor of cognitive than of somatic A-state in this study. Subsequent research has not supported Martens et al.'s original prediction of a stronger relationship between SCAT and somatic A-state (see chapter 6), indicating that these relationships are not stable but are unique to each situation in which they are measured. Particularly because this study was conducted over two back-to-back competitions on the same day, it seems that the saliency of Match 1 performance would override many of the predicted intrapersonal variables' influence on CSAI-2 components in Match 2. This was substantiated when the antecedent variables predicted Match 1 more strongly than they did Match 2 CSAI-2 components. Also, it may be that cognitive A-state was a factor in Match 2 based on expectancies created after Match 1 but that somatic A-state was less a factor in Match 2 due to fatigue or simply the fact that somatic nervousness dissipated after competition began. This can be likened to a basketball player preparing to perform in the second half of a game. Somatic A-state is not nearly as evident as it was before the first half (pre-game jitters are over), but cognitive A-state remains high because the outcome remains uncertain and evaluative threat is still perceived. Thus, this may explain why SCAT could predict initial cognitive and somatic A-state but only cognitive A-state in Match 2.

Also, it is understandable that perceived ability predicted only state self-confidence, as prior research with SCAT demonstrated no relationship between perceived ability and anxiety (see chapter 6). Interestingly, experience predicted cognitive A-state but not somatic A-state, suggesting that experienced athletes can control the worry and negative self-talk better than can less experienced athletes, but all athletes still manifest physical nervousness before competition. It is also significant that no one antecedent strongly predicted all three CSAI-2 components, again supporting the independence of the components.

Self-Efficacy

Supporting Bandura (1977), Yan Lan and Gill (1984) found self-efficacy to be a significant antecedent of anxiety for subjects competing on an experimental task. Self-efficacy was manipulated by controlling the difficulty of the task. Individuals had lower cognitive and somatic A-state and higher state self-confidence when performing the high-efficacious task than when they were performing the low-efficacious task. These findings support the hypothesis that higher self-efficacy leads to lower anxiety. However, these results do not provide evidence for the independence of CSAI-2 components, as all three were significantly affected by the self-efficacy manipulation.

Performance

McAuley (1985) indicated that performance was a significant predictor of post-competitive cognitive A-state and state self-confidence but not of somatic A-state. This finding supports the independence of CSAI-2 components as somatic A-state seems to be more of a preparatory conditioned response to competition that dissipates once the competition is over. Cognitive A-state and state self-confidence, on the other hand, are influenced by the evaluation of previous performance. Particularly, postcompetitive cognitive A-state was negatively related to performance, and postcompetitive state self-confidence was positively related to performance.

Mental Preparation Strategies

Weinberg, Jackson, and Seabourne (1985) had 24 subjects perform under four different mental preparation conditions on four performance tasks. The CSAI-2 was administered before all the tasks. Although performance differences were indicated as subjects performed better in mental preparation conditions than in control conditions, no significant differences emerged in CSAI-2 components. These results indicate that different antecedent conditions represented by the mental preparation strategies were not powerful enough to elicit changes in CSAI-2 components. This may be explained by the fact that gross motor tasks were used (push-ups, pull-ups, sit-ups, standing broad jump) and that the mental preparation strategies used were designed to psych up, or increase the arousal levels of, the subjects. Oxendine (1970) has indicated that higher levels of arousal are appropriate for gross motor tasks when compared to the debilitating effect of anxiety or high arousal on complex motor tasks. In a later study, Weinberg, Seabourne, and Jackson (1987) again found no differences in any of the CSAI-2 components given before karate and muscular endurance performance tests between an arousal induction condition (psych-up), a relaxation condition, and a placebo-control condition. It may be that the contrived experimental settings used in these studies did not provide enough ego threat for the treatments to impact significantly on preperformance anxiety. Further research using different mental preparation strategies is needed in which evaluation apprehension or ego threat is greater. Within the laboratory setting, it would be helpful to replicate these studies using fine motor tasks. Also, to test the matching hypothesis described in chapter 8, research is needed to test the influence of physical and cognitive relaxation techniques on cognitive and somatic A-state.

RELATIONSHIP BETWEEN CSAI-2 COMPONENTS AND MOTOR PERFORMANCE

The "acid test" for any state personality inventory is its ability to predict sport behavior, particularly performance. Experientially, the debilitating effect of anxiety on sport performance is well documented. However, scientific verification of this relationship is more difficult to document due to the myriad factors that impinge on sport performance and the problems associated with the operationalization and measurement of variables. The CSAI-2, as a multidimensional anxiety inventory, should offer more precise measurement to clarify the anxiety-performance relationship.

Theoretical Predictions and Original Research

On the basis of multidimensional anxiety theory, Martens et al. (1982; see chapter 10) predicted that cognitive A-state and state self-confidence would be stronger predictors of performance than would somatic A-state because somatic anxiety manifestations are hypothesized to dissipate at the onset of competition. On the other hand, cognitive A-state and state self-confidence are linked to social evaluation and expectancy, both of which continue throughout the contest. In the first study examining the anxiety-performance relationship in the original CSAI-2 validation research, CSAI-2 components could not predict immediate performance as measured by nine-hole golf scores (see chapter 10). However, Martens and his colleagues felt that the performance measures used in this study lacked the precision necessary to demonstrate accurately the subtle influence of anxiety on performance. Thus, Burton (1988) conducted a second study employing intra-individual performance measures rather than the interindividual measures used in the first study (see chapter 10). Burton also expanded the theoretical framework to account for the relationship between Yerkes and Dodson's (1908) inverted-U theory and CSAI-2 components. On the basis of multidimensional anxiety theory, performance was predicted to decrease linearly with increases in cognitive A-state and to increase linearly with increases in state self-confidence. Also, somatic A-state was predicted to demonstrate an inverted-U relationship with performance. Finally, Burton examined the influence of task variables (task complexity and task duration) in mediating somatic A-state's inverted-U relationship. Specifically, it was predicted that somatic A-state would have greater impact on short-duration tasks than on long-duration tasks and that somatic A-state would have greater impact on tasks of low and high complexity than on tasks of moderate complexity.

The results of the second study, which used more sensitive intraindividual measures, supported the anxiety-performance predictions (Burton, 1988). An inverted-U relationship was found between somatic A-state and performance, a negative linear relationship between cognitive A-state and performance, and a positive linear relationship between state self-confidence and performance. Although task duration results were equivocal, task complexity results were generally congruent with predictions.

Additional Research Examining the Anxiety-Performance Relationship

Subsequent research examining the anxiety-performance relationship using the CSAI-2 may be seen as equivocal, but this equivocality may be attributed to differences in the design and operationalization of key variables. That is, when performance is measured using appropriate intraindividual measures, support for the anxiety-performance relationship is given. Using 14 male collegiate swimmers, Barnes et al. (1986) computed a performance formula based on individual accomplishment compared to previous performance. Although somatic A-state and state self-confidence were not related to performance, cognitive A-state emerged as a significant predictor, accounting for 15% of the total performance variance.

Gould et al. (1987) used intraindividual performance measures and also computed intraindividual CSAI-2 component scores on the basis of procedures designed by Sonstroem and Bernardo (1982). Thirty-seven members of a police training institute participated in a field experiment that included five separate shooting occasions varying in evaluation potential. Polynomial trend analyses indicated that somatic A-state was related to performance in an inverted-U fashion, state self-confidence was negatively related to performance, and cognitive A-state was not related to performance. Although this research is significant in that it accounts for intraindividual CSAI-2 and performance responses across situations of varying threat, the lack of interpretable findings for cognitive A-state and state self-confidence may have resulted from the lack of ego threat in the experiment. The researchers took great pains to increase the evaluation potential inherent in the competitive situation (e.g., inducing competition and giving rewards), but it is doubtful that these police trainees were as ego-involved in their performance and competitive outcomes as collegiate athletes are in their competition. Certainly, Gould et al.'s (1987) unique design needs to be replicated in competitive sport settings.

Other studies examining the anxiety-performance relationship using the CSAI-2 have failed to find significant relationships (Gould et al., 1984; Karteroliotis & Gill, 1987; Krane & Williams, 1987; Maynard & Howe, 1987; McAuley, 1985). However, these studies compared absolute performance scores, which have been shown to confound the documentation of the sensitive relationship between anxiety and performance. Taylor (1987) has provided some support for the task complexity hypotheses examined in the original validation studies. However, the small sample sizes and subjective performance measures used in his study warrant further examination of these relationships. Finally, Murphy et al. (1988) used a modified trait version of the CSAI-2 to determine whether cognitive and somatic competitive A-trait and trait self-confidence were possible mediators of changes in strength performance as a result of emotive imagery. The results indicated that the CSAI-2 subscales were not predictive of any changes in performance.

EFFECT OF INTERVENTION ON THE CSAI-2 COMPONENTS

Crocker et al. (1988) investigated the influence of Smith's (1980) Cognitive-Affective Stress Management Training (SMT) on CSAI-2 components. Elite youth volleyball players were assigned to either a treatment or a control group for 8 weeks. Although the treatment group had fewer negative thoughts in response to stressors and performance was better in a controlled setting, no interpretable differences emerged between groups for any of the CSAI-2 components.

SUMMARY

Although the CSAI-2 is a relatively new inventory, the research that has been conducted with it supports the underlying theory on which it is based. The multidimensionality of the CSAI-2 components is supported by the unique temporal changes of each component as competition nears, the different antecedents that predict each component, and the different relationships of each component with performance. Certainly, many equivocal findings have been indicated, and many questions about the multidimensional nature of anxiety remain. Overall, however, the initial examination of the CSAI-2 as a research tool indicates that it represents a significant contribution to measurement technology in competitive anxiety research. In the next chapter, conclusions are set forth, problems identified, and future research directions outlined for the CSAI-2.

Chapter 13

CSAI-2:
Conclusions, Problems,
and Future Directions

On the basis of the research and writing of Borkovec (1976), Davidson and Schwartz (1976), and Morris, Davis, and Hutchings (1981) supporting the existence of two independent systems of anxiety, the CSAI-2 was developed and validated as a competitive A-state measure of cognitive and somatic anxiety. Surprisingly, through factor analysis a third component emerged in the scale that was independent of the cognitive and the somatic components. This third factor also appeared to be a cognitive component but was opposite of cognitive A-state and thus was labeled state self-confidence. The accumulated evidence for the reliability and validity of the CSAI-2 is substantial yet preliminary, as many questions remain regarding the relationship between anxiety and sport behavior.

CONCLUSIONS DRAWN FROM RESEARCH
USING THE CSAI-2

In chapters 9 and 10, Martens et al. outlined the rigorous psychometric procedures conducted in the development of the CSAI-2. Those procedures resulted in evidence for the discriminability, reliability, concurrent validity, and construct validity of the CSAI-2 as a competitive A-state inventory measuring the sport-specific components of cognitive A-state, somatic A-state, and state self-confidence. Additional support for the concurrent validity of the CSAI-2 has been given by research indicating significant relationships in the predicted direction between the CSAI-2 components and competitive A-trait, attentional style, and state self-confidence.

Although the CSAI-2 components are theorized to be independent, researchers agree that they are likely to be interrelated in certain situations. The completed research indicates that the CSAI-2 components are moderately related across several situations. However, three areas of research provide substantial support for the independence of the CSAI-2 components.

First, differential patterns of responses based on the proximity of competition were noted for the components over time. Some support was found for the theoretical predictions and initial research by Martens et al. that demonstrated that cognitive A-state and state self-confidence remain relatively unchanged before competition, whereas somatic A-state rapidly increases as time to compete nears. Also, the research indicated that intrapersonal and situational factors may influence these changes in components across time.

Second, research has indicated that different antecedent factors predict different CSAI-2 components. Contrary to prediction and previous findings, competitive A-trait was found to be more highly related to cognitive A-state than to somatic A-state. Perceived ability significantly predicted state self-confidence, and experience was the best predictor of cognitive A-state. Performance was a significant predictor of postcompetitive cognitive A-state and state self-confidence but not of somatic A-state. No single antecedent predicted all three CSAI-2 components, thus supporting the independence of the components.

Third, the different relationships between the CSAI-2 components and performance support the multidimensional theory of anxiety. The results are equivocal regarding the exact nature of the anxiety-performance relationship, but overall some theoretical predictions have been confirmed. Martens and his colleagues originally predicted a negative relationship between cognitive A-state and performance, a positive relationship between state self-confidence and performance, and an inverted-U relationship between somatic A-state and performance (see chapter 10). Although those relationships have not been exactly replicated, some evidence exists for the ability of CSAI-2 components to predict performance. The most critical factor in examining the anxiety-performance relationship seems to be the measurement of performance. Prediction has been enhanced in those studies that employ intraindividual performance measures. Similarly, on the basis of the work of Sonstroem and Bernardo (1982) and Gould et al. (1987), it also appears fruitful to compute intraindividual measures of CSAI-2 components to examine more precisely the subtle relationship between anxiety and performance. These methods of operationalization will allow researchers to examine intraindividual patterns of anxiety and performance to test such theories as the inverted-U hypothesis.

PROBLEMS IN CSAI-2 RESEARCH

A major concern is the susceptibility of the CSAI-2 to distortion of responses arising from individuals seeking to present themselves in socially desirable ways. In the original validation research, Martens (1982) modified the cognitive A-state subscale to make it less prone to social desirability distortion (see chapter 9). This modification involved replacing the term *worry* with the less reactive term *concern*. However, some researchers have reported that the term *concern* is confusing to subjects. For example, Barnes et al. (1986) removed Question 1 (''I am concerned about this competition'') from their analyses because the subjects questioned whether this represented worry about competition or whether it asked if the competition was perceived to be important to the subject. Although misinterpretation may occur using the term *concern*, the use of the term *worry* is more problematic because it seems to create greater response distortion due to social desirability. The anti–social desirability instructions were found to reduce response distortion in the original validation research, so it is recommended that these instructions be used whenever the inventory is administered. If investigators have reason to suspect that a particular group may be especially inclined to present themselves as socially desirable, then it is recommended that the short form of the Marlowe-Crowne Social Desirability Scale (Reynolds, 1982) be administered along with the CSAI-2. Individuals scoring high on the social desirability scale should be deleted from the sample.

Another problem in the research is the use of univariate statistical techniques in analyzing the CSAI-2 components. Due to the high intercorrelations between components, multivariate analyses are warranted to account for the interacting effects of the components as dependent variables. Also, it would be helpful for researchers to compute and report the reliability of the CSAI-2 subscales for each particular sample. In this way, correlations may be corrected for attenuation and meta-analytic procedures employed to provide greater statistical precision in anxiety research.

The final problem deals with the use and nonuse of the CSAI-2. Current theory and research has demonstrated that anxiety is multidimensional. Thus, it seems logical that anxiety should be measured on the basis of this multidimensionality. Certainly, researchers are free to choose whichever measures they wish, but the CSAI-2 represents the most current operationalization of A-state in competitive situations. The research reviewed in this section strongly indicates that the future of anxiety research lies in the distinction between the manifestation of somatic and cognitive components and thus in the use of the CSAI-2. For now, no children's version of the CSAI-2 is available, so the CSAI-C is still warranted for that population.

FUTURE DIRECTIONS FOR CSAI-2 RESEARCH

The most obvious future research direction is the continued investigation of the anxiety-performance relationship. A better understanding of the mechanisms that impair performance may be obtained by investigating the separate and interactive functions of cognitive A-state, somatic A-state, and state self-confidence. As stated previously, the continued refinement of anxiety and performance measures will enable researchers to gain greater precision in the analysis of these relationships. It would also seem useful for sport psychologists and motor control researchers to join forces in clarifying the anxiety-performance relationship. For example, it would be interesting to determine whether process errors are more related to cognitive A-state and whether output errors are more related to somatic A-state.

Another methodological problem in studying the anxiety-performance relationship is the temporal proximity of the anxiety and performance measurements. Generally, with self-report measures A-state scores are obtained before and after competition. Frequently, these precompetitive measures of A-state have not predicted performance well, and this is not surprising. Although precompetitive anxiety is common in sport, many athletes report that A-state levels drop quickly once the competition begins. Thus, A-state can fluctuate substantially during a competitive event. If this is true, then it is unlikely that precompetitive A-state measures will be good predictors of performance.

Certainly, it is difficult to monitor A-state during competition using psychological inventories. Although some researchers have turned to miniaturized and telemetric measurements of physiological indicators of A-state, we hope that the use of psychological inventories will not be abandoned. Competitive settings should be sought or created in which anxiety can be measured during the contest. A recommended approach is to place less emphasis on discovering between-group differences and instead to focus on within-subject relationships between critical incidents in the competitive event and CSAI-2 components.

Another major question to be investigated concerns the matching hypothesis: Are certain stress management techniques better for different types of anxiety? Reports of sport psychologists using progressive relaxation methods with athletes are frequent. But if athletes are experiencing high cognitive A-state, will progressive relaxation (a somatic-based treatment) be as effective as will a cognitive-based treatment? Or if athletes experience somatic A-state that is highly conditioned to the situation, will cognitive methods facilitate relaxation as well as will somatic-based methods? It may be that somatic techniques can help reduce cognitive A-state and vice versa. For example, it has been suggested that the successful operant reduction of somatic A-state can lead to highly constructive internal attributions and thereby have a considerable positive impact on reducing cognitive A-state. Perhaps any effective procedure that reduces cognitive or somatic A-state will be effective in reducing both components of anxiety due to their interrelationship in competitive situations. These questions and other stress management issues await scrutiny by researchers.

Additional research investigating the antecedents of both cognitive and somatic A-state in competitive sports is needed. For example, do parents or coaches who are highly evaluative about a youngster's performance create higher cognitive than somatic A-state? Do early failure experiences become associated with or conditioned to certain stimuli in the competitive situation resulting in higher somatic A-state? Which child-rearing factors and coaching methods produce more or less cognitive and somatic A-state in young athletes? By better understanding the causes of cognitive and somatic anxiety, greater effort can be directed at the prevention of anxiety rather than at the treatment of it.

Finally, perhaps the "golden egg" of the CSAI-2 development was the fortuitous discovery of the state self-confidence component. Although this component of the CSAI-2 has been partially validated with the competitive anxiety framework, further research with the subscale is warranted to determine its utility. Self-confidence has long been advocated by athletes, coaches, and sport psychologists as perhaps the most critical psychological skill, yet it remains an area largely uninvestigated in sport psychology research.

Although research in competitive anxiety has a rich tradition in sport psychology, it remains a fertile area for discovery. As long as there is sport, athletes will experience anxiety; and as long as athletes experience anxiety, sport psychologists will try to better understand how anxiety is produced and manifested in competitive situations. It is hoped that the development of SCAT and the CSAI-2 as valid, theoretically grounded measurement tools will facilitate the pursuit of knowledge in competitive anxiety research.

SUMMARY

This chapter has attempted to provide a broad overview of the CSAI-2 research that was reviewed in chapter 12. On the basis of the conclusions set forth, problems have been identified and future research directions outlined. Although the CSAI-2 is a relatively new inventory, the completed research using the scale has indicated the importance of accounting for the multidimensionality of competitive A-state when examining anxiety in sport.

PART V

Concluding With a Theory

Throughout our work on competitive anxiety, we were guided by theory and intuition based on experience in determining the next steps to take. In turn, we constantly sought to develop a better theoretical explanation for predicting competitive anxiety in sport, that is, to explain the cause of competitive anxiety. Part V contains an emerging theory of competitive anxiety that is based on the proposition that the cause of competitive anxiety is an interactive function of uncertainty about the outcome and the importance of the outcome. On the basis of these concepts, a number of predictions are offered to explain certain behaviors in sport. The theory has received very limited empirical scrutiny, but it is our hope that readers will find the propositions sufficiently compelling to test them.

Chapter 14

A Theory of
Competitive Anxiety

A systematic research program on competitive anxiety was initiated by Martens in 1969 and continued until 1984 with the assistance of the coauthors and other doctoral students. Throughout that period our studies of competitive anxiety used an interactional paradigm based on the model of the competitive process presented in chapter 2 (see Figure 2.2). That is, competitive A-trait, as a personality disposition, is hypothesized to interact with potentially many different variables in the objective competitive situation to produce an A-state reaction. This interactional approach is shown in Figure 14.1.

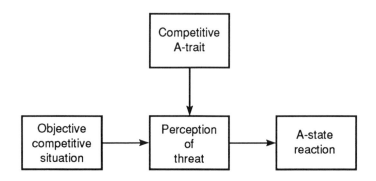

Figure 14.1. Interaction model for competitive-stress process.

Throughout our program of research we worked toward the development of a theory of competitive anxiety. The purpose of this chapter is to present the theory as it now stands. Martens began working on the theory in 1974 and was going to publish it in the *Sport Competition Anxiety Test* monograph, which was released in 1977, but at the last moment chose not to in order to develop the theory further. The theory remains incomplete primarily because it lacks rigorous empirical testing.

We chose to publish the theory as a concluding chapter here because the theory organizes existing evidence and gives direction for future research. We think that the theory has sufficient conceptual merit to warrant consideration by sport psychologists, and we encourage scientists to test the theory empirically.

BASIC PROPOSITIONS

A good theory of competitive anxiety should predict the levels of A-state among people who differ in competitive A-trait in varying competitive situations. To do so, the theory must develop axioms and theorems about the relationships among elements of the competitive situation, the persons in competitive situations, and their responses in the form of varying levels of A-state. But a theory needs to do more—it must specify the causes of competitive anxiety.

Spielberger's (1972b) trait-state theory has been helpful in advancing the study of anxiety but is limited because it fails to specify any of the antecedents that are likely to cause A-state. To date, no other theory has been put forth to explain the causes of competitive anxiety. The theory of competitive anxiety presented here postulates which elements in the objective competitive situation cause the perception of threat.

Uncertainty of the outcome and *Importance of the outcome* are the two constructs proposed to explain how different objective competitive situations affect a person's perception of threat and thus A-state. Stated another way, it is proposed that changes in the objective competitive situation affect the perception of uncertainty and importance of the outcome, which *causes* changes in threat and thus A-state.

Throughout this chapter, the term *threat* will be used, as distinct from A-state, to mean the perception of danger arising from the objective competitive situation. *A-state* will refer to the response made to the perception of danger or threat. This distinction is made to emphasize the importance of perception in determining responses made to the environment.

The important constructs of the theory of competitive anxiety are shown in Figure 14.2. It is postulated that competition is an evaluative process that creates uncertainty about the outcome before the actual competition. The greater the uncertainty and the importance of the outcome, the greater the threat. The relationship between uncertainty and importance is hypothesized to be multiplicative because if either uncertainty or importance is absent, no threat is expected to exist. Thus, Threat is a function of Uncertainty × Importance of the outcome, or, symbolically expressed, $T = f(U \times I)$. For threat to exist there must be substantial uncertainty about an outcome, and the outcome must be important to the person. Hence, as threat increases, it causes increasing A-state responses. Thus, A-state $= f(T) = f(U \times I)$.

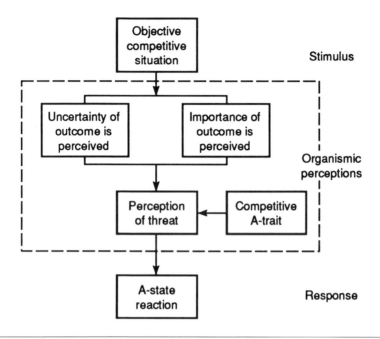

Figure 14.2.   A theory of competitive anxiety.

The perception of threat in competitive situations varies from person to person as a function of previous experiences and individual qualities; that is, individuals differ in competitive A-trait. Research has shown that persons with higher levels of competitive A-trait perceive a greater degree of threat in competitive situations than do persons with lower levels of competitive A-trait (Martens, 1977; Martens & Gill, 1976; Scanlan, 1977, 1978; Scanlan & Passer, 1979b; Simon & Martens, 1977).

Our discussion of the theory will always pertain to the outcome of obtaining a favorable or an unfavorable evaluation with the standard defined by the competitive process to determine a winner or a loser. Of course there are many other potential outcomes from the competitive process besides that of winning and losing that may be important sources of uncertainty. For example, a person may be uncertain about his or her ability to endure, to avoid physical harm, or to remain nonaggressive under potential defeat. Although the concern here is limited to the outcome common to all competitive processes—that of winning and losing—in most cases the relationships developed among the concepts of the competitive anxiety theory can be applied to these other outcomes.

CAUSES OF COMPETITIVE A-STATE

McGrath (1970a) has specified the antecedents of threat and thus A-state in a general form in his conceptual development of the stress process. Stress, he states, "has to do with a (perceived) substantial imbalance between demand and response capability, under conditions where failure to meet demand has important (perceived) consequences" (p. 20); that is, there is *uncertainty* that the demand can be met, and failure to do so is *important*. From this general formulation, a theory of the specific causes of threat in competitive situations was developed.

Uncertainty of the Outcome

Uncertainty, as a scientific construct, has been popular in information theory and psycholinguistics but not particularly in theorizing about anxiety. This is surprising, as uncertainty about future outcomes intuitively appears to be a common denominator among the many sources of A-state that we all experience. In a provocative paper, Kagan (1972) has made an excellent case that the resolution of uncertainty is a basic motive in humans and that the anticipation of this resolution can be extremely threatening. Uncertainty, according to Kagan, is a result of an incompatibility between cognitions, between cognitions and experiences, or between cognitions and behavior.

For example, in a competitive situation, a person may perceive the positive consequences of defeating an opponent of considerable ability but also perceive that defeat is possible and that the loss of self-esteem would accompany failure. A person may also recall that, when competing against others previously, the A-state reaction was very uncomfortable, and one may not want to experience this again. Thus, there is an approach-avoidance conflict, or an incompatibility between cognitions in the first case and between a cognition and experience in the second case. Kagan (1972) refers to the source of uncertainty in this example as the "inability to predict the future, especially if the doubt centers on the experience of potentially unpleasant events like punishment, physical harm, failure, or rejection" (p. 52).

According to Kagan (1972), when uncertainty occurs a primary motive is engaged to resolve it, and if no appropriate responses are immediately available, distress, A-state, fear, shame, or guilt may occur. The primary means for reducing uncertainty is to obtain information that, if appropriate, converts uncertainty to certainty. In competition the actual engagement in the comparison process always eliminates uncertainty about that particular comparison but may or may not eliminate uncertainty about the abilities compared. This point is discussed later in this chapter.

The unexpected events of life—the uncertainty of the future—have been postulated to be anxiety provoking by psychologists throughout the century. Of course not all levels of uncertainty should be expected to be perceived as threatening and thus to yield high levels of A-state. There probably exists some threshold value that uncertainty must reach before it is perceived as threatening, given that the perceiver places some importance on the outcome. In McGrath's terms, this threshold value is attained when the demand *substantially* exceeds the response capability. What this threshold value is, or what is substantial, will vary from person to person. High competitive A-trait persons perhaps have lower threshold values than do low competitive A-trait persons.

In competition, uncertainty about the outcome is inevitable before the performances are compared. In fact, competition may be thought of as structured uncertainty. Although we can have more or less accurate expectations about the outcomes of the comparison process before competing, we can never be certain about the outcomes until the comparison process is completed. Although this structured uncertainty in competition is hypothesized to be a source of threat, it is this same uncertainty that is often thought to be the challenge that makes competition a thrilling experience. Whether the uncertainty is positive (a challenge) or negative (a threat) depends on how the individual perceives that particular situation.

Uncertainty as a Challenge

One criterion for a competitive event being a good contest is that the outcome be reasonably uncertain. In some sports handicap systems are used for the purpose of maximizing uncertainty. The purpose of a handicap is to make an adjustment in competitors' scores based on past performances with the intent to equalize their abilities. The more equal the abilities of the persons competing, the greater the uncertainty about the outcome.

Maximizing uncertainty in competition may be achieved in another way. When selecting an opponent with whom we may wish to compete, we usually prefer a person who is of similar ability. It is not satisfying or challenging to compete with someone who we can easily defeat or who can easily defeat us. Thus, when we compete we seek opponents who have abilities that tend to maximize uncertainty about the outcome.

In some competitive situations, it appears that participants themselves attempt to maximize uncertainty by manipulating the quality of their own performance. For example, when players gain a substantial lead, they may reduce their effort to permit their opponents to stay in the game. Some players, when they believe they can obtain victory relatively easily, may permit their opponents to stay close in the game or even to obtain a lead but then toward the end of the contest will strive to obtain the victory. When a player diminishes his or her effort during the early part of a contest, he or she has implemented a self-imposed handicap. Through this informal handicap, the player with superior ability keeps the outcome relatively uncertain, and this makes the contest more interesting.

Thus, through several means competition is structured to be more uncertain. The rules may structure the scoring so that the initial abilities are equalized, or opponents are selected so that initial abilities are equal, or performance is controlled during the contest to increase uncertainty.

Why do we seek to maximize uncertainty? As suggested, maximum uncertainty increases the likelihood that the contest will be challenging. Berlyne (1960) and Ellis (1973) have proposed that individuals seek some uncertainty in their life—not too much, however, nor too little. What individuals seek is an optimal amount of arousal. It is when the outcome of the competition is perceived to be both highly uncertain and important that arousal is likely to exceed the optimum and threat is perceived. Berlyne also suggested that individuals will seek arousal to experience the satisfaction of reducing or eliminating the arousal; that is, it is rewarding to the person to reduce high levels of arousal successfully. Berlyne called this an *arousal jag*.

Festinger (1954) has suggested another reason for seeking to maximize the uncertainty of the competitive situation. In his social comparison theory, he hypothesizes that we seek others of similar ability because we are seeking to evaluate our own abilities. When we compare ourselves with others of similar ability we are able to learn more about our own abilities than we do when we compare ourselves to persons of discrepant abilities. Persons who compete with the motive to reduce uncertainty about their own abilities (although competing with a person of similar ability will be maximally uncertain before competition) will maximize the reduction of uncertainty about the competitor's abilities. This is so because an opponent of equal ability is maximally informative.

Operationalizing Uncertainty

Uncertainty about winning or losing in competition can be determined by the person's perceived probability of success (Ps) or probability of failure (Pf). The former is a fundamental construct in several other theories, including Atkinson's (1957) risk-taking theory, Crandall's (1974) achievement motivation theory, and Rotter's (1954) social learning theory. In each of these theories and in the theory of competitive anxiety, Ps is conceptualized as an expectancy—a cognitive anticipation aroused by cues in the objective competitive situation that performance of some act will produce a particular consequence. In other words, when a person anticipates competing, he or she determines the probability of obtaining a positive outcome by evaluating the quality of the standard (the demand) with the anticipated performance (response capability).

The relationship between Ps and uncertainty is nonmonotonic, as shown in Figure 14.3. As Ps increases, uncertainty increases to a point at which there is an equal chance of the outcome being positive or negative (Ps = .50). As Ps increases above .50, uncertainty decreases. When Ps is .0 or 1.0, no uncertainty exists.

Importance of the Outcome

The extent to which a person values attaining a favorable outcome defines *importance*. Crandall (1974) has labeled this construct *attainment value* and stated that the concept focuses simultaneously on the individual and on the task and situation at hand. Thus, it is a situation-specific measure of individual differences in perceived value in obtaining a particular outcome. These values may be extrinsic or intrinsic. For example, the expectancy of receiving $100,000 for winning a golf tournament, or the accolades of colleagues for making a game-saving play, or the winning of a gold medal in the Olympics are all extrinsic rewards that

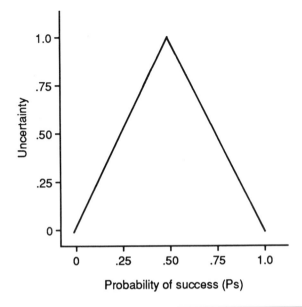

Figure 14.3.   Relationship between uncertainty and probability of success.

usually are valued by competitors. A feeling of competence, personal satisfaction, and increased self-esteem are intrinsic rewards that also are valued by competitors. Thus, importance is a combination of both the intrinsic and the extrinsic values held by the individual for obtaining a positive outcome. An interesting question for future investigation is whether intrinsic or extrinsic rewards interact differently with uncertainty to create different perceptions of threat.

RECIPROCAL INFLUENCE OF UNCERTAINTY AND IMPORTANCE

Atkinson's (1957) theory also contains a value component that he labels the *incentive value of success* (Is). He has hypothesized that Is is a negative linear function of Ps. That is, as Ps increases, Is decreases which is expressed by the equation Is = 1 − Ps. Crandall (1974) took issue with this proposed relationship and argued the following:

> This assumption is based on the notion that the individual should get less "kick" out of succeeding at a task which has been defined to him as easy where his expectancy should be high, than out of one defined as difficult where his expectancy should be low. But, I could just as well reason that I may come to value that which I can do well and to devalue what I am no good at. (p. 9)

Crandall (1974) reported eight different studies in which expectancy and value, when measured separately, were correlated between $-.10$ to $+.25$ (essentially independent). Martens and Greer (1980) found a relationship between Importance and expectancy of $+.09$. These findings thus indicate that Ps and Importance should be measured independently. Because Uncertainty is derived from Ps, Uncertainty and Importance are also thought to be independent when measured across subjects. The Martens and Greer study supports this conclusion with a correlation of $+.10$. Yet there is some reason to believe that Uncertainty and Importance influence each other in certain situations. For example, when Ps is very low, Importance may be diminished as a defense mechanism to cope with the likely failure.

On the other hand, when Importance is extremely high it may influence Uncertainty, as demonstrated in a study reported by Emerson (1966). In a field study in which he was a participant observer in the 1963 ascent of Mount Everest, Emerson observed that when climbers were engaged in the life-and-death struggle to conquer the mountain, the communication among members of the expedition was of the form that maximized uncertainty. He hypothesized that goals tended to be defined in regions of uncertain outcome to maintain high levels of motivation (to maximize the challenge).

When Ps appeared high (optimism) during the expedition, communication tended to remind the climbers that unknown events could reduce Ps. When Ps appeared low (pessimism), such as during a blizzard, the communication would tend to verify that the skills and abilities of the climbers would be able to overcome the hardships.

Emerson (1966) stated it this way:

In group-goal-striving requiring coordinated effort and collective assessment of the environment, communication processes tend to maximize and maintain uncertainty about outcomes through selective transmission of information. Communicated information tends (a) to counteract the prevailing information provided in the environment, and (b) communication feedback tends to counteract the information currently being communicated, thereby sustaining doubt and maintaining collective effort. (p. 213)

Similar events are frequently observed in communication among coaches and athletes before and during competition. When Ps is high, communication will often take the forms of "We can't take this team lightly," "They've beaten some good teams before," and "If they get a lead, they're tough to catch." When Ps is low, communication will more often take the forms of "These guys can be beaten," "They put their pants on just like we do—feet first," and "I saw them get beat once, and we can beat them too."

Often the coach of a team plays the important role of attempting to direct the communication among his or her players so that uncertainty is maximized. The coach seeks to move Ps toward the .50 region, where challenge is high but tempered by the perception that success can be obtained by effort and good performance. When the contest is perceived as important and uncertainty is maximum, the probability of threat being perceived increases.

How uncertainty and importance influence each other in competitive sports needs further study. When one of the constructs affects the other, the proposed relationship of $U \times I = T$ may not hold. At the present, however, the evidence suggests they are independent.

CONSENSUAL VALIDATION

Most readers will recognize the theory of competitive anxiety to be an Expectancy $\times$ Value theoretical derivative. In the absence of direct experimental evidence to support the theory, indirect evidence is reviewed that provides consensual validity.

In one way or another, some psychologists have observed that uncertain situations of importance to a person are threatening. Atkinson (1957), for example, observed that whenever performance is evaluated in relation to some standard of excellence, what constitutes a challenge to achieve for one individual poses the threat of failure to another. That is, one person's challenge is another person's stress. Both the perception of a challenge and the threat of failure have been shown to increase A-state when anticipating competition, although perhaps for quite different reasons, as demonstrated by the differences in cognitive and somatic anxiety discussed in chapter 8.

Berlyne (1960), in discussing anticipatory arousal (which we can equate with anticipatory A-state), wrote that

> anticipatory arousal will, however, depend on more than uncertainty. It will reflect the individual's estimate of how important the impending event is likely to be, how much surprise he must brace himself for, how far it is likely to demand some vigorous action that cannot be identified beforehand, how close an examination it will require. It may take the form of a general alertness or vigilance. If it is particularly intense or combined with the distinctive accompaniments of fear, it will appear as a state of general foreboding, apprehensiveness, or, to give the word a connotation it sometimes has, anxiety. (p. 185)

The .50 Ps situation is potentially more threatening in another way. All situations in which failure is probable are potentially threatening, but some evidence suggests that the situation in which there is a reasonable chance to avoid failure if one performs well is more stressful than is a situation in which little chance exists to change the outcome on the basis of the person's own performance. When individuals perceive that regardless of how well they perform they still most likely will fail, they are less likely to become anxious than they are when they perceive that if they do well they have a chance to obtain a positive outcome. Mechanic (1970) found that when the situation appeared hopeless, individuals accepted their fate. Acceptance of fate is one form of adaptive behavior, and it lessens A-state. Mechanic wrote, ''Those persons who gave the impression of 'having given up' were less tense and anxious than those who were struggling actively against extremely difficult problems'' (p. 113). It appears then that as persons perceive they cannot affect the outcome by their behavior, they psychologically dissociate themselves with the outcome as a means to cope with the inevitable failure they anticipate. The entire line of research on learned helplessness also supports this conclusion.

We may wonder why people compete at all if the competitive process inevitably creates uncertainty and often leads to threat. The answer probably lies in the old adage ''Nothing ventured, nothing gained.'' Competition creates psychological conflict because the individual is motivated simultaneously by two strong, competing drives. The person wishes to obtain the positive outcomes that are intrinsically and extrinsically associated with the competition while wishing to avoid the negative outcomes, such as loss of self-esteem, physical harm, and so on. Thus, a classic approach-avoidance conflict exists when Ps is equal to .50. In this situation the possibility of failure is real, but the incentive value of success is significant. Almost every text that has focused on the antecedents of anxiety has identified the approach-avoidance conflict as a major source of threat and thus A-state.

Significant consensual validity is found also in Berlyne's (1960) theory of psychological conflict (C), which postulates that $C = E \times H$, where E represents the absolute strength of competing responses, which is substantively synonymous with Importance, and H is entropy, or an information theory measure of Uncertainty. Stripped of its elegant terminology, Berlyne's theory postulates that $C = f(U \times I)$. Thus, Berlyne's theory postulates constructs that are the same as the conditions that create conflict and that are postulated to create threat in the theory of competitive anxiety. Therefore, it is logical to assume that as the magnitude of conflict increases so does the magnitude of threat.

REDUCTION OF UNCERTAINTY

When arousal produced by uncertainty exceeds an optimal level, theorists have postulated that a primary motive to reduce uncertainty is activated (e.g., Kagan, 1972). The primary means for reducing uncertainty is to obtain information that, if appropriate, transforms uncertainty to certainty. The reduction of uncertainty by seeking information is the basis of Festinger's (1954) social comparison theory. Festinger has postulated that in the absence of objective standards individuals will seek to compare themselves with others to evaluate their abilities. Those with similar abilities are hypothesized to be more informative than are others.

Because competitive situations are social comparison situations in which abilities are evaluated, uncertainty about abilities can be reduced by competing. Uncertainty about the outcome of the competition can also be reduced before competing by obtaining information about one's own abilities, the opponent's abilities, and other situational factors that may determine the outcome (e.g., weather, condition of equipment, etc.). Indeed, in sport much effort is given to obtaining information about the competitive situation to reduce uncertainty. For example, statistical records are a fetish of most well-organized sports that provide normative information. More immediate and specific types of information are sought frequently through direct opponent observation, or scouting the opponent, which helps reduce uncertainty about the opponent's abilities.

Athletes frequently need information about their own abilities as well. Thus, they engage in competition to determine more accurately their abilities in order to reduce uncertainty when engaging in a subsequent, more important competition. Thus, two sources of information are potentially available in sport situations: normative information (statistics) and experiential information, which is gained through the actual experience on the criterion task.

Persons in anticipation of competition will have varying amounts of information about the performance demands and their own abilities. The quantity and quality of information available are key factors in determining the degree of uncertainty and, in part, importance. Information available before the actual comparison in the competitive process reduces uncertainty about the outcome only when the precompetitive information indicates that Ps is very high or very low. If the precompetitive information indicates that Ps is near .50, uncertainty will increase. Stated differently, when precompetitive information indicates that Ps is near .50, we can say with greater certainty that the outcome is uncertain. In the absence of precompetitive information, we are "uncertain" about Uncertainty.

The information from the comparison always reduces uncertainty about that comparison but not necessarily about the attribute compared in the competition. Uncertainty about the correctness of the outcome for the attribute being compared may remain high if the comparison is perceived to have been inequitable, not representative of the person's ability, or a result of luck or chance.

To determine Ps and thus uncertainty accurately, information is needed about at least four components of the competitive process:

- Information about the quality of the standard to which the performance will be compared
- Information about the self's performance capability
- Estimates of the probability that actual performance will approximate performance capability
- Estimates of the probability that actual performance will determine performance outcome

Information About the Standard

In some cases the person may know precisely the behavioral demand before competing. This is usually the case when competing against a preestablished standard. For example, a shot putter wishes to break his former best throw of 65 ft or a pole vaulter is trying to establish a new world record of 20 ft. Behavioral demand can also be accurately known when the temporality of the comparison process is contiguous but not when it is simultaneous. When performance is contiguous (i.e., Person X performs and then Person Y, not X and Y simultaneously) Person Y has the advantage of knowing the precise behavioral demands for that comparison. This frequently occurs in such events as gymnastics, diving, and skiing.

In competition in which the comparison process occurs simultaneously (e.g., auto racing, tennis, baseball, wrestling, or handball), the competitor must estimate the quality of the standard. In any sport in which the competitor directly interacts, the comparison standard cannot be accurately known in advance.

Response Capability

Response capability refers to the self's (not opponent's) perceived ability for producing a particular response or behavior. Response capability is subjectively determined by the self on the basis of previous experiences in comparable situations. In some competitive situations a person may have had few similar experiences from which to evaluate his or her ability. The inability to determine accurately self's ability and thus Ps is a source of uncertainty.

Although it is more common to not have accurate information about the standard when the standard is an opponent, individuals sometimes have little information about their own ability to exceed the standard. When they lack information about both the standard and their own ability, it is not possible to arrive at an estimate of Ps in which they have much confidence. Not knowing how one might fare is a source of uncertainty, and if the outcome is of considerable importance, uncertainty may be a source of substantial threat. Individuals who have weak or low self-esteem are especially likely to perceive greater uncertainty about their own ability and thus higher A-state (Scanlan & Passer, 1978).

Actual Performance

Although athletes may have quite accurate information about the standard and their own ability, they cannot be certain they will be able to produce the response they are capable of making. Performance is ephemeral; it varies widely because it is determined by many factors, ability being only one. In sport one of the great mysteries is why one day an athlete performs so well and the next day performs so poorly. If we could unravel this mystery and know how to always display our best performance, the sport world would be drastically changed because there would be little uncertainty about the outcomes. Those athletes with better abilities would always emerge victorious. Indeed, it is uncertainty about whether a person can perform up to his or her ability that makes competitive sport intriguing. When a person competes against opponents, the intrigue is who will perform closest to his or her ability, all other things being equal.

Ability may be conceptualized as an estimate of a person's potential for optimal performance under favorable conditions. Ability is a person's capacity to perform. Actual performance may be hypothesized to be a function of Potential Performance − (Errors + Motivation Losses).

Seldom do people perform to their potentials, that is, their abilities. Instead, people make errors because they are imperfect and their motives to perform optimally vary. In fact, the A-state so frequently associated with precompetition is thought to affect adversely the motivational state of the performer. For those who fear failure more than they value the intrinsic and extrinsic rewards of success, they may opt to not compete at all if given that choice.

Thus, because actual performance is ephemeral and only in part determined by ability, there is uncertainty whether actual performance will approach potential performance. We often hear an athlete say, "Just as long as I don't embarrass myself and I play up to my ability." This statement reflects the athlete's concern about the discrepancy between actual performance and potential performance.

Performance Outcome

The fourth source of uncertainty is the discrepancy between performance and performance outcome. In all competitive sports a person's performance is not the only determinant of performance outcome. Performance outcome is in part determined by external factors, including the performance of opponents, judgments by officials, weather conditions, the physical condition of equipment or the playing surface, and chance occurrences. Thus, performance outcome is a function of actual performance and external factors. For example, a batter in baseball may hit the ball very well but be out because the shortstop had taken a certain position and made a diving attempt to catch a line drive. On another occasion the batter swings, and the ball squirts off the end of the bat, spins along the first baseline, and is unplayable by anyone. The outcome is a single. In the first case the performance was good but the outcome poor, and in the second case the performance was poor but the outcome good.

Although in some competitive sports the discrepancy between performance and performance outcome is minimal, in others it may be substantial. Thus, although athletes perceive that they have the ability to exceed the standard, they also recognize that their performance is ephemeral and that external factors may affect the outcome. To the extent that the objective competitive situation indicates that the performance outcome may be determined by external factors that are beyond the control of the performer, uncertainty about the performance outcome will increase.

Conclusions and Questions Regarding Uncertainty

Although experienced players such as professional athletes experience increased A-state levels before competition, it is usually thought that these A-state levels are lower than those of less experienced players. It is understandable why this should be so. In general, experienced competitors have more information about each of the four factors. Whether the comparison occurs simultaneously or contiguously, they know what the standard is. Professional athletes usually compete against the same opponents frequently or have available to them accurate information about the opponent's ability.

Experienced athletes of course should know well what they are capable of doing and how variable they are in terms of their actual performance approximating their potential performance. And with experience, athletes obtain a good idea about the probability of their performance, rather than external factors, determining the outcome. On the other hand, experienced athletes frequently compete with opponents of near-equal ability and play for important outcomes, making the situation more threatening.

In summary, Ps in a competitive situation is an estimate based on the content and availability of information about the four components of the comparison process just reviewed. Specifically, Ps is a function of the content and availability of information about the discrepancy between

- the standard (S) and the self's ability (A),
- the self's ability (A) and actual performance (P), and
- actual performance (P) and performance outcome (O).

In symbolic form, then, uncertainty may be expressed as $U = f(Ps) = f([S - A] + [A - P] + [P - O])$.

From this discussion, two types of competitive uncertainty can be identified and may be helpful in future research:

- Certain uncertainty
- Uncertain uncertainty

When the standard and self's ability are known and the perceived discrepancies among potential performance, actual performance, and performance outcome are small, then Ps should determine Uncertainty. When Ps is in the midrange (+.50), Uncertainty will be high. Under these conditions "certain" uncertainty exists. When there is a lack of information about one or more of the four factors discussed previously, Ps is less accurate in estimating performance outcome. In this case "uncertain" uncertainty exists.

From these speculations about how Ps is estimated and about certain and uncertain uncertainty, several interesting questions arise:

- Is uncertainty and thus A-state higher in sports for which the discrepancy between performance and performance outcome is large?
- Are sports that rely on judgments by humans to determine the outcome more stressful due to of the greater Uncertainty arising from subjective scoring than are sports that are scored objectively?

- Is certain uncertainty more or less threatening than uncertain uncertainty?
- Are sports for which the temporality of the comparison process is simultaneous more or less threatening than those for which the process in contiguous?

REDUCTION OF IMPORTANCE

Importance is determined by the individual's perception of the value of the rewards potentially attainable in the particular situation. Those rewards may be either extrinsic or intrinsic. Importance may be reduced by removing available extrinsic rewards (e.g., trophies, medals, and social recognition). In other words, the objective competitive situation can be changed by withdrawing the availability of extrinsic rewards. It is impossible, however, to remove all potential extrinsic rewards because the other competitors are always a source of potential social reinforcement.

The importance of extrinsic and intrinsic rewards may also be diminished by changing one's perception or value system about the significance of these rewards. Some athletes "live and die" by how well they play sports; a poor performance brings on great despair and a good performance immense joy. Their feelings of self-worth and competence are closely linked to how they play sports. Techniques such as cognitive behavior modification may be suitable for helping to reduce the importance a person places on the value of the competitive outcome if they are experiencing high levels of A-state.

QUESTIONS REGARDING COMPETITIVE A-TRAIT

Competitive A-trait is theorized to be a construct that predicts how individuals differ in their perceptions of threat in objective competitive situations. The value of competitive A-trait, as measured by SCAT (Martens, 1977), in predicting A-state responses in competitive situations has been well established (Martens, 1977; Martens & Gill, 1976; Scanlan, 1977, 1978; Scanlan & Passer, 1979b; Simon & Martens, 1977). Yet many questions about competitive A-trait remain unanswered, mainly about its causes and how it interacts with specific situational factors in the competitive environment:

- Do persons high in competitive A-trait perceive greater uncertainty, importance, or both in the objective competitive situation than do persons low in competitive A-trait?
- Do persons high in competitive A-trait perceive a wider range of competitive situations as threatening than do persons low in competitive A-trait? (We know that they respond with a greater degree of A-state in the same situation.)
- What are the causes of high competitive A-traits: previous failure, physical harm, embarrassment, parental pressure, coach intimidation, unrealistic goals,

weak self-concept? Although it is reasonable to conclude that an accumulation of experiences in competitive situations, combined with inherited differences, are the major determinants of high competitive A-traits, a better understanding of the specific causes is needed in helping athletes manage their anxiety. For example, it appears worthwhile to investigate whether competitive A-trait can predict A-states better by developing a new scale that contains a cognitive and a somatic component of competitive A-trait. It may also be helpful to search for other components of competitive A-trait to investigate the causes of competitive A-state.

- Is fear of failure more or less threatening than fear of physical harm among athletes who differ in competitive A-trait? One study (Endler, 1978) has suggested that fear of physical harm is not a frequent source of competitive stress.

STRESS MANAGEMENT AND THE THEORY OF COMPETITIVE ANXIETY

A wide range of stress management procedures have been developed over the last decade, and many of these are being used with athletes. If future research supports the competitive anxiety theory (or some modification thereof), it should have implications for the effectiveness of stress management procedures. Because the theory places the cause of stress on *perceptions* of uncertainty and importance, the techniques most likely to reduce high levels of A-state will be those that change these perceptions. This suggests that various cognitive stress management techniques will be more efficacious. Straightforward relaxation methods, hypnosis, and transcendental meditation may be found to be effective, but only by indirectly affecting the perception of uncertainty and importance.

In short, the better we understand the causes of competitive A-state, the better our stress management procedures will be. In turn, the more we know about which stress management procedures are effective, the better we will understand the causes of competitive stress.

SUMMARY

The theory of competitive anxiety is parsimonious, can be operationalized, and implicates a number of testable hypotheses. At present it lacks direct experimental verification, but such is the nature of a new theory. We invite sport psychologists to test the theory and, as is inevitable with all theories, to replace it with a better one.

Appendix A

Published Empirical Studies Using SCAT[3]

Albrecht & Feltz, 1987

Anderson & Williams, 1987

Auvergne, 1983

Betts, 1982

Biddle & Jamieson, 1988

Blais & Vallerand, 1986

Broughton & Perlstrom, 1986

Brustad, 1988

Brustad & Weiss, 1987

Burhans, Richman, & Bergey, 1988

Cheatham & Rosentswieg, 1982

Colley, Roberts, & Chipps, 1985

Cooley, 1987

Crocker, Alderman, & Smith, 1988

Dothwaite & Armstrong, 1984

Durtschi & Weiss, 1984

Feltz & Albrecht, 1986

Fisher & Zwart, 1982

Furst & Tenenbaum, 1984

Gerson & Deshaies, 1978

Gill, 1988

Gill, Dzewaltowski, & Deeter, 1988

Gill & Martens, 1977

Gould, Horn, & Spreeman, 1983a

Gould, Horn, & Spreeman, 1983b

Gould, Petlichkoff, & Weinberg, 1984

Gravelle, Searle, & St. Jean, 1982

Gray & Haring, 1984

Hanin, 1982

Hanson & Gould, 1988

Hellstedt, 1987

Hogg, 1980

Huband & McKelvie, 1986

Karteroliotis & Gill, 1987

Koyama, Inomata, & Takeda, 1980

Krotee, 1980

Lanning & Hisanaga, 1983

Magill & Ash, 1979

Martens, Burton, Rivkin,
 & Simon, 1980

Martens & Gill, 1976

Martens, Gill, & Scanlan, 1976

[3]Complete references for these studies are included in the reference list of this book.

Martens, Rivkin, & Burton, 1980

Martens & Simon, 1976a

Maynard & Howe, 1987

McKelvie & Huband, 1980

McKelvie, Valliant, & Asu, 1985

Miller & Miller, 1985

Murphy & Woolfolk, 1987

Ostrow & Ziegler, 1978

Owie, 1981

Passer, 1983

Passer & Seese, 1983

Poteet & Weinberg, 1980

Power, 1982

Rainey, Conklin, & Rainey, 1987

Rainey & Cunningham, 1988

Riddick, 1984

Robinson & Carron, 1982

Rupnow & Ludwig, 1981

Scanlan, 1977

Scanlan, 1978

Scanlan & Lewthwaite, 1984

Scanlan & Lewthwaite, 1988

Scanlan & Passer, 1977

Scanlan & Passer, 1978

Scanlan & Passer, 1979a

Scanlan & Passer, 1979b

Scanlan & Passer, 1981

Scanlan & Ragan, 1978

Segal & Weinberg, 1984

Simon & Martens, 1977

Smith, 1980

Smith, 1983

Sonstroem & Bernardo, 1982

Stadulis, 1977

Taylor, 1987

Thirer, Knowlton, Sawka,
  & Chang, 1978

Thirer & O'Donnell, 1980

Vealey, 1986

Wandzilak, Potter, & Lorentzen, 1982

Wark & Wittig, 1979

Watson, 1986

Weinberg, 1978

Weinberg, 1979

Weinberg & Genuchi, 1980

Willis, 1982

Wittig, 1984

Wittig, Duncan, & Schurr, 1987

Appendix B

Annotated Bibliography of Doctoral Dissertations Using SCAT[4]

Blacksmith, W.A. (1977). The effect of systematic desensitization on pre-match anxiety states among collegiate wrestlers (Doctoral dissertation, West Virginia University, 1977). *Dissertation Abstracts International*, **38**, 1974A.

Using 26 collegiate wrestlers as subjects, SCAT was found to be significantly correlated with the Wrestling Self-Inventory (WSI, a wrestling-specific A-trait scale) ($r = .70$) and also with the State-Trait Anxiety Inventory (STAI) ($r = .30$). The STAI was a better predictor of noncompetitive A-state than was SCAT or the WSI, but the WSI and SCAT were better predictors of precompetitive A-state than was the STAI.

Brik, J. (1984). The effects of EMG biofeedback training and relaxation training on self-reported measures of trait anxiety and sports competition anxiety (Doctoral dissertation, Oregon State University, 1984). *Dissertation Abstracts International*, **45**, 1071A.

The effect of a 6-week progressive relaxation and biofeedback monitoring program on locus of control, general A-trait, competitive A-trait, and various physiological measures was examined. Subjects were 36 male collegiate varsity track-and-field athletes divided into one of four treatment groups: cassette tape Quieting Response program, Quieting Response program with augmented EMG biofeedback, EMG

---

[4]Many of the entries in this bibliography were based on dissertation abstracts. Thus, it should not be considered a critical review of the dissertation research. Rather, the purpose of this bibliography is to provide a quick reference for readers. The entries focus mainly on how SCAT was used in the studies.

feedback alone, and listening to music of choice (control). Although EMG measures were significantly reduced through training, no differences were found among groups on any of the psychological measures.

Britton, S.E. (1986).   Identifying specific cognitive and affective attributes of female junior elite gymnasts (Doctoral dissertation, Boston University, 1986). *Dissertation Abstracts International*, **46**, 4442B.

This study attempted to identify differences between female junior elite gymnasts and female nonathletes the same age ($N = 105$) in intelligence and competitive trait anxiety. Gymnasts were significantly higher in competitive A-trait than were nonathletes in the same age-group. No relationship was found between intelligence and competitive A-trait.

Brustad, R.J. (1987).   Affective outcomes in competitive youth sport: The influence of intrapersonal and socialization factors (Doctoral dissertation, University of Oregon, 1986). *Dissertation Abstracts International*, **47**, 2499A.

This study examined the influence of intrapersonal and social factors on positive affect (enjoyment) and negative affect (competitive A-trait) experienced during competitive youth sport participation. Two hundred and seven youth sport subjects completed self-report measures of self-esteem, perceived basketball competence, intrinsic motivation, perceived parental pressure, and frequency of evaluative and performance worry. For boys, high competitive A-trait was predicted by low self-esteem and frequent performance and evaluative worries. For girls, high competitive A-trait was predicted by low self-esteem, low perceived competence, and frequent performance worries.

Buckles, T.M. (1986).   The effects of visuo-motor behavior rehearsal on competitive performance tasks, anxiety, and attentional style (Doctoral dissertation, University of Tennessee, 1985). *Dissertation Abstracts International*, **46**, 3283A.

Ten female college basketball players were divided into a visuomotor behavior rehearsal (VMBR) group and a no-treatment group to assess the effects of a 5-mo VMBR program on competitive A-trait, competitive A-state, attentional style, and performance. VMBR facilitated performance on a closed task and decreased somatic competitive A-state (CSAI-2) but had no effect on attentional style (TAIS) or competitive A-trait.

Bump, L.A. (1987).   Empathy in coaches and its influence on athletes (Doctoral dissertation, University of Illinois, 1986). *Dissertation Abstracts International*, **47**, 2499A.

The purpose of this study was to study the relationship between coaches' empathy and athletes' social support, satisfaction, and performance. SCAT was used to operationalize accurate empathy by comparing coaches' predictions of athletes' competitive A-trait levels with the athletes' actual competitive A-trait levels. Coaches who were higher in accurate empathy displayed better communication ability than did coaches lower in accurate empathy. Also, athletes coached by coaches who were higher in accurate empathy displayed better communication ability than did athletes who were coached by coaches lower in accurate empathy.

Burton, D. (1984).   Evaluation of goal-setting training on selected cognitions and performance of collegiate swimmers (Doctoral dissertation, University of Illinois, 1983). *Dissertation Abstracts International*, **45**, 116A.

A 5-month goal-setting training (GST) program was conducted with 30 collegiate swimmers to ascertain the effects of systematic goal setting on selected cognitions and swimming performance. As compared to non-GST swimmers ($n = 35$), GST swimmers demonstrated more optimal cognitions and performance. Although non-GST swimmers were higher in competitive A-trait than were GST swimmers, this difference was not statistically significant. SCAT was also used as a measure of competitive A-trait in the psychological profile of the GST swimmers to aid in understanding the individual goal-setting needs of the swimmers.

Ettenger, R.H. (1985).   The effects of feedback on competitive anxiety and motor performance (Doctoral dissertation, University of Southern California, 1985). *Dissertation Abstracts International*, **46**, 352A.

High and low competitive A-trait subjects ($N = 106$) were randomly assigned to a success or a failure feedback group. Subjects putted 10 golf balls, were given either success or failure feedback, and then putted 10 more balls. A-state (STAI) was assessed before the first set of putts and after the feedback treatment. High competitive A-trait subjects exhibited greater posttest A-state in the failure feedback condition than they did in the success feedback condition. Also, high competitive A-trait subjects exhibited greater posttest A-state than did low competitive A-trait subjects.

Goodspeed, G.A. (1984).   Effects of comprehensive self-regulation training on state anxiety and performance of female gymnasts (Doctoral dissertation, Boston University, 1984). *Dissertation Abstracts International*, **44**, 3009A.

In two experiments, the effects of self-regulation training on A-state (STAI) and gymnastics performance were assessed. SCAT was employed as a baseline competitive A-trait measure. In Study 1 ($n = 9$), the training had no effect on state anxiety, but performance was improved when compared to the previous season. However, this study lacked a control group. In Study 2 ($n = 16$), a self-regulation group was compared to a control group. No differences were found between groups in A-state or performance.

Hamilton, S.A. (1986).   Cognitive-behavioral training of basketball players: Professional and peer training (Doctoral dissertation, West Virginia University, 1985). *Dissertation Abstracts International, 47*, 835A.

From a pool of 25 male and female collegiate basketball players, better free throw shooters ($n = 6$) were compared to poorer free throw shooters ($n = 7$) in performance, competitive A-trait, competitive A-state (CSAI), and three performance anxiety measures (the Social Avoidance and Distress Scale [SADS], the Personal Report of Confidence of a Speaker [PRCS], and the Suinn Test Anxiety Behavior Scale [STABS]). Also, cognitive-behavioral training was compared to peer training in increasing free throw proficiency. Poorer free throw shooters were higher in competitive A-trait than were better free throw shooters, but no pre- or post-treatment changes were found. SCAT was not significantly correlated with the SADS, PRCS, or STABS.

Harris, A.J. (1981).   A cognitive-behavioral program to improve bowling performance (Doctoral dissertation, University of Southern Mississippi, 1981). *Dissertation Abstracts International, 42*, 2057B.

Twenty-five high competitive A-trait experienced male and female bowlers were randomly assigned to a cognitive-behavioral treatment group or a control group. Treatment subjects participated in a 7-week program involving systematic desensitization and covert rehearsal. Treatment subjects bowled significantly better than did control subjects, but no differences in competitive A-trait were found between groups.

Hisanaga, B.W. (1983).   Coaches, relaxation training, and sports performance: A field study (Doctoral dissertation, Indiana University, 1982). *Dissertation Abstracts International, 43*, 2893A.

The relationship among competitive A-trait, relaxation training, and performance was examined in 24 female high school volleyball players. Competitive A-trait accounted for 62% of the variance in performance and relaxation training for 16% of the variance in competitive A-trait.

Horsfall, J.S. (1979).   Interrelationships among autonomic, self-report and behavioral measures of competitive arousal (Doctoral dissertation, University of Northern Colorado, 1979). *Dissertation Abstracts International, 40*, 2542A.

Fifty-one male physical education majors completed a complex maze task during which self-report competitive A-state (CSAI), physiological A-state, and performance were measured. Self-report competitive A-trait was assessed by SCAT. Multiple regression analyses indicated that the combination of physiological A-state and competitive A-trait explained 20% of the variance in performance. Competitive A-trait was significantly correlated with competitive A-state ($r = .41$, $p < .003$).

Houseworth, S.D. (1984).   Relative contributions of achievement motivation and attributions to performance outcome upon competitive athletic performance (Doctoral dissertation, Southern Illinois University, 1983). *Dissertation Abstracts International, 44*, 2093A.

The relationship between different measures of achievement motivation and causal attributions was examined using 121 male and female collegiate swimmers and divers. SCAT was employed as a measure of fear of failure. No relationship was indicated between any of the measures of achievement motivation and causal attributions.

Jennings, L.M. (1989).   The differences in the variables of attention, anxiety and mental imagery in golf and tennis players (Doctoral dissertation, Fordham University, 1988). *Dissertation Abstracts International, 49*, 2858B.

The purpose of this study was to compare anxiety, attention, and imagery in golf and tennis players in an attempt to determine whether athletes in different sports rely on different cognitive perceptual variables. Subjects were 31 golfers and 29 tennis players, all of whom were nationally ranked amateurs. All subjects were administered SCAT, the Cognitive Somatic Anxiety Questionnaire (CSAQ), and the Test of Attentional and Interpersonal Style (TAIS). No differences were found between groups in competitive A-trait. Also, the groups did not differ on cognitive anxiety, but golfers were lower in somatic anxiety than were tennis players.

Kjoss, H.B. (1984).   Prediction of sport competitive state anxiety among coaches and athletes (Doctoral dissertation, University of Northern Colorado, 1983). *Dissertation Abstracts International, 44*, 3009A.

The ability of coaches and athletes to predict each others' precompetitive anxiety was examined. The findings indicated that athletes were more accurate at predicting coaches' anxiety than were the coaches in predicting athletes' anxiety. Competitive A-trait was significantly related to competitive A-state (CSAI). Also, a significant relationship was found between the empathy level of coaches and their ability to predict anxiety in their athletes.

Lacey, A.E. (1984).   The effects of competition on psychological, physiological, and behavioral parameters of anxiety: An examination of the validity of the CSAI-2 (Doctoral dissertation, University of Iowa, 1983). *Dissertation Abstracts International, 44*, 3629A.

Eighty females were paired according to ability on a video-game task and assessed on the basis of baseline measures of heart rate, competitive A-trait, and A-trait (CSAQ) as well as pre-, mid-, and postcompetitive measures of heart rate, competitive A-state (CSAI-2), and A-state (Worry-Emotionality Inventory [WEI]). The results indicated that the physiological and psychological measures of anxiety were not related. Results provided evidence for the concurrent and construct validity of the CSAI-2.

Lewthwaite, R. (1986).   The nature of threat perception in competitive trait anxiety: The endangerment of important goals (Doctoral dissertation, University of California, Los Angeles, 1985). *Dissertation Abstracts International*, **46**, 4453-4454B.

The relationship between competitive A-trait and associated threat perception was examined in 102 9- to 15-year-old soccer players. A conceptual framework for competitive trait anxiety was proposed with the central prediction that competitive A-trait is a function of threat appraisal, which occurs when children perceive that important personal goals are endangered through sport competition. The measurement of competitive A-trait was expanded in the study, as both the somatic and the cognitive manifestations of competitive A-trait and the frequency and the intensity of these constructs were measured. Correlational analyses indicated weak to moderate support for the hypothesized relationship between indicants of competitive A-trait and a summary measure of threat to important goals. Multiple regression analyses indicated that competitive achievement factors and effort and mastery achievement goals were the strongest predictors of the competitive A-trait indicants.

Martin, T.R. (1978).   A comparison of the effect of trait anxiety levels on the performance of a complex motor response time task as a function of pre-stimulus delay (Doctoral dissertation, West Virginia University, 1978). *Dissertation Abstracts International*, **38**, 7212A.

The effect of competitive A-trait on the performance of a motor response time task was examined. Undergraduate students who scored in the upper and the lower 20 percentiles of SCAT ($N = 72$) were selected as subjects. The results indicated that experience, prestimulus delay period, competition, and competitive A-trait were related to performance of a complex motor task.

McClean, E. (1984).   The relationship of attentional style and anxiety patterns to performance tendencies in intercollegiate basketball competition (Doctoral dissertation, University of Tennessee, 1984). *Dissertation Abstracts International*, **45**, 1103A.

Two male collegiate basketball players completed the TAIS and SCAT in a noncompetitive situation and then completed the STAI immediately after 10 intercollegiate games. The coach rated the athletes' performances in each of the games. Attentional style was related to performance, but competitive A-trait was not. Competitive A-trait was not consistently related to A-state as measured by the STAI.

McSweeney, F.P. (1984).   Hemispheric EEG lateralization and achievement motivation in average and elite male and female adolescent distance runners (Doctoral dissertation, Rutgers University, 1983). *Dissertation Abstracts International*, **45**, 359B.

The relationship between hemispheric functioning and competitive A-trait was examined using 38 adolescent distance runners. Subjects completed SCAT and were recorded on an EEG while watching a video presentation of a triathlon competition. Measures were taken during the film as well as before and after the film. No relationship was found between EEG measures and competitive A-trait.

Millhouse, J.A. (1981).   Cognitive control of competitive anxiety (Doctoral dissertation, West Virginia University, 1980). *Dissertation Abstracts International*, **41**, 4640B.

The effectiveness of two cognitive-behavioral techniques in reducing anxiety and facilitating performance was investigated. Nine collegiate track-and-field athletes were randomly assigned to a cognitive restructuring (CR) group, a cognitive restructuring with self-monitoring instructions (CRSMI) group, and a control (C) group. Pre-, post-, and follow-up measures were taken using SCAT. Self-report ratings of anxiety, perceived physiological anxiety, confidence, and excitement were taken before five track meets. Both treatment groups reduced competitive A-trait on the post and follow-up SCAT measures to a greater extent than did the control group. These differences also were found in the ratings of self-reported anxiety and perceived physiological anxiety.

Moulds, E.E. (1979).   Selected physiological measures of arousal of high- and low-trait-anxiety females during competition (Doctoral dissertation, Louisiana State University, 1978). *Dissertation Abstracts International*, **39**, 6635A.

The relationship between A-state (STAI), competitive A-trait, and selected physiological measures of arousal was examined using 30 subjects competing on a video game. No significant differences were found between high and low competitive A-trait subjects on the three physiological measures of arousal. High competitive A-trait subjects were higher than were low competitive A-trait subjects on both the pre- and the postcompetitive A-state measures.

Nault, L.P. (1981).   The effect of achievement motivation and perceived relative ability on risk-taking behavior and motor performance (Doctoral dissertation, University of Southern California, 1981). *Dissertation Abstracts International*, **41**, 4645A.

Sixty male college students were subdivided as Ms and Maf on the basis of scores on SCAT and the Mehrabian Achievement Scale for Males and performed a bodily balance task. It was predicted that regardless of perceived ability, Ms subjects would select tasks of intermediate difficulty and that Maf subjects would select tasks of intermediate difficulty as their perceived ability increased. Neither prediction was supported, but Ms subjects performed better than did Maf subjects.

Pierce, W.J. (1980).   Psychological perspectives of youth sport participants and nonparticipants (Doctoral dissertation, Virginia Polytechnic Institute and State University, 1980). *Dissertation Abstracts International,* **41,** 2500A.

To determine the relationship between stress and participation in youth sports, 436 children in Grades 6 through 11 and 106 youth sport participants completed the Sport Participation Questionnaire and SCAT. The primary source of stress for youth sport participants was concern with skills. All subjects selected fear of a poor individual performance as their greatest source of stress. Little variation was found between participants, nonparticipants, and former participants on sources of stress and competitive A-trait.

Schloder, M.E. (1988).   Effects of teaching styles on performance, anxiety, and attitude toward instruction of college novice swimmers (Doctoral dissertation, Arizona State University, 1987). *Dissertation Abstracts International,* **49,** 458A.

The effects of an authoritarian teaching style versus a liberal/eclectic teaching style on the performance, anxiety, and attitude of 84 college novice swimmers were examined. No differences in competitive A-trait as measured by SCAT were indicated between groups. A significant relationship was indicated between SCAT and the Autonomic Perception Questionnaire ($r = 24$). Female subjects were higher in competitive A-trait than were males.

Seabourne, T.G. (1984).   The effect of individualized, non-individualized, and package cognitive intervention strategies on karate performance (Doctoral dissertation, North Texas State University, 1983). *Dissertation Abstracts International,* **44,** 3332A.

The effectiveness of different cognitive intervention strategies on karate performance, competitive A-trait, A-state, and attentional profile was examined using 43 male karate students. Subjects were randomly assigned to individualized, non-individualized, package, placebo control, and control groups. All treatment groups practiced their cognitive strategies over a 15-week period that included handouts, mini-strategies, manipulation checks, and interviews. No significant differences were found among groups on any of the psychological measures, although some performance differences were found.

Smith, D.E. (1987).   Evaluation of an imagery training program with intercollegiate basketball players (Doctoral dissertation, University of Illinois, 1987). *Dissertation Abstracts International,* **48,** 336A.

An imagery training program was conducted for 12 members of a male collegiate basketball team over the course of a season, and changes in physical and psychological skills were assessed. Two other teams were used as control groups for the study. No differences were found in competitive A-trait or competitive A-state

(CSAI-2) between the treatment and the control athletes. SCAT was included as a measure in the psychological profiles of the treatment subjects to aid the investigator in understanding the competitive A-trait levels of athletes to individualize the imagery treatments.

Spiker, D.D. (1983). An assessment and treatment of precompetitive state anxiety among collegiate baseball players (Doctoral dissertation, West Virginia University, 1982). *Dissertation Abstracts International*, **43**, 3841A.

Members of a collegiate baseball team ($N = 22$) were given SCAT and the CSAQ on two occasions. By averaging and combining SCAT and CSAQ scores, 9 high competitive A-trait subjects were retained in the study. The CSAI and Present Affect Reactions Questionnaire III (PARQIII) were administered to these 9 subjects under noncompetitive and precompetitive conditions. By averaging and combining CSAI and PARQIII scores, 2 high competitive A-state subjects were retained in the study. The effectiveness of cognitive restructuring and progressive relaxation training in reducing competitive A-state was then examined.

Vasser, B.W. (1984). An investigation of the effect of relaxation, attentional control strategies and conation training on female students' locus of control and state-trait anxiety (Doctoral dissertation, University of Pittsburgh, 1984). *Dissertation Abstracts International*, **45**, 1302A.

The effects of relaxation training, attentional control training, and conation training on selected psychological constructs were examined. Fifty-three high school students were divided into experimental and control groups. Differences between groups were found for locus of control, but no significant differences between groups were indicated for competitive A-trait, attentional style (TAIS), or A-state (STAI).

Voss, R.R. (1982). The effects of participation in new games workshops on competitive A-trait and achievement motivation of adults (Doctoral dissertation, Florida State University, 1982). *Dissertation Abstracts International*, **42**, 5057A.

This study was conducted to determine the effect of new-games workshop participation on adults' competitive A-trait and achievement motivation. Subjects ($N = 142$) completed SCAT and Mehrabian's Motivation to Achieve Test (MAT) before and after workshop participation. The only significant difference found was that females scored higher in competitive A-trait on both the pretest and the posttest than did males.

Wagner, D.B. (1984). Sports anxiety reduction techniques to improve golf performance (Doctoral dissertation, Hofstra University, 1983). *Dissertation Abstracts International*, **45**, 1275B.

Male high school golfers ($N = 51$) were randomly assigned to five conditions: relaxation, imaginal rehearsal, thought-stopping/self-instruction, thought stopping/ neutral statements, and an attention control group. Each treatment group received 6 hours of instruction in five sessions over a 4-week period. Subjects were pre- and posttested on SCAT and the STAI. None of the treatments had any effect on self-reported anxiety. Some treatment effects on performance were noted.

Wolfe, J.E. (1980).   Anthropometrical, physiological and psychological measures to predict performance in cross-country skiing (Doctoral dissertation, University of Northern Colorado, 1979). *Dissertation Abstracts International*, **40**, 4478A.

The relationships among competitive A-trait, lean body weight, physical work capacity, and cross-country skiing performance in 75 skiers were examined. Using multiple regression analyses, lean body weight, physical work capacity, and competitive A-trait were found to be significant predictors of performance for males.

Zimet, L. (1985).   Children's sport trait anxiety and professionalized sport attitude in three racially different communities (Doctoral dissertation, University of Maryland, 1984). *Dissertation Abstracts International*, **46**, 518A.

The relationship among competitive A-trait, sport attitude, and various individual and demographic factors was examined. Children in Grades 3 through 6 ($N = 740$) completed SCAT and the Webb scale. Gender and community type had the greatest effects on competitive A-trait, as girls were higher in competitive A-trait than were boys, and nonrural subjects were higher in competitive A-trait than were rural subjects. Competitive A-trait and sport attitude were not related.

Zwart, E.F. (1987).   Attentional and anxiety responses of athletes to mental training techniques (Doctoral dissertation, Syracuse University, 1985). *Dissertation Abstracts International*, **47**, 2504A.

This study explored changes in competitive A-trait, attentional style, and performance in 13- to 15-year-old swimmers ($N = 30$) after exposure to the Super- learning mental training program. The treatment consisted of a 6-week program of relaxation training, positive affirmation, breathing exercises, and mental rehearsal. SCAT and the TAIS were adminstered pre- and posttreatment. Competitive A-trait was significantly lower after exposure to the training program. There was also greater improvement in performance in low competitive A-trait athletes than in high competitive A-trait athletes.

Appendix C

Published Empirical Studies Using the CSAI-2[5]

Albrecht & Feltz, 1987

Barnes, Sime, Dienstbier, & Plake, 1986

Burton, 1988

Crocker, Alderman, & Smith, 1988

Gould, Petlichkoff, Simons, & Vevera, 1987

Gould, Petlichkoff, & Weinberg, 1984

Karteroliotis & Gill, 1987

Krane & Williams, 1987

Maynard & Howe, 1987

McAuley, 1985

Murphy, Woolfolk, & Budney, 1988

Taylor, 1987

Vealey, 1986

Weinberg, Jackson, & Seabourne, 1985

Weinberg, Seabourne, & Jackson, 1987

Yan Lan & Gill, 1984

---

[5]Complete references for these studies are included in the reference list of this book.

References

Albrecht, R.R., & Feltz, D.L. (1987). Generality and specificity of attention related to competitive anxiety and sport performance. *Journal of Sport Psychology*, **9**, 231-248.

Alderman, R.B. (1976). *The Alberta Incentive Motivation Inventory*. Edmonton: University of Alberta.

Allen, M.J., & Yen, W.M. (1979). *Introduction to measurement theory*. Monterey, CA: Brooks/Cole.

Alpert, R., & Haber, R.N. (1960). Anxiety in academic achievement situations. *Journal of Abnormal and Social Psychology*, **61**, 207-215.

American Psychological Association. (1974). *Standards for educational and psychological tests*. Washington, DC: Author.

Anderson, M.B., & Williams, J.M. (1987). Gender role and sport competition anxiety: A re-examination. *Research Quarterly for Exercise and Sport*, **58**, 52-56.

Anderson, N.H. (1970). Function measurement and psychophysical judgment. *Psychological Review*, **77**, 153-170.

Atkinson, J.W. (1957). Motivational determinants of risk-taking behavior. *Psychological Review*, **64**, 359-372.

Atkinson, J.W., & Feather, N.T. (1966). *A theory of achievement motivation*. New York: Wiley.

Auvergne, S. (1983). Motivation and causal attribution for high and low achieving athletes. *International Journal of Sport Psychology*, **14**, 85-91.

Bandura, A. (1977). Self-efficacy: Toward a unifying theory of behavioral change. *Psychological Review*, **84**, 191-215.

Bandura, A. (1978). The self-system in reciprocal determinism. *American Psychologist*, **37**, 334-348.

Barnes, M.W., Sime, W., Dienstbier, R., & Plake, B. (1986). A test of construct validity of the CSAI-2 questionnaire on male elite college swimmers. *International Journal of Sport Psychology*, **17**, 364-374.

Barratt, E.S. (1972). Anxiety and impulsiveness: Toward a neuro-psychological model. In C.D. Spielberger (Ed.), *Anxiety: Current trends in theory and research* (Vol. 1, pp. 195-222). New York: Academic Press.

Bem, S.L. (1974). The measurement of psychological androgyny. *Journal of Consulting and Clinical Psychology*, **42**, 155-162.

Bem, S.L. (1978). *The short Bem Sex Role Inventory*. Palo Alto, CA: Consulting Psychologists.

Berlyne, D.E. (1960). Conflict, arousal, and curiosity. New York: McGraw-Hill.

Betts, E. (1982). Relation of locus of control to aspiration level and to competitive anxiety. *Psychological Reports*, **51**, 71-76.

Bialer, I. (1961). Conceptualization of success and failure in mentally retarded and normal children. *Journal of Personality*, **29**, 303-320.

Biddle, S.J.H., & Jamieson, K.I. (1988). Attribution dimensions: Conceptual clarification and moderator variables. *International Journal of Sport Psychology*, **19**, 47-59.

Blais, M.R., & Vallerand, R.J. (1986). Multimodal effects of electromyographic biofeedback: Looking at children's ability to control precompetitive anxiety. *Journal of Sport Psychology*, **8**, 283-303.

Borkovec, T.D. (1976). Physiological and cognitive processes in the regulation of anxiety. In G. Schwartz & D. Shapiro (Eds.), *Consciousness and self-regulation: Advances in research* (Vol. 1, pp. 261-312). New York: Phelem Press.

Bowers, K.S. (1973). Situationism in psychology: An analysis and a critique. *Psychological Review*, **80**, 307-336.

Broadhurst, P.L. (1957). Emotionality and the Yerkes-Dodson law. *Journal of Experimental Psychology*, **54**, 345-352.

Broughton, R.S., & Perlstrom, J.R. (1986). PK experiments with a competitive computer game. *Journal of Parapsychology*, **50**, 193-211.

Brustad, R.J. (1986). *Affective outcomes in competitive youth sport: The influence of intrapersonal and socialization factors*. Unpublished doctoral dissertation, University of Oregon, Eugene.

Brustad, R.J. (1988). Affective outcomes in competitive youth sport: The influence of intrapersonal and socialization factors. *Journal of Sport and Exercise Psychology*, **10**, 307-321.

Brustad, R.J., & Weiss, M.R. (1987). Competence perceptions and sources of worry in high, medium, and low competitive trait-anxious young athletes. *Journal of Sport Psychology*, **9**, 97-105.

Bunker, L.K., & Rotella, R. (1980). Achievement and stress in sport: Research findings and practical suggestions. In W.F. Straub (Ed.), *Sport Psychology: An analysis of athlete behavior* (pp. 104-125). Ithaca, NY: Mouvement.

Burhans, R.S., Richman, C.L., & Bergey, D.B. (1988). Mental imagery training: Effects on running speed performance. *International Journal of Sport Psychology*, **19**, 26-37.

Burton, D. (1988). Do anxious swimmers swim slower? Reexamining the elusive anxiety-performance relationship. *Journal of Sport and Exercise Psychology*, **10**, 45-61.

Buss, A.H. (1962). Two anxiety factors in psychiatric patients. *Journal of Abnormal and Social Psychology*, **65**, 426-427.

Carden, R.L. (1979). *The relationship of locus of control and extraversion to test anxiety and test impulsiveness*. Unpublished master's thesis, Middle Tennessee State University, Murfreesboro.

Carron, A.V. (1980). *Social psychology of sport*. Ithaca, NY: Mouvement.

Carson, R.C. (1969). *Interaction concepts of personality*. Chicago: Aldine.

Cattell, R.B. (1957). *The IPAT anxiety scale*. Champaign, IL: Institute for Personality and Ability Testing.

Cattell, R.B., & Cattell, M.D. (1969). *Junior-senior high school personality questionnaire*. Champaign, IL: Institute for Personality and Ability Testing.

Cheatham, T., & Rosentswieg, J. (1982). Validation of the Sport Competition Anxiety Test. *Perceptual and Motor Skills*, **55**, 1343-1346.

Colley, A., Roberts, N., & Chipps, A. (1985). Sex-role identity, personality, and participation in team and individual sports by males and females. *International Journal of Sport Psychology*, **16**, 103-112.

Cooley, E.J. (1987). Situational and trait determinants of competitive state anxiety. *Perceptual and Motor Skills*, **64**, 767-773.

Cooley, E.J., & Spiegler, M.D. (1980). Cognitive versus emotional coping responses as alternatives to test anxiety. *Cognitive Therapy and Research*, **4**, 159-166.

Costill, D.L. (1985). Practical problems in exercise physiology research. *Research Quarterly for Exercise and Sport*, **56**, 378-384.

Cox, R.H. (1985). *Sport psychology: Concepts and applications*. Dubuque, IA: Wm. C. Brown.

Cox, R.H. (in press). Relationship between performance in women's volleyball and selected psychological measures. In L. VanderVelden & J.H. Humphrey (Eds.), *Psychology and sociology of sport: Current and selected research* (Vol. 2). New York: AMS Press.

Crandall, V. (1974). *Achievement motivation: The Crandall model*. Paper presented at the University of Illinois Seminar, Urbana.

Cratty, B.J. (1983). *Psychology in contemporary sport: Guidelines for coaches and athletes* (2nd ed.). Englewood Cliffs, NJ: Prentice-Hall.

Crocker, P.R.E., Alderman, R.B., & Smith, F.M.R. (1988). Cognitive-affective stress management training with high performance youth volleyball players: Effects on affect, cognition, and performance. *Journal of Sport and Exercise Psychology*, **10**, 448-460.

Crowne, D.P., & Marlowe, D. (1960). A new scale of social desirability independent of psychopathology. *Journal of Consulting Psychology*, **24**, 349-354.

Davidson, R.J. (1978). Specificity and patterning in biobehavioral systems. *American Psychologist*, **33**, 430-436.

Davidson, R.J., & Schwartz, G.E. (1976). The psychobiology of relaxation and related states: A multi-process theory. In D. Mostofsky (Ed.), *Behavioral control and modification of physiological activity* (pp. 399-442). Englewood Cliffs, NJ: Prentice-Hall.

Deffenbacher, J.L. (1977). Relationship of worry and emotionality to performance on the Miller Analogies Test. *Journal of Educational Psychology*, **69**, 191-195.

Deffenbacher, J.L. (1978). Worry, emotionality, and task-generated interference in test anxiety: An empirical test of attentional theory. *Journal of Educational Psychology*, **70**, 248-254.

Deffenbacher, J.L. (1980). Worry and emotionality in test anxiety. In I.G. Sarason (Ed.), *Test anxiety: Theory, research and applications* (pp. 111-128). Hillsdale, NJ: Erlbaum.

Deffenbacher, J.L., & Dietz, S.R. (1978). Effects of test anxiety on performance, worry, and emotionality in naturally occurring exams. *Psychology in the Schools*, **15**, 446-450.

Deffenbacher, J.L., Mathis, H., & Michaels, A.C. (1979). Two self-control procedures in the reduction of targeted and nontargeted anxieties. *Journal of Counseling Psychology*, **26**, 120-127.

Deffenbacher, J.L., Michaels, A.C., Michaels, T., & Daley, P.C. (1980). Comparison of anxiety management training and self-control desensitization. *Journal of Counseling Psychology*, **27**, 232-239.

DeWitt, D.J. (1980). Cognitive and biofeedback training for stress reduction with university athletes. *Journal of Sport Psychology*, **2**, 288-294.

Doctor, R.M., & Altman, F. (1969). Worry and emotionality as components of test anxiety: Replication and further data. *Psychological Reports*, **24**, 563-568.

Dothwaite, P.K., & Armstrong, M.R. (1984). An investigation into the anxiety levels of soccer players. *International Journal of Sport Psychology*, **15**, 149-159.

Duda, J.L. (1985). Goals and achievement orientations of Anglo and Mexican-American adolescents in sport and the classroom. *International Journal of Intercultural Relations*, **9**, 131-155.

Duda, J.L. (1986). A cross-cultural analysis of achievement motivation in sport and the classroom. In L. VanderVelden & J. Humphrey (Eds.), *Current selected research in the psychology and sociology of sport* (pp. 117-131). New York: AMS Press.

Durtschi, S.K., & Weiss, M.R. (1984). Psychological characteristics of elite and nonelite marathon runners. In D.M. Landers (Ed.), *Sport and elite performers* (pp. 73-80). Champaign, IL: Human Kinetics.

Ellis, A. (1969). *Reason and emotion in psychotherapy*. New York: Lyle Stuart.

Ellis, M.J. (1973). *Why people play*. Englewood Cliffs, NJ: Prentice-Hall.

Emerson, R.M. (1966). Mount Everest: A case study in communication feedback and sustained group goal-striving. *Sociometry*, **29**, 213-227.

Endler, N.S. (1978). The interaction model of anxiety: Some possible implications. In D.M. Landers & R.W. Christina (Eds.), *Psychology of motor behavior and sport—1977* (pp. 332-351). Champaign, IL: Human Kinetics.

Endler, N.S., Hunt, J.M., & Rosenstein, A.J. (1962). An S-R inventory of anxiousness. *Psychological Monographs*, **76**(Whole No. 536).

Ewing, M.E. (1981). *Achievement orientations and sport behavior of males and females*. Unpublished doctoral dissertation, University of Illinois.

Feltz, D.L. (1982). Path analysis of the causal elements of Bandura's theory of self-efficacy and an anxiety-based model of avoidance behavior. *Journal of Personality and Social Psychology* **42**, 764-781.

Feltz, D.L., & Albrecht, R.R. (1986). Psychological implications of competitive running. In M.R. Weiss & D. Gould (Eds.), *Sport for children and youths* (pp. 225-230). Champaign, IL: Human Kinetics.

Feltz, D.L., Landers, D.M., & Raeder, U. (1979). Enhancing self-efficacy in high-avoidance motor tasks: A comparison of modeling techniques. *Journal of Sport Psychology*, **1**, 112-122.

Fenz, W.D. (1975). Coping mechanisms and performance under stress. In D.M. Landers (Ed.), *Psychology of sport and motor behavior-2* (pp. 3-24). University Park: Pennsylvania State University, College of Health, Physical Education, and Recreation.

Fenz, W.D., & Epstein, S. (1967). Gradients of physiological arousal in parachutists as a function of an approaching jump. *Psychosomatic Medicine*, **29**, 33-51.

Fenz, W.D., & Jones, G.B. (1972). Individual differences in physiologic arousal and performance in sport parachutists. *Psychosomatic Medicine*, **34**, 1-8.

Festinger, L. (1954). A theory of social comparison processes. *Human Relations*, **7**, 117-140.

Fisher, A.C., Horsfall, J.S., & Morris, H.H. (1977). Sport personality assessment: A methodical re-examination. *International Journal of Sport Psychology*, **1**, 76-86.

Fisher, A.C., & Zwart, E.F. (1982). Psychological analysis of athletes' anxiety responses. *Journal of Sport Psychology*, **4**, 139-158.

Furst, D.M., & Tenenbaum, G. (1984). The relationship between worry, emotionality, and sport performance. In D.M. Landers (Ed.), *Sport and elite performers* (pp. 89-96). Champaign, IL: Human Kinetics.

Gerson, R., & Deshaies, P. (1978). Competitive trait anxiety and performance as predictors of precompetitive state anxiety. *International Journal of Sport Psychology*, **9**, 16-26.

Gill, D.L. (1986a). Competitiveness among females and males in physical activity classes. *Sex Roles*, **15**, 233-247.

Gill, D.L. (1986b). *Psychological dynamics of sport*. Champaign, IL: Human Kinetics.

Gill, D.L. (1988). Gender differences in competitive orientation and sport participation. *International Journal of Sport Psychology*, **19**, 145-159.

Gill, D.L., & Deeter, T.E. (1988). Development of the Sport Orientation Questionnaire. *Research Quarterly for Exercise and Sport*, **59**, 191-202.

Gill, D.L., Dzewaltowski, D.A., & Deeter, T.E. (1988). The relationship of competitiveness and achievement orientation to participation in sport and nonsport activities. *Journal of Sport and Exercise Psychology*, **10**, 139-150.

Gill, D.L., & Martens, R. (1977). The role of task type and success-failure in group competition. *International Journal of Sport Psychology*, **8**, 160-177.

Goldfried, M.R., Lineham, M.M., & Smith, J.L. (1978). Reduction of test anxiety through cognitive restructuring. *Journal of Consulting and Clinical Psychology*, **46**, 32-39.

Goleman, D. (1971). Meditation as meta-therapy: Hypotheses toward a proposed fifth state of consciousness. *Journal of Transpersonal Psychology*, **3**, 1-25.

Gould, D., Horn, T., & Spreeman, J. (1983a). Competitive anxiety in junior elite wrestlers. *Journal of Sport Psychology*, **5**, 58-71.

Gould, D., Horn, T., & Spreeman, J. (1983b). Sources of stress in junior elite wrestlers. *Journal of Sport Psychology*, **5**, 159-171.

Gould, D., & Petlichkoff, L. (1988). Psychological stress and the age-group wrestler. In E.W. Brown & C.F. Branta (Eds.), *Competitive sports for children and youth* (pp. 63-73). Champaign, IL: Human Kinetics.

Gould, D., Petlichkoff, L., Simons, J., & Vevera, M. (1987). Relationship between Competitive State Anxiety Inventory—2 subscale scores and pistol shooting performance. *Journal of Sport Psychology*, **9**, 33-42.

Gould, D., Petlichkoff, L., & Weinberg, R.S. (1984). Antecedents of, temporal changes in, and relationships between CSAI-2 subcomponents. *Journal of Sport Psychology*, **6**, 289-304.

Gould, D., & Weinberg, R. (1985). Sources of worry in successful and less successful intercollegiate wrestlers. *Journal of Sport Behavior*, **8**, 115-127.

Gravelle, L., Searle, R., & St. Jean, P. (1982). Personality profiles of the Canadian women's national volleyball team. *Volleyball Technical Journal*, **7**, 13-17.

Gray, J.J., & Haring, M.J. (1984). Mental rehearsal for sport performance: Exploring the relaxation-imagery paradigm. *Journal of Sport Behavior*, **7**, 68-78.

Griffin, M.R. (1972). An analysis of state and trait anxiety experienced in sports competition at different age levels. *Foil* (Spring), 58-64.

Hahnloser, R.M. (1974). A comparison of cognitive restructuring and progressive relaxation in test anxiety reduction. *Dissertation Abstracts International*, **35**, 1444A. (University Microfilms No. 74-18, 897)

Hall, E.G., & Erffmeyer, E.S. (1983). The effect of visuo-motor behavior rehearsal with videotaped modeling on free throw accuracy of intercollegiate female basketball players. *Journal of Sport Psychology*, **5**, 343-346.

Hamilton, S.A., & Fremouw, W.J. (1985). Cognitive-behavioral training for college basketball free-throw performance. *Cognitive Therapy and Research*, **9**, 479-484.

Hanin, Y.L. (1982). Adaptation of the Sport Competition Anxiety Test. *The Questions of Psychology*, **3**, 136-141. (From *Journal of Sport Psychology*, **4**, 308-309)

Hanson, T.W., & Gould, D. (1988). Factors affecting the ability of coaches to estimate their athletes' trait and state anxiety levels. *The Sport Psychologist*, **2**, 298-313.

Harter, S. (1978). Effectance motivation reconsidered: Toward a developmental model. *Human Development*, **21**, 34-64.

Harter, S. (1979). *Perceived competence scale for children* (Form O) [Manual]. Denver: University of Denver.

Hellstedt, J.C. (1987). Sport psychology at a ski academy: Teaching mental skills to young athletes. *The Sport Psychologist*, **1**, 56-68.

Highlen, P.S., & Bennett, B.B. (1979). Psychological characteristics of successful and unsuccessful elite wrestlers: An exploratory study. *Journal of Sport Psychology*, **1**, 123-137.

Hogg, J.M. (1980). Anxiety and the competitive swimmer. *Canadian Journal of Applied Sport Sciences*, **5**, 183-187.

Holroyd, K.A. (1978). Effectiveness of an "attribution therapy" manipulation with test anxiety. *Behavior Therapy*, **9**, 526-534.

Holroyd, K.A., Westbrook, T., Wolf, M., & Badhorn, E. (1978). Performance, cognition and physiological responding in test anxiety. *Journal of Abnormal Psychology*, **87**, 442-451.

Huband, E.D., & McKelvie, J.S. (1986). Pre and post game state anxiety in team athletes high and low in competitive trait anxiety. *International Journal of Sport Psychology*, **17**, 191-198.

Hunter, J.E., Schmidt, F.L., & Jackson, G.B. (1982). *Meta-analysis: Cumulating research findings across studies*. Beverly Hills, CA: Sage Publications.

Iso-Ahola, S.E., & Hatfield, B. (1986). *Psychology of sports: A social psychological approach*. Dubuque, IA: Wm. C. Brown.

Jaspen, N. (1946). Serial correlation. *Psychometrika*, **11**, 23-30.

Johnston-O'Connor, E.J., & Kirschenbaum, D.S. (1986). Something succeeds like success: Positive self-monitoring for unskilled golfers. *Cognitive Therapy and Research*, **10**, 123-136.

Kagan, J. (1972). Motives and development. *Journal of Personality and Social Psychology*, **22**, 51-66.

Kaplan, R.M., McCordick, S.M., & Twitchell, M. (1979). Is it the cognitive or the behavioral component which makes cognitive-behavior modification effective in test anxiety? *Journal of Counseling Psychology*, **26**, 371-377.

Karteroliotis, C., & Gill, D.L. (1987). Temporal changes in psychological and physiological components of state anxiety. *Journal of Sport Psychology*, **9**, 261-274.

Kerlinger, F.N. (1973). *Foundations of behavioral research* (2nd ed.). New York: Holt, Rinehart and Winston.

Kirkland, K., & Hollandsworth, J.G. (1980). Effective test taking: Skills-acquisition versus anxiety-reduction techniques. *Journal of Consulting and Clinical Psychology*, **48**, 431-439.

Kirschenbaum, D.S., & Bale, R.M. (1980). Cognitive-behavioral skills in golf: Brain power golf. In R.M. Suinn (Ed.), *Psychology in sports: Methods and applications* (pp. 334-343). Minneapolis: Burgess.

Kirschenbaum, D.S., Ordman, A.M., Tomarken, A.J., & Holtzbauer, R. (1982). Effects of differential self-monitoring and level mastery on sports performance: Brain power bowling. *Cognitive Therapy and Research*, **6**, 335-342.

Kirschenbaum, D.S., Wittrock, D.A., Smith, R.J., & Monson, W. (1984). Criticism inoculation training: Concept in search of strategy. *Journal of Sport Psychology*, **6**, 77-93.

Klavora, P. (1978). An attempt to derive inverted-U curves based on the relationship between anxiety and athletic performance. In D.M. Landers & R.W. Christina (Eds.), *Psychology of motor behavior and sport* (pp. 369-377). Champaign, IL: Human Kinetics.

Kolonay, B.J. (1977). *The effects of visuo-motor behavior rehearsal on athletic performance.* Unpublished master's thesis, City University of New York, Hunter College.

Koyama, S., Inomata, K., & Takeda, T. (1980). Competitive anxiety of tennis players in varying situations. *Japanese Journal of Sport Psychology, 7,* 1. (From *International Journal of Sport Psychology,* 1982, *13,* 278-279.)

Krane, V., & Williams, J.M. (1986). *Relationship of cognitive anxiety, somatic anxiety, and self confidence to performance in male and female track and field athletes.* Unpublished manuscript, University of Arizona, Tucson.

Krane, V., & Williams, J.M. (1987). Performance and somatic anxiety, cognitive anxiety, and confidence changes prior to competition. *Journal of Sport Behavior, 10,* 47-56.

Kroll, W. (1979). The stress of high performance athletics. In P. Klavora & J.V. Daniel (Eds.), *Coach, athlete, and sport psychologist* (pp. 211-219). Champaign, IL: Human Kinetics.

Krotee, M.L. (1980). The effects of various physical activity situational settings on the anxiety level of children. *Journal of Sport Behavior, 3,* 158-164.

Landers, D.M., & Boutcher, S.H. (1986). Arousal-performance relationships. In J.M. Williams (Ed.), *Applied sport psychology: Personal growth to peak performance* (pp. 163-184). Palo Alto, CA: Mayfield.

Lane, J.F. (1980). Improving athletic performance through visuo-motor behavior rehearsal. In R.M. Suinn (Ed.), *Psychology in sports: Methods and applications* (pp. 316-320). Minneapolis: Burgess.

Lanning, W., & Hisanaga, B. (1983). A study of the relation between the reduction of competition anxiety and an increase in athletic performance. *International Journal of Sport Psychology, 14,* 219-227.

Layman, E.M. (1978). Meditation and sports performance. In W.F. Straub (Ed.), *Sport psychology: An analysis of athlete behavior* (pp. 266-273). Ithaca, NY: Mouvement.

Lehrer, P.M., Schoicket, S., Carrington, P., & Woolfold, R.L. (1980). Psychophysiological and cognitive responses to stressful stimuli in subjects practicing progressive relaxation and clinically standardized meditation. *Behavior Research and Therapy, 18,* 293-303.

Levy, N.A. (1958). A short form of the children's manifest anxiety scale. *Child Development, 29,* 153-154.

Lewin, K. (1935). *A dynamic theory of personality.* New York: McGraw-Hill.

Lewthwaite, R. (1986). The nature of threat perception in competitive trait anxiety: The endangerment of important goals (Doctoral dissertation, University of California, Los Angeles, 1985). *Dissertation Abstracts International, 46,* 4453-4454B.

Lewthwaite, R. (1988). *Threat perception in competitive trait anxiety: The endangerment of important goals.* Manuscript submitted for publication.

Liebert, R.M., & Morris, L.W. (1967). Cognitive and emotional components of test anxiety: A distinction and some initial data. *Psychological Reports*, **20**, 975-978.

Maehr, M.L., & Nicholls, J.G. (1980). Culture and achievement motivation: A second look. In N. Warren (Ed.), *Studies in cross-cultural psychology* (pp. 221-267). New York: Academic Press.

Magill, R.A., & Ash, M.J. (1979). Academic, psycho-social, and motor characteristics of participants and non-participants in children's sport. *Research Quarterly*, **50**, 230-240.

Magnusson, D. (1966). *Test theory*. Reading, MA: Addison-Wesley.

Mahoney, M.J., & Avener, M. (1977). Psychology of the elite athlete: An exploratory study. *Cognitive Therapy and Research*, **1**, 135-141.

Mandler, G., & Sarason, S.B. (1952). A study of anxiety and learning. *Journal of Abnormal and Social Psychology*, **47**, 166-173.

Martens, R. (1974). Arousal and motor performance. In J.H. Wilmore (Ed.), *Exercise and sport sciences review* (Vol. 2, pp. 155-188). New York: Academic Press.

Martens, R. (1975a). *Social psychology and physical activity*. New York: Harper & Row.

Martens, R. (1975b). The paradigmatic crisis in American sport personology. *Sportwissenschaft*, **5**, 9-24.

Martens, R. (1976). Competition: In need of a theory. In D.M. Landers (Ed.), *Social problems in athletics* (pp. 9-17). Urbana: University of Illinois Press.

Martens, R. (1977). *Sport competition anxiety test*. Champaign, IL: Human Kinetics.

Martens, R. (1979). About smocks and jocks. *Journal of Sport Psychology*, **1**, 94-99.

Martens, R. (1988). Competitive anxiety in children's sports. In R.M. Malina (Ed.), *Young athletes: Biological, psychological, and educational perspectives* (pp. 235-244). Champaign, IL: Human Kinetics.

Martens, R., Burton, D., Rivkin, F., & Simon, J. (1980). Reliability and validity of the Competitive State Anxiety Inventory (CSAI). In C.H. Nadeau, W.C. Halliwell, K.M. Newell, & G.C. Roberts (Eds.), *Psychology of motor behavior and sport—1979* (pp. 91-99). Champaign, IL: Human Kinetics.

Martens, R., Burton, D., Vealey, R.S., Bump, L.A., & Smith, D.E. (1982, May). Competitive state anxiety inventory-2. Symposium conducted at the meeting of the North American Society for the Psychology of Sport and Physical Activity (NASPSPA), College Park, MD.

Martens, R., & Gill, D.L. (1976). State anxiety among successful and unsuccessful competitors who differ in competitive trait anxiety. *Research Quarterly*, **47**, 698-708.

Martens, R., Gill, D.L., & Scanlan, T.K. (1976). Competitive trait anxiety, success-failure and sex as determinants of motor performance. *Perceptual and Motor Skills*, **43**, 1199-1208.

Martens, R., Gill, D., Simon, J.A., & Scanlan, T.K. (1975, October). Competitive anxiety: Theory and research. In *Mouvement: Proceedings of the*

Seventh Canadian Psychomotor Learning and Sport Psychology Symposium (pp. 289-292). Quebec City, PQ: Association of Professionals of Physical Activity of Quebec.

Martens, R., & Greer, D. (1980). *Precompetitive stress among high school wrestlers.* Unpublished manuscript.

Martens, R., Rivkin, F., & Burton, D. (1980). Who predicts anxiety better: Coaches or athletes? In C.H. Nadeau, W.R. Halliwell, K.M. Newell, & G.C. Roberts (Eds.), *Psychology of motor behavior and sport—1979* (pp. 84-90). Champaign, IL: Human Kinetics.

Martens, R., & Simon, J.A. (1976a). Comparison of three predictors of state anxiety in competitive situations. *Research Quarterly, 47,* 381-387.

Martens, R., & Simon, J.A. (1976b). *Competitive trait anxiety as a predictor of precompetitive state anxiety.* Unpublished manuscript, University of Illinois.

Maynard, I.W., & Howe, B.L. (1987). Interrelations of trait and state anxiety with game performance of rugby players. *Perceptual and Motor Skills, 64,* 599-602.

McAuley, E. (1985). State anxiety: Antecedent or result of sport performance. *Journal of Sport Behavior, 8,* 71-77.

McGrath, J.E. (1970a). A conceptual formulation for research on stress. In J.E. McGrath (Ed.), *Social and psychological factors in stress* (pp. 1-13). New York: Holt, Rinehart and Winston.

McGrath, J.E. (1970b). Major methodological issues. In J.E. McGrath (Ed.), *Social and psychological factors in stress* (pp. 14-29). New York: Holt, Rinehart and Winston.

McKelvie, S.J., & Huband, D.E. (1980). Locus of control and anxiety in college athletes and non-athletes. *Perceptual and Motor Skills, 50,* 819-822.

McKelvie, S.J., Valliant, P.M., & Asu, M.E. (1985). Physical training and personality factors as predictors of marathon time and training injury. *Perceptual and Motor Skills, 60,* 551-566.

Mechanic, D. (1970). Some problems in developing a social psychology of adaptation to stress. In J.E. McGrath (Ed.), *Social and psychological factors in stress* (pp. 104-123). New York: Holt, Rinehart and Winston.

Mehrabian, A. (1968). Male and female scales of the tendency to achieve. *Educational and Psychological Measurement, 28,* 493-502.

Meichenbaum, D. (1977). *Cognitive-behavior modification: An integrated approach.* New York: Plenum.

Mellstrom, M., Jr., Cicala, G.A., & Zuckerman, M. (1976). General versus specific trait anxiety measures in the prediction of fear of snakes, heights, and darkness. *Journal of Consulting and Clinical Psychology, 44,* 83-91.

Meyers, A.W., Cooke, C.J., Cullen, J., & Liles, L. (1979). Psychological aspects of athletic competitors: A replication across sports. *Cognitive Therapy and Research, 3,* 361-366.

Meyers, A.W., & Schleser, R. (1980). A cognitive behavioral intervention for improving basketball performance. *Journal of Sport Psychology, 2,* 69-73.

Meyers, A.W., Schleser, R., Cooke, C., & Cuvillier, C. (1979). Cognitive contributions to the development of gymnastics skills. *Cognitive Therapy and Research*, **3**, 75-85.

Miller, B.P., & Miller, A.J. (1985). Psychological correlates of success in elite sportswomen. *International Journal of Sport Psychology*, **16**, 289-295.

Mischel, W. (1968). *Personality and assessment*. New York: Wiley.

Mischel, W. (1973). Toward a cognitive social learning reconceptualization of personality. *Psychological Review*, **80**, 252-283.

Morgan, W.P. (1978, April). The mind of a marathoner. *Psychology Today*, pp. 38-49.

Morris, L.W., Brown, N.R., & Halbert, B. (1977). Effects of symbolic modeling on the arousal of cognitive and affective components of anxiety in preschool children. In C.D. Spielberger & I.G. Sarason (Eds.), *Stress and anxiety* (Vol. 4). Washington, DC: Hemisphere.

Morris, L., Davis, D., & Hutchings, C. (1981). Cognitive and emotional components of anxiety: Literature review and revised worry-emotionality scale. *Journal of Educational Psychology*, **73**, 541-555.

Morris, L.W., & Engle, W.B. (1981). Assessing various coping strategies and their effects on test performance and anxiety. *Journal of Clinical Psychology*, **37**, 165-171.

Morris, L.W., & Fulmer, R.S. (1976). Test anxiety (worry and emotionality) changes during academic testing as a function of feedback and test importance. *Journal of Educational Psychology*, **68**, 817-824.

Morris, L.W., Harris, E.W., & Rovins, D.S. (1981). Interactive effects of generalized and situational expectancies on cognitive and emotional components of social anxiety. *Journal of Research in Personality*, **15**, 302-311.

Morris, L.W., & Liebert, R.M. (1970). The relationship of cognitive and emotional components of test anxiety to physiological arousal and academic performance. *Journal of Consulting and Clinical Psychology*, **35**, 332-337.

Morris, L.W., & Liebert, R.M. (1973). Effects of negative feedback, threat of shock, and level of trait anxiety on the arousal of two components of anxiety. *Journal of Counseling Psychology*, **20**, 321-326.

Morris, L.W., & Perez, T.J. (1972). Effects of interruption on emotional expression and performance in a testing situation. *Psychological Reports*, **31**, 559-564.

Morris, L.W., Smith, L.R., Andrews, E.S., & Morris, N.C. (1975). The relationship of emotionality and worry components of anxiety to motor skills performance. *Journal of Motor Behavior*, **7**, 121-130.

Murphy, S.M., & Woolfolk, R.L. (1987). The effects of cognitive interventions on competitive anxiety and performance on a fine motor skill accuracy task. *International Journal of Sport Psychology*, **18**, 152-166.

Murphy, S.M., Woolfolk, R.L., & Budney, A.J. (1988). The effects of emotive imagery on strength performance. *Journal of Sport and Exercise Psychology*, **10**, 334-345.

Nicholls, J. (1984). Conceptions of ability and achievement motivation. In R. Ames & C. Ames (Eds.), *Research on motivation in education: Student motivation* (Vol. 1, pp. 64-92). New York: Academic Press.

Nideffer, R.M. (1976). Test of attentional and interpersonal style. *Journal of Personality and Social Psychology*, **34**, 394-404.

Nie, N.H., Hull, C.H., Jenkins, J.G., Steinbrenner, K., & Bent, D.H. (1975). *Statistical package for the social sciences* (2nd ed.). New York: McGraw-Hill.

Noel, R.C. (1980). The effect of visuo-motor behavior rehearsal on tennis performance. *Journal of Sport Psychology*, **2**, 221-226.

Osarchuk, M.M. (1976). A comparison of a cognitive, a behavior therapy, and a cognitive-and-behavior therapy treatment of test anxious college students (Doctoral dissertation, Adelphi University, 1974). *Dissertation Abstracts International*, **36**, 3619B. (University Microfilms No. 76-14, 25)

Ost, L.G., Jerremalm, A., & Johansson, J. (1981). Individual response patterns and the effects of different behavioral methods in the treatment of social phobia. *Behavioral Research and Therapy*, **19**, 1-16.

Ostrow, A.C., & Ziegler, S.G. (1978). Psychometric properties of the Sport Competition Anxiety Test. In B. Kerr (Ed.), *Human performance and behaviour* (pp. 139-142). Calgary, AB: University of Calgary.

Owie, I. (1981). Influence of sex-role standards in sport competition anxiety. *International Journal of Sport Psychology*, **12**, 289-292.

Oxendine, J.B. (1970). Emotional arousal and motor performance. *Quest*, **13**, 23-32.

Paivio, A., & Lambert, W.E. (1959). Measures and correlates of audience anxiety. *Journal of Personality*, **27**, 1-17.

Parks, S. (1980). *Self-consciousness and test anxiety*. Unpublished master's thesis, Middle Tennessee State University, Murfreesboro.

Passer, M.W. (1982). Children in sport: Participation motives and psychological stress. *Quest*, **33**, 231-244.

Passer, M.W. (1983). Fear of failure, fear of evaluation, perceived competence, and self-esteem in competitive-trait-anxious children. *Journal of Sport Psychology*, **5**, 172-188.

Passer, M.W. (1984). Competitive trait anxiety in children and adolescents. In J.M. Silva & R.S. Weinberg (Eds.), *Psychological foundations of sport* (pp. 130-144). Champaign, IL: Human Kinetics.

Passer, M.W. (1988). Determinants and consequences of children's competitive stress. In F.L. Smoll, R.A. Magill, & M.J. Ash (Eds.), *Children in sport* (3rd ed., pp. 153-177). Champaign, IL: Human Kinetics.

Passer, M.W., & Seese, M.D. (1983). Life stress and athletic injury: Examination of positive versus negative events and three moderator variables. *Journal of Human Stress*, **9**, 11-16.

Peper, E., & Schmid, A. (1983). The use of electrodermal biofeedback for peak performance training. *Somatics*, **4**, 16-18.

Petlichkoff, L.M. (1986, October). *Psychological characteristics of successful and less successful elite sailors*. Paper presented at the Annual Meeting of the Association for the Advancement of Applied Sport Psychology, Jekyll Island, GA.

Poteet, D., & Weinberg, R. (1980). Competition trait anxiety, state anxiety, and performance. *Perceptual and Motor Skills*, **50**, 651-654.

Power, S.L. (1982). An analysis of anxiety levels in track and field athletes of varying ages and abilities. *International Journal of Sport Psychology*, **13**, 258-267.

Rainey, D.W., Conklin, W.E., & Rainey, K.W. (1987). Competitive trait anxiety among male and female junior high school athletes. *International Journal of Sport Psychology*, **18**, 171-180.

Rainey, D.W., & Cunningham, H. (1988). Competitive trait anxiety in male and female college athletes. *Research Quarterly for Exercise and Sport*, **59**, 244-247.

Reynolds, W.M. (1982). Development of reliable and valid short forms of the Marlowe-Crowne social desirability scale. *Journal of Clinical Psychology*, **38**, 119-125.

Riddick, C.C. (1984). Comparative psychological profiles of three groups of female collegians: Competitive swimmers, recreational swimmers, and inactive swimmers. *Journal of Sport Behavior*, **7**, 160-174.

Rinehart, R.E. (1981). *Relationship of anticipatory anxiety to swimming performance as measured by catecholemine levels and psychological inventory.* Unpublished master's thesis, University of Arizona, Tucson.

Roberts, G.C., Spink, K.S., & Pemberton, C.L. (1986). *Learning experiences in sport psychology.* Champaign, IL: Human Kinetics.

Robinson, T.T., & Carron, A.V. (1982). Personal and situational factors associated with dropping out versus maintaining participation in competitive sport. *Journal of Sport Psychology*, **4**, 364-378.

Rosenthal, R. (1968). Experimenter expectancy and the reassuring nature of the self hypothesis decision procedure. *Psychological Bulletin*, **70**(Monograph Suppl.), 30-47.

Rotter, J.B. (1954). *Social learning and clinical psychology.* Englewood Cliffs, NJ: Prentice-Hall.

Rotter, J.B. (1966). Generalized expectancies for internal versus external control of reinforcement. *Psychological Monographs*, **80**(1, Whole No. 609).

Rupnow, A., & Ludwig, D.A. (1981). Psychometric note on the reliability of the Sport Competition Anxiety Test: Form C. *Research Quarterly for Exercise and Sport*, **52**, 35-37.

Ryckman, R.M., Robbins, M.A., Thornton, B., & Cantrell, P. (1982). Development and validation of a physical self-efficacy scale. *Journal of Personality and Social Psychology*, **42**, 891-900.

Safrit, M.J., Costa, M.G., & Hooper, L.M. (1986). The validity generalization model: An approach to the analysis of validity studies in physical education. *Research Quarterly for Exercise and Sport*, **57**, 288-297.

Sarason, I.G. (1975a). Test anxiety and the self-disclosing coping model. *Journal of Consulting and Clinical Psychology*, **43**, 148-153.

Sarason, I.G. (1975b). Test anxiety, attention and the general problem of anxiety. In C.D. Spielberger & I.G. Sarason (Eds.), *Stress and anxiety* (Vol. 1, pp. 165-187). Washington, DC: Hemisphere.

Sarason, S.B., Davidson, K.S., Lighthall, F.F., Waite, R.R., & Ruebush, B.K. (1960). *Anxiety in elementary school children.* New York: Wiley.

Scanlan, T.K. (1975). *The effect of competition trait anxiety and success-failure on the perception of threat in a competitive situation.* Unpublished doctoral dissertation, University of Illinois.

Scanlan, T.K. (1977). The effects of competition trait anxiety and success-failure on the perception of threat in a competitive situation. *Research Quarterly*, **48**, 144-153.

Scanlan, T.K. (1978). Perceptions and responses of high- and low-competitive trait-anxious males to competition. *Research Quarterly*, **49**, 520-527.

Scanlan, T.K. (1984). Competitive stress and the child athlete. In J.M. Silva & R.S. Weinberg (Eds.), *Psychological foundations of sport* (pp. 118-129). Champaign, IL: Human Kinetics.

Scanlan, T.K. (1986). Competitive stress in children. In M.R. Weiss & D. Gould (Eds.), *Sport for children and youths* (pp. 113-118). Champaign, IL: Human Kinetics.

Scanlan, T.K. (1988). Social evaluation and the competition process: A developmental perspective. In F.L. Smoll, R.A. Magill, & M.J. Ash (Eds.), *Children in sport* (3rd ed., pp. 138-152). Champaign, IL: Human Kinetics.

Scanlan, T.K., & Lewthwaite, R. (1984). Social psychological aspects of competition for male youth sport participants: I. Predictors of competitive stress. *Journal of Sport Psychology*, **6**, 208-226.

Scanlan, T.K., & Lewthwaite, R. (1985). Social psychological aspects of competition for male youth sport participants: III. Determinants of personal performance expectancies. *Journal of Sport Psychology*, **7**, 389-399.

Scanlan, T.K., & Lewthwaite, R. (1986). Social psychological aspects of competition for male youth sport participants: IV. Predictors of enjoyment. *Journal of Sport Psychology*, **8**, 25-35.

Scanlan, T.K., & Lewthwaite, R. (1988). From stress to enjoyment: Parental and coach influences on young participants. In E.W. Brown & C.F. Branta (Eds.), *Competitive sports for children and youth* (pp. 41-48). Champaign, IL: Human Kinetics.

Scanlan, T.K., Lewthwaite, R., & Jackson, B.L. (1984). Social psychological aspects of competition for male youth sport participants: II. Predictors of performance outcomes. *Journal of Sport Psychology*, **6**, 422-429.

Scanlan, T.K., & Passer, M.W. (1977). The effects of competition trait anxiety and game win-loss on perceived threat in a natural competitive setting. In D.M. Landers & R.W. Christina (Eds.), *Psychology of motor behavior and sport—1976* (pp. 157-160). Champaign, IL: Human Kinetics.

Scanlan, T.K., & Passer, M.W. (1978). Factors related to competitive stress among male youth sport participants. *Medicine and Science in Sport*, **10**, 103-108.

Scanlan, T.K., & Passer, M.W. (1979a). Factors influencing the competitive performance expectancies of young female athletes. *Journal of Sport Psychology*, **1**, 212-220.

Scanlan, T.K., & Passer, M.W. (1979b). Sources of competitive stress in young female athletes. *Journal of Sport Psychology*, **1**, 151-159.

Scanlan, T.K., & Passer, M.W. (1981). Determinants of competitive performance expectancies of young male athletes. *Journal of Personality*, **49**, 60-74.

Scanlan, T.K., & Ragan, J.T. (1978). Achievement motivation and competition: Perceptions and responses. *Medicine and Science in Sports*, **10**, 276-281.

Schmidt, F.L., & Hunter, J.E. (1977). Development of a general solution to the problem of validity generalization. *Journal of Applied Psychology*, **62**, 529-540.

Schmidt, F.L., Hunter, J.E., Pearlman, K., & Hirsh, H.R. (1985). Forty questions about validity generalization and meta-analysis. *Personnel Psychology*, **38**, 697-798.

Schmidt, F.L., Hunter, J.E., & Urry, J.E. (1976). Statistical power in criterion-related validation studies. *Journal of Applied Psychology*, **61**, 473-485.

Schwartz, G.E., Davidson, R.J., & Goleman, D.J. (1978). Patterning of cognitive and somatic processes in the self-regulation of anxiety: Effects of meditation versus exercise. *Psychosomatic Medicine*, **40**, 321-328.

Segal, J.D., & Weinberg, R.S. (1984). Sex, sex role orientation, and competitive trait anxiety. *Journal of Sport Behavior*, **7**, 153-159.

Silva, J.S. (1982). Performance enhancement through cognitive intervention. *Behavior Modification*, **6**, 443-463.

Simon, J.A., & Martens, R. (1977). SCAT as a predictor of A-states in varying competitive situations. In D.M. Landers & R.W. Christina (Eds.), *Psychology of motor behavior and sport—1976* (Vol. 2, pp. 146-156). Champaign, IL: Human Kinetics.

Simon, J.A., & Martens, R. (1979). Children's anxiety in sport and nonsport evaluative activities. *Journal of Sport Psychology*, **1**, 160-169.

Smith, C.A., & Morris, L.W. (1976). Effects of stimulative and sedative music on two components of test anxiety. *Psychological Reports*, **38**, 1187-1193.

Smith, C.A., & Morris, L.W. (1977). Differential effects of stimulative and sedative music on anxiety, concentration and performance. *Psychological Reports*, **41**, 1047-1053.

Smith, C.P. (1969). The origin and expression of achievement-related motives in children. In C.P. Smith (Ed.), *Achievement-related motives in children* (pp. 102-150). New York: Russell Sage Foundation.

Smith, R.E. (1980). A cognitive-affective aproach to stress management training for athletes. In C.H. Nadeau, W.R. Halliwell, K.M. Newell, & G.C. Roberts (Eds.), *Psychology of motor behavior and sport—1979* (pp. 54-72). Champaign, IL: Human Kinetics.

Smith, T. (1983). Competition trait anxiety in youth sport: Differences according to age, sex, race and playing status. *Perceptual and Motor Skills*, **57**, 1235-1238.

Sonstroem, R.J. (1984). An overview of anxiety in sport. In J.M. Silva & R.S. Weinberg (Eds.), *Psychological foundations of sport* (pp. 104-117). Champaign, IL: Human Kinetics.

Sonstroem, R.J., & Bernardo, P. (1982). Intraindividual pregame state anxiety and basketball performance: A re-examination of the inverted-U curve. *Journal of Sport Psychology*, **4**, 235-245.

Spielberger, C.D. (1966a). The effects of anxiety on complex learning and academic achievement. In C.D. Spielberger (Ed.), *Anxiety and behavior* (pp. 361-398). New York: Academic Press.

Spielberger, C.D. (1966b). Theory and research on anxiety. In C.D. Spielberger (Ed.), *Anxiety and behavior* (pp. 3-20). New York: Academic Press.

Spielberger, C.D. (1972a). Anxiety as an emotional state. In C.D. Spielberger (Ed.), *Anxiety: Current trends in theory and research* (Vol. 1, pp. 23-49). New York: Academic Press.

Spielberger, C.D. (1972b). Conceptual and methodological issues in anxiety research. In C.D. Spielberger (Ed.), *Anxiety: Current trends in theory and research* (Vol. 2, pp. 481-493). New York: Academic Press.

Spielberger, C.D. (1973). *Preliminary test manual for the State-Trait Anxiety Inventory for Children*. Palo Alto, CA: Consulting Psychologists.

Spielberger, C.D., Gonzalez, H.P., Taylor, C., Algaze, B., & Anton, W.D. (1978). Examination stress and test anxiety. In C.D. Spielberger & I.G. Sarason (Eds.), *Stress and anxiety* (Vol. 5, pp. 167-191). New York: Hemisphere/Wiley.

Spielberger, C.D., Gorsuch, R.L., & Lushene, R.L. (1970). *Manual for the State-Trait Anxiety Inventory*. Palo Alto, CA: Consulting Psychologists.

Stadulis, R.E. (1977). Need achievement, competition preference and evaluation seeking. In D.M. Landers & R.W. Christina (Eds.), *Psychology of motor behavior and sport—1976* (pp. 113-122). Champaign, IL: Human Kinetics.

Suinn, R. (1977). Behavioral methods at the Winter Olympic Games. *Behavior Therapy*, **8**, 283-284.

Tatsuoka, M.M. (1971). *Multivariate analysis*. New York: Wiley.

Taylor, J. (1987). Predicting athletic performance with self-confidence and somatic and cognitive anxiety as a function of motor and physiological requirements in six sports. *Journal of Personality*, **55**, 139-153.

Taylor, J.A. (1953). A personality scale of manifest anxiety. *Journal of Abnormal and Social Psychology*, **48**, 285-290.

Thirer, J., Knowlton, R., Sawka, M., & Chang, T.J. (1978). Relationship of psycho-physiological characteristics to perceived exertion and levels of anxiety in competitive swimmers. *Journal of Sport Behavior*, **1**, 169-173.

Thirer, J., & O'Donnell, L.A. (1980). Female intercollegiate athletes' trait-anxiety level and performance in a game. *Perceptual and Motor Skills*, **50**, 18.

Thompson, J.G., Griebstein, M.G., & Kuhlenschmidt, S.L. (1980). Effects of EMG biofeedback and relaxation training in the prevention of academic underachievement. *Journal of Counseling Psychology*, **27**, 97-106.

Titley, R.W. (1980). The loneliness of a long distance kicker. In R.M. Suinn (Ed.), *Psychology in sports: Methods and applications* (pp. 321-327). Minneapolis: Burgess.

Unestahl, L.E. (1986). Self-hypnosis. In J.M. Williams (Ed.), *Applied sport psychology: Personal development to peak performance* (pp. 285-300). Palo Alto, CA: Mayfield.

Vale, J.W., & Vale, C.A. (1969). Individual differences and general laws in psychology: A reconciliation. *American Psychologist*, **24**, 1093-1108.

Vealey, R.S. (1986). Conceptualization of sport-confidence and competitive orientation: Preliminary investigation and instrument development. *Journal of Sport Psychology*, **8**, 221-246.

Wandzilak, T., Potter, G., & Lorentzen, D. (1982). Factors related to predictability of pre-game state anxiety. *International Journal of Sport Psychology*, **13**, 31-42.

Wark, K.A., & Wittig, A.F. (1979). Sex role and sport competition anxiety. *Journal of Sport Psychology*, **1**, 248-250.

Watson, D., & Friend, R. (1969). Measurement of social-evaluative anxiety. *Journal of Consulting and Clinical Psychology*, **33**, 448-457.

Watson, G.G. (1986). Approach-avoidance behaviour in team sports: An application to leading Australian national hockey players. *International Journal of Sport Psychology*, **17**, 136-155.

Weinberg, R.S. (1977). Anxiety and motor behavior: A new direction. In R.W. Christina & D.M. Landers (Eds.), *Psychology of motor behavior and sport—1976* (pp. 132-139). Champaign, IL: Human Kinetics.

Weinberg, R.S. (1978). The effects of success and failure on the patterning of neuromuscular energy. *Journal of Motor Behavior*, **10**, 53-61.

Weinberg, R.S. (1979). Anxiety and motor performance: Drive theory vs. cognitive theory. *International Journal of Sport Psychology*, **10**, 112-121.

Weinberg, R.S., & Genuchi, M. (1980). Relationship between competitive trait anxiety, state anxiety, and golf performance: A field study. *Journal of Sport Psychology*, **2**, 148-154.

Weinberg, R.S., Gould, D., & Jackson, A. (1979). Expectations and performance: An empirical test of Bandura's self-efficacy theory. *Journal of Sport Psychology*, **1**, 320-331.

Weinberg, R.S., Gould, D., & Jackson, A. (1980). Cognition and motor performance: Effect of psyching-up strategies on three motor tasks. *Cognitive Therapy and Research*, **4**, 238-245.

Weinberg, R.S., Gould, D., & Jackson, A. (1981). Relationship between duration of the psych-up interval and strength performance. *Journal of Sport Psychology*, **3**, 166-170.

Weinberg, R.S., Jackson, A., & Seabourne, T. (1985). The effects of specific and nonspecific mental preparation strategies on strength and endurance performance. *Journal of Sport Behavior*, **8**, 175-180.

Weinberg, R.S., Seabourne, T.G., & Jackson, A. (1981). Effects of visuo-motor behavior rehearsal, relaxation and imagery on karate performance. *Journal of Sport Psychology*, **3**, 228-238.

Weinberg, R.S., Seabourne, T., & Jackson, A. (1987). Arousal and relaxation instructions prior to the use of imagery. *International Journal of Sport Psychology*, **18**, 205-214.

Weiner, B. (1974). *Achievement motivation and attribution theory*. Morristown, NJ: General Learning Press.

Weiner, B. (1979). A theory of motivation for some classroom experiences. *Journal of Educational Psychology*, **71**, 3-25.

Weiner, E.A., & Stewart, B.J. (1984). *Assessing individuals: Psychological and educational tests and measurements*. Boston: Little Brown.

Weiss, M. (1988). *Relationships between competitive state anxiety, state self confidence, and rifle shooting performance for elite junior shooters*. Unpublished manuscript, University of Oregon, Eugene.

Weiss, M., Bredemeier, B., & Shewchuk, R. (1985). An intrinsic/extrinsic motivation scale for the youth sport setting: A confirmatory factor analysis. *Journal of Sport Psychology*, **7**, 75-91.

Wenz, B.J., & Strong, D.J. (1980). An application of biofeedback and self-regulation procedures with superior athletes: The fine tuning effect. In R.M. Suinn (Ed.), *Psychology of sports: Methods and applications* (pp. 328-333). Minneapolis: Burgess.

Willis, J.D. (1982). Three scales to measure competition-related motives in sport. *Journal of Sport Psychology*, **4**, 338-353.

Wine, J.D. (1971). Test anxiety and direction of attention. *Psychological Bulletin*, **76**, 92-104.

Wine, J.D. (1980). Cognitive-attentional theory of test anxiety. In I.G. Sarason (Ed.), *Test anxiety: Theory, research and applications* (pp. 349-385). Hillsdale, NJ: Erlbaum.

Wittig, A.F. (1984). Sport competition anxiety and sex role. *Sex Roles*, **10**, 469-472.

Wittig, A.F., Duncan, S.L., & Schurr, K.T. (1987). The relationship of gender, gender-role endorsement and perceived physical self-efficacy to sport competition anxiety. *Journal of Sport Behavior*, **11**, 192-199.

Yan Lan, L., & Gill, D.L. (1984). The relationships among self-efficacy, stress responses, and a cognitive feedback manipulation. *Journal of Sport Psychology*, **6**, 227-238.

Yerkes, R.M., & Dodson, J.D. (1908). The relation of strength of stimulus to rapidity of habit-formation. *Journal of Comparative Neurology and Psychology*, **18**, 459-482.

Zuckerman, M. (1960). The development of an affect adjective check list for the measurement of anxiety. *Journal of Consulting Psychology*, **24**, 457-462.

Author Index

Subject Index

A

Achievement Anxiety Test (AAT), 133-134
Achievement motivation and competitive anxiety, 30-31, 71, 77-78, 82-83, 98-99, 109
Activation, 6
Affect Adjective Checklist (AACL), 134-136
Alberta Incentive Motivation Inventory, 82-83
Anxiety-performance hypothesis, 155, 160, 166-173, 205-206, 210-212
Arousal. *See also* Inverted-U hypothesis
    anticipatory, 225
    definition of, 6, 10
    jag, 222
    SCAT and, 38, 90-91
    somatic anxiety and, 149
    task type and, 162
Attention
    cognitive anxiety and, 124, 126, 151, 160, 172
    competitive trait anxiety and, 72, 92, 104, 115
    CSAI-2 components and, 194-195

B

Bem Sex Role Inventory (BSRI), 74-75
Biofeedback, 48-49, 92, 100-101, 196

C

Children's Manifest Anxiety Scale Short Form (CMAS), 26-27
Cognitive anxiety. *See also* Cognitive competitive state anxiety
    definition of, 6, 9, 120
    somatic anxiety and, 121-126
Cognitive appraisal, 15
Cognitive competitive state anxiety. *See also* Competitive State Anxiety Inventory-2 (CSAI-2)
    ability differences in, 143-150
    antecedents of, 202-204, 210
    attention and, 194-195
    competitive trait anxiety and, 88-89, 107, 133, 143-150, 194
    CSAI-2 components and, 136-137, 139, 145, 196-200, 210
    development of CSAI-2 subscale measuring, 127-140
    gender differences in, 143-150
    intervention and, 204, 206
    performance and, 155-173, 203-206, 210-212
    physiological arousal and, 196
    self-confidence and, 195
    sport type and, 142-150
    temporal changes in, 150-155, 199-202, 212
Cognitive competitive trait anxiety, 94, 104
Cognitive paradigm, 14-15
Cognitive-somatic anxiety distinction
    antecedents of anxiety using, 122-123
    definitions used in, 6
    independence of constructs in, 122-126, 136-139, 150-155

About the Authors

Rainer Martens is the developer of the Sport Competition Anxiety Test (SCAT), the first instrument to assess sport-specific anxiety. A sport psychologist for more than 20 years and a professor in the Department of Kinesiology at the University of Illinois, Dr. Martens is widely recognized for his research on competitive anxiety. He lectured on the subject in the Soviet Union as the first American sport psychologist to visit that country. Dr. Martens is the past president of the North American Society for the Psychology of Sport and Physical Activity and the recipient of the Distinguished Alumnus Award from Emporia State University. He is the author of numerous books on coaching and sport psychology and is president of Human Kinetics Publishers. Away from his professional responsibilities, Dr. Martens enjoys jogging, biking, and handball.

Robin S. Vealey is an assistant professor in the Department of Physical Education, Health, and Sport Studies at Miami University in Oxford, Ohio. She earned her PhD in sport psychology at the University of Illinois, where she concentrated her research on competitive anxiety and self-confidence under the direction of Dr. Martens. Dr. Vealey serves on the executive board of the Association for the Advancement of Applied Sport Psychology and the editorial boards of the *Journal of Sport and Exercise Psychology, The Sport Psychologist,* and the *Journal of Applied Sport Psychology.* She enjoys a variety of sports and fitness activities, including racquetball, basketball, golf, biking, and swimming. As an accomplished athlete, Dr. Vealey admits to firsthand knowledge of competitive anxiety!

Like his coauthor Robin Vealey, Damon Burton studied for his PhD under the tutelage of Dr. Martens at the University of Illinois. His research activities focused heavily on the development and validation of the CSAI-2, as well as a goal-setting program designed to reduce anxiety among collegiate swimmers. Dr. Burton is an associate professor of sport psychology at the University of Idaho.